"IN THEIR OWN WORDS"

"IN THEIR OWN WORDS"

Derbyshire Cricketers in Conversation

Steve Dolman

First published by Pitch Publishing, 2016

Pitch Publishing
A2 Yeoman Gate
Yeoman Way
Worthing
Sussex
BN13 3QZ
www.pitchpublishing.co.uk

© 2016, Steve Dolman

ISBN 978-1-78531-139-0

Typesetting and origination by Pitch Publishing
Printed by Bell & Bain, Glasgow, Scotland

Contents

Foreword 9

Introduction 11

Author's note 16

Walter Goodyear (1938–1982). 17

Edwin Smith (1951–1971) 38

Harold Rhodes (1953–1969) 54

Keith Mohan (1957–1958) 70

Peter Eyre (1959–1972) 80

Brian Jackson (1963–1968). 89

Bob Taylor MBE (1963–1984) 98

Peter Gibbs (1966–1972) 109

Tony Borrington (1971–1980). 122

Alan Hill (1972– 1986) 134

Colin Tunnicliffe (1973–1983). 151

Geoff Miller OBE (1973–1990) 163

John Wright OBE (1977–1988) 175

Devon Malcolm (1984–1997) 188

Kevin Dean (1996–2008) 201

Graeme Welch (2001–2006) 210

James Pipe (2006–2009) 221

Wayne Madsen (2009–present) 232

Chris Grant (2010–present) 243

Epilogue. 254

To Mum and Dad, for your early encouragement of my interest in the greatest of games and for your lifetime support.

And to my wife Sylvia and children, Stephen and Rachel, just for being there. I simply couldn't have done it without you.

Foreword

AS AN inquisitive player, always looking to improve, I am very aware of what is being said in the media and on social forums. In 2009, when I started my Derbyshire career, I came across the Peakfan Blog and it was different to most fan pages and blogs I had seen. I noticed that unlike the other sites, which mainly criticise and bemoan performances, Peakfan's blog is honest, supportive and fair.

I got to know Steve as an almost mythical character before I actually got to know him properly, face to face. I say mythical because of the way 'Peakfan' is talked about in the dressing room. Steve's *nom de plume* is heard as a whisper from time to time in the change-room, and his opinions are seen as being balanced and positive. This shows a great deal of respect for the club, the team and the individuals involved.

Having got to know Steve over my time at Derbyshire, he is a loyal and honourable man with Derbyshire County Cricket Club running through his veins. His values and support are what make him so likeable and I certainly have enjoyed getting to know him.

This book is a great opportunity to read about Steve's passion for Derbyshire cricket and includes amazing stories and anecdotes from some of the people, on and off the field, who have shaped Derbyshire into such a special club.

As a captain, the book will allow me to gain further insight into the history that has forged our great club. It has given me a greater perspective on the role I have, to make sure that when I finish playing, I leave the club in a better place than when I arrived.

Steve, thank you for your passion, enthusiasm, support and friendship. I'm sure you have enjoyed your research into this book. I certainly have enjoyed getting to know you better and look forward to sharing more of Derbyshire County Cricket Club's history with you.

Wayne Madsen
Club Captain
Derbyshire County Cricket Club

Introduction

I FIRST watched Derbyshire County Cricket Club in 1968. It was 26 August, the last day of a three-day game against Yorkshire and one that saw the county battling to save the match in the final session. It was not to be the last time I saw such a struggle, but in the years that followed I became hooked on the game of cricket and the fortunes of 'my' county.

On balance, the intervening period has seen more bad times than good, yet my interest and support has never waned. Moving from our home in Ripley across the border into Nottinghamshire changed nothing, nor did a subsequent spell in Manchester for further education. Making my life in Scotland caused logistical issues, but I retained both the accent and my love of the county of my birth.

Six years ago, I started the Peakfan Blog on Derbyshire cricket and in the intervening time have made contact with former players and conducted occasional interviews on their lives and careers. What I found interesting was that those chats unearthed many stories that had never previously appeared in written form. The response from blog followers was very positive and it set me thinking that an oral history of the county's post-war years might have some merit.

Occasionally a worthy tome on a journeyman professional will emerge in cricket literature, but by and large, books are on the biggest names, those whose careers have occupied the columns of newspapers and, in this modern era, the many social media channels. Such names, after all, will sell.

The journeyman professional rarely gets the chance to tell his tales, unless at an occasional cricket dinner or cricket society meeting. The relish with which those early participants recounted their stories convinced me that there was something worthwhile in a bigger project and it started to gain momentum.

Having a background in oral history from a previous career, I was well aware of the importance of gathering these memories, or risk losing them forever. Those involved were patient, understanding and engaging, as they recalled people and events of up to 70 years before.

The interview with the doyen of groundsmen, Walter Goodyear, turned out to be the first he had ever given, at the age of 98. I asked for an hour of his time, sat with him in his home for four and ended up having regular chats by telephone as he remembered other stories he thought may be of interest. They were, every last one of them – though some of the more scurrilous have had to be omitted for fairly obvious reasons. He may well be the last man with first-hand recall of the legendary – some might say infamous – Bill Bestwick, who in his final years walked his dog around the boundary at Derby, passing comment on the action to all and sundry as he did so. The thought that with one man I was linked to 19th-century cricket has stayed with me.

What became increasingly evident was that the older generation, almost without exception, were delighted to chat, while players from more recent decades were in some cases more reluctant. There are scars that still run deep and I had to respect that.

As word spread about my project, bigger names agreed to be interviewed. So many, in fact, that I had to introduce unexpected selection criteria. Those who made the final cut are the ones who had been involved in the biggest stories, or whose lives and careers I felt of the greater interest to the reader and to posterity. Some had post-cricket careers that enhanced their claim for inclusion. I was, in short, looking for new stories and a different angle to those that I already knew. To a man, the participants in this book delivered handsomely, but I apologise unreservedly to those for whom there was simply no room.

I ended up with a good cross-section of players from each decade of the post-war era and my gratitude to each is duly recorded. To sit talking cricket, with people who I have spent much of my life watching from afar, has been a dream come true and none of them left me disappointed with the interaction. As things turned out, five of them were playing in that first game I saw at Chesterfield, something that dawned on me as the book progressed and which emphasises the effect that first experience had on a small, bespectacled and star-struck schoolboy.

The finished product is book-ended by two men who have made major off-field contributions, whose involvement added value to the project and made it more about the club and not just the cricket.

Each subject, in turn, has seen their finished interview and approved it. Sometimes things look different on the printed page than when spoken and I wanted to ensure that they were happy with the final version and had the option to edit, correct or omit. They rarely did, which in itself was gratifying. Some of the comments are surprising and very honest, but they were each happy to have them recorded.

I would like to thank club captain Wayne Madsen, a man who swapped Durban for Derbyshire and so clearly loves his adopted home, for kindly agreeing to write a foreword. The club is very close to his heart and that comes through very clearly in the words that he has written. He is both an outstanding cricketer and man and it has been a pleasure to get to know and become friends with him, his delightful wife Kyla and his extended family over recent seasons.

Special thanks also go to Peter Gibbs, then secretary of the club's former players' association, as well as to Harold Rhodes, who was willing to answer questions and provide important background on his era. Tony Borrington has also been of invaluable assistance and I am indebted to him for his interest and support. It was he who told me never to underestimate the interest an old cricketer had in discussing his career. Both sage and propitious words, as it turned out.

I would also like to thank Edwin Smith, the subject of my first book, both for contacts and for his friendship. I have learned much from him about county cricket in the first quarter-century after the war. Car trips, where he pointed out former haunts and player homes, as well as time spent at the County Ground, where he showed me the location of old landmarks, were priceless. So too were his endless collection of stories, a number of which were recalled too late for his biography, but thankfully in time to appear here.

The result is a series of interviews that cover Derbyshire County Cricket Club's history from 1945 to 2015. Truth be told, thanks to the astonishing recall of Walter Goodyear, it goes back to the side that won the County Championship in 1936, but the majority of the book covers the post-war era.

It reveals the truth about stories that made the news over that period, recounted by those who were closest to those stories, or made them. Some will surprise, others will make you laugh and hopefully all of them will be of interest. My interest in how players 'arrive' in the county game and in certain individuals in the club's history resulted in some replication, but the ends, I think, justify the means.

The hardest part was editing down hours of chat to a workable size, but I hope my final selection gives a flavour of life on the county cricket circuit over the post-war years. I have tried, in the writing, to capture the way that those involved speak, so local vernacular creeps in on occasion.

I would like to thank the *Derby Telegraph*, in association with the Cricket Derbyshire Heritage Project, for the photographs, which are used with permission. Special thanks go to Mark Eklid and Colston Crawford at the newspaper for their assistance in gathering them together. Thanks also to Chris Airey and Neil Bates at Derbyshire County Cricket Club, whose assistance throughout has been invaluable and appreciated.

Special thanks also go to Paul and Jane Camillin at Pitch Publishing for their advice and support.

They quickly got back to me when I approached them with my idea for the book and I hope that the finished product repays their faith.

Finally, thanks to Martin Edwards, an outstanding writer and good friend, for his encouragement of my writing, on my blog and elsewhere, over recent years. Also to Martin and David Booth of Office Care, whose sponsorship of my blog and its layout over several years has helped to take it to a new level.

INTRODUCTION

To everyone whose stories are recounted in the book – thank you for the memories. It was my very great pleasure to meet you all, just as it has been to watch you over all those summers.

Author's note

The dates after the name of each player are when they began and ended their playing careers with the county. Those for Walter Goodyear and Chris Grant refer to their involvement with the club.

Walter Goodyear (1938–1982)

WALTER GOODYEAR was the groundsman's groundsman, a man who had forgotten more about his art than most ever know. From 1932, when he started work at Queens Park, Chesterfield, to 1982, when he retired, he prepared wickets specifically, as you will read, for Derbyshire's rich array of seam bowlers.

They weren't so much Derbyshire wickets as 'Walter wickets'. He knew what the club wanted and prepared them impeccably. Anyone winning the toss would fancy a bowl, the extra grass offering early help to any seam bowler worthy of the name and willing to bend his back. For much of his time the county did very well, because the conveyor belt of quick bowling talent kept producing the goods… Copson, the Popes, Gladwin, Jackson, Rhodes, Jackson again, Ward, Hendrick…the list went on. Yet you could get runs on them too, because when the 'green' went off it, the wickets were simply good for cricket.

Walter Goodyear is 99 now but still as sharp as a tack. Old age doesn't come alone, as the saying goes, but he is philosophical about his lot, despite losing both his wife and son to accidents that perhaps could and should have been prevented. He is refreshingly honest and funny – wonderful company, in short. How he got to that age without any interview requests remains a mystery, because his recollections are like gold dust to the oral historian.

Before I met him, I managed to speak to Steve Birks, now groundsman at Trent Bridge and one of the most respected in the game. He got a start as a groundsman under Walter Goodyear, spending 12 months with him at the County Ground from 1981 to 1982.

'He was the biggest single influence on my career, without a doubt,' Steve said. 'He was quite a fearsome character and a lot of people were frankly terrified of him. But he took me under his wing and I remember he would tell me to fetch my flask and we'd go out on the square and have our lunch, or a tea break. If you listened to him, you couldn't help but learn, because he knew it all.'

Steve joined the ground staff from a Youth Training Scheme, making such an impression as to being the one from that scheme that Walter still remembers with a great deal of fondness.

Did he have any particular memories?

'I loved the guy to bits and he remains one of the greatest characters I have met in the game. The play that Peter Gibbs did a few years back, *Arthur's Hallowed Ground,* was Walter to the life. It was brilliantly done and captured him as he really was. The man is a legend in our circles and anything I have achieved in the game of cricket owes a great deal to Walter Goodyear.'

He is the last man standing. No one else survives from pre-war Derbyshire cricket and if they did, it is unlikely that their memory would be as acute as his. A groundsman at both Chesterfield and Derby in his time, he is also a decorated war hero, fighting at Anzio and in the north African desert. He is one of the last of the legendary Desert Rats and it was a very great honour to meet him.

In the course of our first chat, I found out that his best friend during the war was my late uncle, my Dad's brother Bill. It was an extraordinary and unexpected coincidence, but then Walter Goodyear is, by any standards, an extraordinary man.

Walter, can you tell me about your early life?

I was born at Chesterfield on 1 February 1917 and brought up in Southwell at a doctor's house. My Mum was a char lady and we were there until I was five, when I moved to Hasland, near Chesterfield, with my Mum. My Dad was a farmer, then went on the railway. I had a sister but she died when she was young from peritonitis.

My father was very bad-tempered – you might even say vicious – and my three brothers and I got some rough treatment at times. I got the brunt of his anger and I was picked on, to be honest.

> **You took a job as assistant at Chesterfield cricket ground at Queens Park in 1932 when you were just 16. How did that come about?**

Well, I went on the park at 14, then went to the pit for a while, as so many did. I was then asked to go back to Chesterfield, specifically to help out on the cricket ground. I worked with Fred Pope, who was, of course, the father of our bowlers, George and Alf.

There was plenty of work on at that time. There was a first and second team, a Wednesday side and a Thursday police team. All those wickets needed preparation but they were marvellous years. I should never have left, if I'm honest, as I enjoyed it much more than Derby. I was employed by the Chesterfield corporation and not by the cricket club.

I was 'King Dick' there. A friend of mine called me recently and told me that he had been listening to a piece on the local radio. Someone had said that I was the most important person in Chesterfield in 1938! I used to wind the market hall clock, the parish church clock, help out councillors and do various bits of charity work.

When I moved to Derby, I had to go into digs and if I am honest, I never settled there as much as at Chesterfield. I still love Queens Park.

> **It was a golden era for Derbyshire cricket. Were you a fan at that time?**

I was never a cricket fan. It was just a job and when you're out of work you do anything to get money coming in. That's what I was happy to do, until the day that I retired.

> **Was there much difference in pitch and ground preparation between Derby and Chesterfield?**

I had a hand roller at Chesterfield and a motor roller at Derby! The one at Chesterfield was 15cwt. Two of us had to push it, though I did it alone sometimes when there was no one else about. It used to pull your guts out, but it certainly kept you fit.

At Derby there was much more than cricket. There was Derby Amateurs football club, five hockey teams, the National Westminster Bank with different teams – it was a constant battle to keep the ground in a decent condition. All the teams wanted to play as late as they could to prolong their season. I was forever replacing divots and trying to keep the ground half decent for the cricketers, who needed the best surface, of course.

So how long was your working day?

I would often leave for the ground at 5am, then go home for lunch around one. Then I would work until perhaps 10pm in the summer. I was a workaholic, but it kept the money coming in for my wife and son. That's the way I looked at it.

How did the move to Derby in 1938, when you took over as head groundsman, come about?

Harry Fletcher, the groundsman at Derby, died and Stan Worthington, our all-rounder, lodged with him. On Stan's recommendation I was offered the job outright, no interview or anything. I only saw it as a short-term thing though. I should have gone back home to Chesterfield after the war and I regret not doing that, as I've said.

It was a racecourse then as well. Mr Smedley was the racecourse manager. He gave me decent money for working on it, but he also gave me a paddock ticket for the course, as a thank you for what I had done. Now, I wasn't interested in horse racing at all, but a friend of mine was commissionaire at the Regal Cinema at Chesterfield and he moved to do the same job at the one in Derby. I told him to give the paddock ticket to the cinema manager, so he could come to the racing whenever he wanted. In return, I got complimentary tickets for the cinema whenever I wanted!

The cinema was in East Street, halfway up on the left-hand side. The Derby Building Society is there now. I also got to go to the theatre, and to the Hippodrome for free too. Old Walter did all right out of that and I had to wheel and deal throughout my days.

Were there many differences between the two squares and the way they played?

Chesterfield was much easier to manage. The thatch was better – you had to rake cricket grounds to get the turf to the texture you wanted – and of course the surrounds were much nicer. The drainage at Derby was dreadful and the water went down a seven-inch pipe that stopped at the pavilion. Whenever it rained, it used to back up and flood, but there was never any money to sort it.

A few years ago they wanted to excavate the square at Derby and they dug down around ten inches to do so. Once they had it dug out, they went for lunch and came back an hour later. It was full of water! There's a very high water table there and that was always an issue until they spent some money on the drainage.

I could take you to Derby now and show you where there's a well on the ground. It dates from the time before the Grandstand Hotel, when there was a farmhouse there. The well belonged to the farm. It is covered with large slabs of concrete, so nobody's likely to fall down it in a hurry!

Author note: On a visit to the ground last summer, I asked current groundsman Neil Godrich about this. He showed me where the well is, not too far inside the boundary in front of the Gateway Centre. If we're ever a fielder short, that's the first place to look.

By all accounts it wasn't a very nice ground at that time?

Ooh no. It was depressing to look at. It was always cold, even in the summer. Other teams didn't like that and ours weren't that keen either! Especially the batsmen, who always knew when they came to Derby that they would get a green wicket with plenty of grass left on it.

They didn't have a choice though. They got MY wicket and for a long time I prepared them for Les Jackson. People used to turn up for matches and ask me how it would play. My answer was usually the same, 'If we win the toss we'll put the buggers in and Les will have three or four wickets before lunch.'

He usually did, you know. If he didn't, I was for it!

It never turned much at Derby. Chesterfield did, but only later in the summer did it ever turn much at Derby. Mind you, Tommy Mitchell could spin it there. He could spin it on anything.

How many staff did you have there?

Staff? You must be joking! There was a bloke named Joe Thomson who helped me when he could, but everything else was down to Walter. Whether it was moving or relaying the square, I had to do it all myself. I had 32 acres to maintain, all of it on my own for most of the time.

I subsequently helped Joe Thomson by getting him to Chesterfield to work on the ground at Clay Cross and put some money in his pocket. There were the ground staff boys, but with a few exceptions their hearts weren't in it and they were in too big a hurry to get home to be that much use.

Later on I got some help but it was youngsters off the dole – they weren't interested, with the exception of one. That was Steve Birks, who has gone on to become a very well-regarded groundsman at Trent Bridge, of course. He was a good lad, willing to listen and to graft.

Were there opportunities for you to move?

I could have gone to Lord's in 1977. Donald Carr asked me if I would be interested in moving down there, but I told him that I was too old by that stage – I was 60.

I said he should go to Nottingham and get Jim Fairbrother, which he did. Jim was a very good groundsman.

Did you ever get asked to prepare specific kinds of wickets by the captains? Did that change as time went on?

My wickets were always green tops for the Derbyshire seamers. Walter Robins came with Middlesex in 1947 and took me out to have a look at the wicket, which was green, as always. He told me it looked damp and had too much grass. I told him it didn't.

He wasn't at all happy and said that if he won the toss he was going to get it cut. I told him, 'You bloody well won't, it's my wicket.'

So he went off to see our club secretary, Will Taylor, who gave me his backing and then he came back out, saying, 'Okay you win, Walter… so what's going to happen?'

I told him they would lose two wickets for 20 but probably make 300. I also told him to leave out his spinner, the long-serving Jim Sims, in favour of a young seamer, Norman Hever. He subsequently went to Glamorgan where he played in their championship-winning side of 1948 and never forgot that I got him picked for that game! Norman later became groundsman at Northamptonshire and we got to know each other very well.

Robins, being the strong character that he was, kept Sims in the side too and he took seven wickets in the match!

Did any Derbyshire captains ask you to go out to the wicket with them?

Some did, earlier on in particular, but a few captains later on thought that they knew it all and didn't need any help from me.

Who were the best Derbyshire captains of your experience?

Captain G.R. Jackson in the 1930s was the best by a mile. He was a gentleman and a really good captain, something he'd done in the army, of course. He called a spade a spade and you knew where you stood with him. Arthur Richardson was very good too, while post-war, Donald Carr and Guy Willatt were both excellent men to work with.

You had other involvement in the club too, I understand?

Oh, I got involved in no end of stuff. Players used to lodge with me and the wife. Harold Rhodes, Reg Carter, John Kelly, Arnold Hamer – they all stayed with us in our back bedroom at times.

I got a reputation around the club as a 'Mr Fixit'. In 1952, when they were visiting Derby, I got Fred Perry and Dan Maskell to do a tennis exhibition at the ground. They were doing some work for the council and I crossed a palm or two to get them over to the County Ground. I never did get paid for that, nor for a lot of other things over the years.

There were some real characters in the side of the 1930s. I'd like to mention some names to you. Arthur Richardson?

He was an absolute gentleman. You know, when the Australians came to Derby with Bradman in 1948, we had the biggest crowd in the club's history. There were 17,000 there on the first day and close to five figures on the others – and the club forgot to pay me!

I went to Arthur Richardson, who was on the club committee at the time and he wrote me a cheque for £20 and told me to take it to my bank. I didn't have a bank account, so he gave me the cash himself. It shows you the way the club was run around that time.

Will Taylor?

He did a lifetime of work with the club but he guarded the finances as if they were his own, which I suppose they were to some extent. We had to submit our expenses to him each month and the first time I was asked for these, I spoke to my wife, to see what I should ask for.

She said that I'd had to pay for different things, including the papers being delivered to the ground, so we worked out a figure of £5. Then the next time, I doubled it to ten. I quickly worked out that he didn't like to be seen as 'tight' when other people were with him, so I made a point of going for my expenses when someone else was there.

I eventually got him up to nearly £20. You did what you had to do, because the money I was paid was barely enough to get by on.

There's a story I have heard – maybe apocryphal – regarding you and Mr Taylor.

[Laughs] That one! Oh, it was true. Mr Taylor did a lot of good for Derbyshire cricket as secretary for over 50 years, but he and I didn't see eye to eye all the time. He had an office that was at the top of the old stand at Derby and one day – it was a match day – he came out of it and shouted across to where I was working on the ground.

'Goodyear!' He bellowed it and everyone heard, including me.

Now, keep in mind that I had fought in the war and didn't much like people talking down to me any more, especially when there was a ground full of people. I just turned round to the pavilion and shouted back at him.

'Bollocks.'

I walked on and he shouted again. This time it was, 'Walter!'

So I turned around and shouted back 'Yes, Mr Taylor?'

He never called me by my surname again.

Denis Smith?

Denis and I got on brilliantly. We got on well when he was a player, but when he became coach we had a lot of fun. He always had his pipe on the go – you rarely saw him without it – and we never had a cross word. I also knew where he was from the plume of smoke from that pipe!

I remember one time he broke my finger by accident and I'd to go to the hospital to get it splinted. The next day I dropped something when I was trying to protect my injured finger and it landed on his foot and broke his toe! We had some laughs about that, I can tell you.

He was a grand bloke. Not many people know that he coached Derek Randall, the Nottinghamshire batsman. His Mum used to bring him down to the County Ground for evening sessions with Denis.

He liked four nets for practice. Two had more grass for the seamers, while two were shaved for the spin bowlers. He liked players to work hard in the nets, there was no room for slacking and he soon told anyone who did.

I missed Denis when he retired.

Stan Worthington?

He was a lovely man and I saw him a lot. Before the war, he asked me to go to Clipstone and take over as groundsman at the football ground there, where his Dad was a manager. I didn't fancy leaving home and so turned him down, but there were no hard feelings.

After the war, when Stan came out of the army, one of the first things he did was to come down to the ground and help me strip down the motorised roller. He was an electrician and a first-class mechanic and we got it cleaned up so it ran beautifully. It saved Will Taylor a lot of money for a new one, so he was pleased with that!

He was coach at Lancashire for ten years and he coached in India for a while. I asked him not to go there because of his health and he was a bag of bones when he got back home.

When he was at Lancashire, he turned up for a game one day in his car with three of their committee men and the gate man wouldn't let them in – the county coach! I told the gate man, bluntly, not to be so silly – or words to that effect – and told Stan where to park. He'd played for us all those years and wasn't even recognised. Unbelievable!

The gate men were often pretty strict, I remember that.

Because most of them didn't use their brains. The best was Percy Fendall, who worked for years on the Nottingham Road gate. One time he gave me a shout and said there were Derby County footballers wanted to get in and wanted to know what to do. I went over and there were 20-odd of them!

I was a regular at the Baseball Ground and knew them all, but there was a bloke from Spondon with them who I knew wasn't. He'd also nicked my new shovel when I was working at Quarndon one time, so I made sure that he paid and the rest got in for nowt.

Les Townsend?

Les was a terrific cricketer and was good to watch, but he kept himself to himself. He didn't mix that much with other people.

Harry Elliott?

He was a top bloke and a marvellous wicketkeeper. He didn't miss much and he was a good coach too. He was another who called a spade a spade and didn't miss anyone who messed him about, but I liked him.

He was older than Derbyshire ever knew, you know. When he signed for the county after the First World War he told them he was born in 1895, when in fact it was 1891. He reckoned they'd not have given him a chance at that age, but he went on to play up to the Second World War. They made him coach in 1947 and he came back and played a few games that year, at the age of 56, as it turned out.

You know, nobody knew about his real age until a reunion of the championship-winning side in 1967? He kept it quiet all those years.

George and Alf Pope?

They were from Brimington, near Chesterfield. Their Dad, as I've said, was a groundsman and all the brothers played the game. They even had a net in the back garden when they were growing up!

Alf was a lovely fella. I lodged with him for a few years when I first came to Derby and we got on very well. He was good company and his house on Nottingham Road was really handy for the cricket ground.

When George was ruled out for most of the championship summer in 1936, Arthur Richardson told Alf that it would mean he had to do a lot more bowling as stock bowler. Alf's reply was the kind that Les Jackson would have later made, 'I like bowling, skipper.'

George was harder, very competitive. He used to play quick bowlers like Brian Close did in later years. If they bounced him, he used to take it on the chest and glare down the wicket at them, as if to say, 'Is that the best you've got?'

With the ball he was very aggressive and he always had something to say. He mellowed as time went on, but he always enjoyed bowling on my green tops. Being a middle-order player, he often got in when the early colour had gone and he scored a lot of runs too, whereas Alf was basically a bowler pure and simple, who clumped it occasionally.

Their brother Harold was a decent cricketer too, but never got established as a county bowler with his leg spin.

Tommy Mitchell?

Tommy was perhaps the most colourful character of them all. He could be very abrupt with some people and I don't think he had much time for me, because I prepared wickets for seam bowlers rather than him. I was a young lad at the time and he didn't think I knew better than him, an older, experienced professional. Maybe he was right. But he was a fine bowler and probably turned it more on an unhelpful wicket than any of his contemporaries. An odd one might go astray, but when he got it right, he was lethal.

He was quite a joker but wasn't so keen when the joke was played on him. He was also very aware of his value and turned down a return to the county after the war because he could make more money at the pit. Will Taylor offered to make the money up for him, but Tommy said it was a matter of principle and went into the leagues to get extra money.

There's a lot of stories about Tommy and not all of them are printable. There was one time when at the end of a county season, he was offered a short-term engagement to go as professional to Blackpool for a few games, where he was a great success.

Sometime that October, his wife contacted Will Taylor to ask when Tom's engagement there was going to finish. Mr Taylor didn't know what to say, as the season had finished several weeks earlier!

Bill Copson?

He was a very good bowler, but Bill didn't have much to do with me. I was a young groundsman and he had played for England.

Later in life we got on better, when he became a first-class umpire, but in his playing days our paths rarely crossed.

Who were the characters of that side?

[Laughs] Oh, they all were. There's some stories that you couldn't possibly print I'm afraid. There was one player who was released by Mr Taylor because of a supposed dalliance with the daughter of a senior club official. Nothing happened, they only dated, but Mr Taylor disapproved and the player had to go. He was even taken off team pictures of the period.

It has never been mentioned before, but everyone knew what had happened and it was a waste, because the bloke could play and might have been a fine cricketer for us.

There was another too, who wasn't the most sociable. When he got a car he had the back seats taken out of it so he didn't get asked to give lifts!

But Denis Smith and Stan Worthington were my favourites. We were firm friends for the rest of their days. As groundsman, you don't really get all that close to many people, but they were wonderful men.

Funnily enough, my wife knew all the wives very well because she cleaned the ladies' toilets at the ground. We were invited to social events, but that was generally the only time that I had close dealings with the players, with a few exceptions.

In 1939 war broke out. What did that mean for you?

I was in the army for six full years, from 1940 to 1946. I was N/T Sergeant in the 14 Sherwood Foresters and served in north Africa as part of the Desert Rats, as well as fighting at Anzio, among many others.

It was terrible and I lost a lot of friends. I made a lot too though and we worked together, helped each other and somehow I got through it. Six long years. A lot of good people didn't get through it.

What happened to the ground in wartime?

I'll tell you. I was in Stan Worthington's house at Mickleover when war was declared on the Sunday at 12 o'clock, with Alf Pope, as it happened. When I got to the ground on the Monday morning, Will Taylor asked me to go to his office and said I was no longer required. I was effectively chopped off at the knees and they made a chap named Jackie Mays in charge of the ground. They could get him to do the job cheaper, you see.

I did all I could do and went and got a job with the parks department under Mr Wells at Alvaston Park Lake, until I was conscripted in 1940.

And what happened after the war – how did you come back?

I came back on a month's leave in August 1946. At the camp I was at, there were five other cricket groundsmen and they were all brought home in the June of that year, to return to their former duties.

There was a match on at Derby in the August, a three-day game against Gloucestershire and I was asked to go and see Will Taylor. I asked him why he hadn't applied to have me brought home in the June with the others and he was very evasive.

He asked me what I thought of the wicket and I told him that the game wouldn't last three days as it was sub-standard. The condition of that wicket, the square and the ground as a whole was shocking. I was right, it finished inside two days!

I was asked to come back and I had to choose between the cricket club and an opportunity at the parks department on a similar wage. I opted for the cricket club, but to be honest I wondered many times over the years whether I made the right decision.

> **The late 1940s saw a fresh crop of players emerge, spearheaded by the legendary Les Jackson and Cliff Gladwin. Can you tell me about them?**

Cliff was from Doe Lea, near Chesterfield, and travelled through to games or to the ground with his very good friend, Eric Marsh. He was a lovely man Cliff, but he could get annoyed if people dropped catches off him and woe betide them if they misfielded.

He was a very fine and accurate bowler, but after he retired from playing he went to Lilleshall to get his cricket coaching badge. He failed and it finished his interest in cricket, especially when people who weren't in the same league as a player managed to pass.

He took to growing chrysanthemums and won a lot of prizes in doing so, while he also ran a sports shop in Chesterfield for a few years.

The last time that I saw him, he came to me with an engine for a Qualcast lawnmower and asked if I had any contacts at the company, who might help to get it repaired.

I knew the managing director there very well and he took one look at it and chucked it in a skip! Then he gave me a brand new one to give to Cliff.

He passed away soon afterwards, far too early, really.

Les came along for his trial at the County Ground and Harry Elliott asked him to bowl against the skipper, Eddie Gothard. He'd already made it known to people that he didn't rate Les at all and played a few balls fairly easily – and Eddie wasn't a great bat.

Now, Harry Elliott rated Les and told him he wasn't bowling quick enough. So Les started to bend his back, rattled Eddie's stumps a few times and bruised him a few times more. That was really the start of it all for him.

When he first started he used to have to get up at 5.30am and get a bus to Chesterfield from Whitwell. Then he'd get a train to Derby and then another bus to the ground. He'd have his breakfast in the end room of the pavilion and did this until he had enough money to afford a car.

He made his debut for Derbyshire at Abbeydale Park in Sheffield against Kent in 1947 – that was one of our grounds then. He turned up with his boots and cricket clothes in a carrier bag. He didn't do anything special but he took a wicket.

The following year it all started for Les and he became the leader of the attack for the next 15 years. He was a lovely man and I never had a cross word with him.

You know, one day he came off at the end of play and took off a cricket boot, then tossed it to me. It was full of blood.

'I'd a nail come through the sole this morning Wal…can you get it sorted for me?'

He'd bowled nearly all day, with a nail sticking in his foot! Can you imagine them doing that today?

I borrowed someone's bicycle and took it to a cobbler on East Street.

He was just closing up, but when I told him I'd got Les Jackson's boot for repair, he opened up again and sorted it, so I could take it back to him for the next day's play.

It wasn't just about sorting the ground, for Walter.

The era of uncovered wickets must have been challenging for groundsmen?

Ooh, yes! We used to cover an area 4ft 6in in front of the popping crease and the rest was left open to the elements. The umpires had to decide when play was possible and the bowlers were always more keen to get on with it than the batsmen!

There was a touring side playing at Chesterfield and the rest came to Derby to practice in the nets. They were fine in the morning, but Jack Ikin from Lancashire, who was doing some coaching, asked me to leave the covers off when they went for their lunch, even though the rain was threatening.

Well, it duly came down for about an hour and when they went back out the wickets were 'sticky'. They didn't like it at all.

Who were the stand-outs, apart from Cliff and Les, in that team?

Arnold Hamer was a fantastic batsman. I loved watching him bat and he lodged with my wife and I on occasions. I was with him when he got released and he was really upset. He cried and I could understand why. He deserved better after what he'd done for the county, although he was getting on a bit by that time.

John Kelly was another nice bat. He was a quiet lad, but a good team man. I remember him getting into a row with Denis Smith one time, just for giving a woman a lift in his car! There was nothing going on, but Denis reckoned he shouldn't have been doing it, that it wasn't professional.

Did the batsmen say much to you about the seam-friendly pitches of the period?

They used to say, 'Leave the grass on it for Les, Wal.' They just wanted to win and realised that the more was in it for bowlers, the better chance we had. After the first hour the green had gone and if you could bat, you could score runs.

Albert Lightfoot of Northamptonshire was a character and I remember him telling me that I should put some holes in the wicket at the end of the day, so they could have a game of snooker! That's how good it was.

Mind you, I caught him that night, about eight o'clock it was. They were round having a drink at the Grandstand Hotel and Albert came on to the ground. I caught him peeing on the wicket…he wanted a bit of life in it for their bowlers!

We were good mates, Albert and me, so I didn't report it.

Players used to drink together then, of course, and sometimes the journalists joined them. I remember giving John Arlott a lift to the station after his last visit to the County Ground. They'd presented him with a bottle of whiskey and he was pleased with that.

Did you retain involvement in other grounds?

No, I had enough to do at Derby. They all had a groundsman and if he asked for advice, he got it. All I had to do was make sure the stands were taken around the grounds and I had to put them up and take them down again.

I had all the pieces lettered and numbered and I could put four up in about an hour, but if others did it, they took a lot longer. Sometimes these stands were rented out to places and I remember taking them to Repton School on occasion and setting them up there.

If we played at Buxton I got a couple of ground staff lads to go with me. We used to get Brooks Removals from Derby to take them up and we'd go with them in the van.

How did your budget change over the years?

I didn't really have one! I used to buy marl, which was quite expensive, and fertiliser. There was a farmer on the committee for a long time, Bob Green, and he used to send me bags of fertiliser as he knew I didn't have much money to buy what I needed.

I remember one time a committee man came and told me that I'd spent hardly any money on the ground. I told him straight, 'That's because there is no money.' I used to scrounge whatever I needed.

People would come and drop me a lorry of top soil and I'd give them a drink.

That's how I operated and how I kept going as long. It was the same with lorries of tarmac for the road into the ground – give them a drink and they'd see you right.

One time I 'borrowed' a flock of sheep from a local farmer. It was ahead of a visit from a civil servant, who wanted to see we justified getting agricultural diesel, which we got free. Once he had seen the sheep and signed to say we could get it, the sheep went back! I knew all the dodges.

I saved the club a fortune over the years and hardly anyone appreciated or understood what I did and how I did it.

Hardly anyone?

Except for Eddie Gothard. He was a gentleman. He used to hold lavish parties at his home, Mickleover House, and my wife and I were always first on the guest list. Denis Smith, too. We were regulars because Eddie acknowledged what both of us did for the club. Mind you, he had a dog named Jim and you'd to watch, because he'd bite your backside if you turned your back on him!

One time Denis and I went out there and Eddie had a blockage in his toilet – he had a septic tank in the garden. Denis and I had to find out where it was blocked, following the pipe. We were tapping away, tapping away – and then this thing burst! We were covered in you know what…we mended the pipe, got it all sorted for him. He was a gentleman, Mr Gothard, and made sure we were rewarded appropriately for it.

I just wish he hadn't been as old when he made his debut in first-class cricket.

He wasn't a great cricketer at that level, but by crikey he had guts – AND he was one of the few men who could say that he bowled Donald Bradman.

What was your salary as groundsman?

Not enough! When I came to Derby from Chesterfield, it was on the understanding that I would get £5 a week. I got three. When I came out of the army after the war, they said they were giving me a raise and took me to £4. It was chicken feed, though the club never had any money, of course.

That's why I used to do so many 'foreigners' – extra jobs, or 'homers'. There's not a ground in Derbyshire that I haven't worked on over the years, but I only got told off for going on one.

There's an unwritten rule in cricket that as a groundsman you don't go on someone else's ground without asking permission first. I got told off at Darley Dale for doing that and it was right. You had to wait for an invitation. I'd have given anyone who went to look at mine short shrift, if they'd not asked in advance.

Who were the players you most remember from the 1960s and 1970s?

Ian Hall was a grand bloke. I knew his father, Ben, who was a school master, very well. His grandfather used to come and give me a hand at Cromford Meadows, where I did a lot of work with Ray Buxton, the father of Derbyshire all-rounder Ian. My wife used to go away picking blackberries with Mrs Buxton, Ian's mother – we had no end of jam each year!

TV personality Leslie Crowther used to bring a showbiz team to play at Cromford each year. He was a keen cricketer and the games were usually well-attended. It was at one of those that Ray Buxton sadly died of a heart attack. It was a terrible shame. Going to their house was like going home.

Ian Buxton was another lovely man. I was saddened to hear of his death a few years back.

Peter Gibbs wrote a play, *Arthur's Hallowed Ground*, in which the lead character is a groundsman.

That was me. He sat where you are right now and wrote it.

So you saw it then? What did you think?

I liked it. He had me off to a 'T'. Oh aye, it was Walter all right. There were a few things that were added in – I never had a dog, for example, but the things he did…I used to go and hide myself away, keep out of the road when I had the chance. Especially when Will Taylor was looking for me!

Author note: I also spoke to Peter Gibbs, who confirmed that Walter was the inspiration for the piece, but that it was a composite of others he encountered over the years.

When Will Taylor finally retired, Major Douglas Carr took over, brother of Donald. Were relations between the two of you better?

Major Carr had been in the army, just like me. He always treated me with respect and we got on famously.

It was in that period that we started to run advertisements. We never had any at Derby, so I went to Harry Bedford, the manager of the Gaumont Cinema, and asked him to make me a banner of forthcoming cinema attractions.

This would have been in the mid-1960s. I fastened it on to the railings and it was very successful.

Then the club cottoned on to the idea and started charging for advertising boards around the ground.

They did all right out of it, but the cinema couldn't afford it, so stopped. I lost out on a complimentary ticket that I had, but my son used to use that and go with his mates, so I didn't lose too much!

You were groundsman of the year in 1970. It must have been a thrill to get it in the club's centenary year?

I was. I knew nothing about it, until the Lancashire chairman stood up at the end of the centenary dinner and announced that I'd won it. I was sat at my table and felt quite overwhelmed after all those years. I'd to go to Edgbaston to collect the award.

What was the prize?

I got £100 and the trophy for a year. It then got passed on to the winner the following year. My name went up on a board at Lord's too, so it was a nice honour to be recognised in such a way.

Eddie Barlow came along and changed things in the mid-1970s. How did you get on with him?

He was a lovely bloke and a terrific player. I liked him a lot and he told me to keep preparing wickets the way that I always had. By that stage there was a clear divide between players and ground staff, but Eddie was a fine man and did a lot for the club.

Were things as good in that era?

Oh yes. By that stage old Walter normally got his way with things! There were some good lads around at that time. Geoff Miller was one – he came from near where I was born – and so too was Mike Hendrick. He used to like my wickets, because there was plenty in them for him for the first few overs.

Colin Tunnicliffe was another who I got on well with. A good bowler and I knew his father very well. In fact I bought a couple of cars off him over the years, when he worked for Kennings, as a car salesman.

WALTER GOODYEAR (1938–1982)

▎ When did you finish with Derbyshire?

[In] 1982. I was 65 and to be honest I was glad to get out. Mind you, I didn't retire. I took on three jobs – groundsman at Belper, at Quarndon and at Stone, in Staffordshire. The money I got from the three balanced the books – I was no worse off than I was at Derby.

▎ Do you still see any of the old players?

Harold Rhodes and his wife pop over regularly – they're very good to me – and I see Bob Taylor and his wife from time to time. Ian Buxton used to come over, so did Les Jackson, but I have outlived most of them.

▎ Were you a keen gardener outside of work, with a bowling green for a lawn?

I hated gardening, always have. Too much like work. I kept my garden tidy, but that's all.

▎ Only Will Taylor has exceeded your time at the club. That must be a source of pride?

Well, I only joined the club in 1938 as my time at Chesterfield didn't really count. It was 44 years, less the war years. So only 38 years.

Edwin Smith
(1951–1971)

EDWIN SMITH is a Derbyshire legend. It is not a status that one acquires easily; in Edwin's case it was down to bowling over 13,000 overs for the county, over a career that ran from 1951 to 1971.

He took 100 wickets in a season once, in 1955, but spinners rarely do that on Derbyshire pitches and certainly not when you're coming on after the legendary Cliff Gladwin and Les Jackson. Edwin normally got on as second change after Derek Morgan and there were many times when there wasn't much left by that point.

When the great pair retired, they were replaced by Harold Rhodes and Brian Jackson. More bowlers who often took out the top order and a good part of the middle, leaving Edwin to feast on the scraps that remained. If they failed, it was usually a good batting wicket and his role would then become that of stock bowler, keeping it quiet, but not missing the chance of winkling one out with his off-spin variations.

There were certain tracks around the county circuit where spin was the road to success, of course, and that's where he was expected to cash in – and usually did. He took five in an innings on 51 occasions and year after year took between 60 and 90 wickets, ending his career with 1,217 of them at under 25 runs each. As for the economy rate, he went for less than two and a half runs an over, the benchmark of parsimony by which the very best Derbyshire bowlers have been judged.

I saw Edwin bowl on many occasions, but wish I could turn the clock back and see him again with the benefit of experience. I was 12 when he retired and in the naivety of youth was more taken by the pace of Alan Ward and Harold Rhodes, little realising the consummate guile that made Edwin one of the best off-spin bowlers in the country, this at a time when there were a lot more of them to admire and enjoy than there are today.

If he was playing now he would walk into the England team, as a cunning bowler who imparted strong spin between his index and middle fingers. He was a master of flight, line and length and when you're considering the greatest Derbyshire spinners, then he has to be included in the discussions. It is a tribute to his skill that when we signed the great Indian spinner Srinivasan Venkataraghavan in the mid-1970s, my Dad watched the new overseas signing for a few overs then shook his head.

'He's all right,' he said. 'But he's no Edwin Smith.' Praise indeed.

He could bat, too, and often fought bravely in a rearguard action. He regularly got between 500 and 700 runs a summer, had a safe pair of hands and ended up as county coach for several seasons. A man of parts, for sure.

He is also thoroughly engaging company. He has a ready and regular laugh and a remarkable recall for the players and events of the past, together with an astonishing collection of memorabilia. Only seven Derbyshire bowlers have taken more than 1,000 first-class wickets and of them, only Edwin and Derek Morgan survive. Through the time spent researching his 2015 biography, which came from this interview, I got to know both him and his wife Jean very well.

It was my very great pleasure to do so.

Edwin, you were born at Grassmoor, near Chesterfield in 1934 and live there today. Did you never move away?

Yes, we did. My wife and I were married in 1956 and moved on Good Friday, 1957, to Ashgate. We lived there for 41 years, but moved back to Grassmoor in 1998, as we'd seen a bungalow we liked and thought it was the right time to move, with our daughters moving out.

What are your earliest cricket memories?

I suppose that would be 1949, when I was playing for Grassmoor second team. I never usually bowled and then we got to the last three games of the season and the skipper, Wilf Hawkins, asked me to do so. I marked out a run to bowl medium pace, but he told me, 'No – bowl off spin, like you do in the nets.'

In the first match I took 4-0, in the second I took 5-17 and in the third I took 6-10. After that I was seen as a bowler and everything developed from there.

When did you first start getting coaching?

There was some basic coaching at Grassmoor, but it wasn't until I got to the county side that I got what you'd call 'proper' coaching. In 1950, my bowling carried on where I had left off in 1949 and I went to Clay Cross for trials with Derbyshire under-17s, which were being conducted by the county's former wicketkeeper, Harry Elliott.

I played against Yorkshire under-17s and took 1-10 in 11 overs. Will Taylor, the club secretary, was there and he offered me a three-month trial with the club. I actually made my first-team debut for the county before I played for the second team. That doesn't happen very often!

That was against Hampshire at Chesterfield in June 1951, when you were just 17. What are your memories of that game?

The players were very welcoming and they all did their best to put me at ease. I had a decent bowl and finished up with 19-3-67-1. My first wicket was Vic Cannings, who I had caught at deep square leg by John Kelly. It was all very exciting and I just hoped I would get another crack of it before too long.

You didn't play another game until August of that year, in an extraordinary game against Worcestershire, also at Queens Park?

Oh, it was a right turner! For some reason Bert 'Dusty' Rhodes didn't do well on it, so they gave me a go and it started to grip and turn. I bowled Don Kenyon when they were 53/1 and then batsmen kept coming in and going out quickly and it was hard to take it all in. They were all out for 78.

I remember Cliff Gladwin coming up to me, perhaps after I had my fifth or sixth wicket and saying, 'Cometh the hour, Edwin, cometh the man.' He'd used that before, when playing for England before the war during a tight finish in South Africa, but I was overjoyed that all this was happening to me at 17, in my second game in first-class cricket.

I finished with 8-21 in ten overs, but we still got beaten by over a hundred runs – and I was dropped for the next game!

You replaced Bert Rhodes in the Derbyshire side. How much help was he to a young spinner?

To be honest, I didn't see much of him. He was pretty much winding down as a first-class cricketer and retired in 1952, becoming a very good and well-respected umpire. He had been an excellent player, though losing six summers to the war, and the battle to replace him in the side was between me and a left-arm spinner named Reg Carter. Bert was, somewhat strangely, recalled to the side for a short time after his retirement, yet slowly but surely I was seen as the first-choice spin bowler.

Who else helped you in those crucial formative years?

There were a lot of people. Denis Smith was senior professional when I started and he was perfect for the role. Then there was Charlie Elliott and of course Cliff Gladwin. Cliff was a very tetchy player on the field and played to win, but he was a lovely man off it who couldn't do enough to help you.

Denis was a character and his gruff persona hid a mischievous sense of humour. I remember he came back to a hotel we were staying in at one away game and told me to come with him to the local snooker hall up the road. Apparently there was a lad there who fancied himself as a bit of a player and had been building himself up to anyone who cared to listen. Denis told him he had a mate who would give him a good game, knowing that I played a lot and was a pretty good player.

When we got back there, the bloke had scarpered!

So you played a lot of snooker?

Oh yes! I started playing for Grassmoor in 1948 and still do. My highest break is 130. Over the years I have won dozens of competitions, trophies, holidays – the lot!

There was reputedly a strong Derbyshire dressing room at that time?

There was – and people were not slow in giving opinions if they felt it would improve you as a player, or the side as a whole. But it was a happy place and we all got on so well. Not like more recent Derbyshire dressing rooms, when there seemed to be people leaving every winter and they seemed to be falling out all the time over the slightest thing.

We went away each September and looked forward to seeing each other again when we started back in the spring. There weren't too many changes to the side in the 1950s, so you knew you'd see people again the next summer. People didn't move around at that time.

Were you ever tempted to move?

There was an opportunity for me to do so in the mid-1950s, when Jock Livingston asked me to go and play for Northamptonshire. The wickets there would have been ideal for a spinner, but I have always been a strong believer in people playing for the county of their birth. I'd have had to qualify to play for them and I never wanted to play for anyone other than Derbyshire.

Were you conscious of the need to give nothing away as a Derbyshire bowler? Were things different for you as a spinner than for the seamers?

We were, yes. Cliff used to say that if we scored 250 we'd win more than we lost, because he and Les were often unplayable, especially when rain fell on the uncovered wickets of the day. Derek Morgan was an excellent first change, then there was my off spin and Donald Carr's slow left-arm. We fancied our chances in the field, but sometimes came up short with the bat and that cost us at times.

That attack was rarely 'collared' though and there was no such thing as cheap runs against us.

There were a lot of good spinners at that time though?

There were so many, particularly off-spinners. You'd struggle to name three good ones in the county game today, but there were three at Gloucestershire at the same time! John Mortimore, David Allen and 'Bomber' Wells. They were all very fine bowlers. Tom Goddard had only recently retired there too.

Then there was the great Jim Laker at Surrey, as well as the very underrated Eric Bedser. Yorkshire had Ray Illingworth and Brian Close, Middlesex had Fred Titmus and Lancashire had Roy Tattersall.

They were all top bowlers and it was a magical time to play the game.

Did you get together at the end of a day's play?

Oh yes. There was a spin bowlers' union, I suppose. We'd sit down with a pint and talk over the day's play, chat about different players on the circuit and how we bowled to them. You learned a lot from these sessions – as you had to do, picking the brains of people who were so good at their craft, of course.

The next few years were steady consolidation and you got your cap in 1954. A big moment?

I got used to the idea of being a county player and getting paid for it. I took regular wickets, but I was also under no misapprehension that I had to perform. I got my cap for consistent performances and it was a very proud day, but it didn't make a lot of difference money-wise. In fact, there was a school of thought that you were better off without it, as you otherwise got match money.

When I got my cap, it took my salary to £400 a summer. My wife earned more than that, working in the weaving shed at Robinson's in Chesterfield!

Through the 1950s you got 70–90 wickets regularly at mid-20s average. Good going for a bowler, when there was often little left after Cliff and Les?

That's absolutely right! There was one wicket at Northampton in the mid-50s and when we got there it looked really green. There was little difference from the rest of the square and the outfield. When we went out to see it up close, it was just grass clippings on top of sand. It was obviously going to turn square and I fancied my chances.

The thing was, so did Les and Cliff. Les bowled from 11.30am to 12.50pm and when Cliff got a little tired, he cut down his pace and bowled off-cutters, so I didn't get on at all!

For many who never saw you, tell me about your action/ delivery/style.

I used to take a six-pace run-up and liked to flight the ball and get good purchase. I used to turn it quite a bit, but had a lot of trouble with my spinning finger, as a lot did at that time.

You don't hear so much of that today.

That's because most of them don't turn it. They roll it, rather than tweaking it between their first two fingers. Jim Laker had the same problem and we used a similar method to sort it. I developed a callus on my middle finger, but the inside of my index finger used to split. There was an old woman in our village, Mrs Hart, who had lost the tip of one of her fingers and she told me to use Friars' Balsam.

I used to put it on my finger each night and it used to harden the skin, so you could bowl without too much pain the next day.

What was it like to play in the same side as Cliff and Les?

It was really special and you were conscious that you were playing alongside the best. They were very different as people. Like I said earlier, Cliff could be very aggressive and abrupt on the pitch, but was lovely off it. Les was always the same, on and off the pitch and the two of us became very good friends, right up to the time of his death.

Les was always philosophical if things went wrong. Cliff would swear if you dropped a catch off him, but Les just shrugged his shoulders and carried on as if it never happened.

They both just wanted to bowl. I've seen Les bowl all morning and Cliff finish with the new ball then switch to off-cutters and even off spin! They were very fit and would have happily bowled all day. Cliff would come off the field at intervals and know exactly how many runs he had conceded and how many overs he had bowled. He encouraged us to do the same and reckoned that if you couldn't remember you had conceded too many.

Both were outstanding cricketers and men. They helped to settle you down as a young player and would come up to me, tell me to take my time, get my field right and not to worry. It meant a lot to me when I was a young lad of 17 and they continued to be helpful, even as I gained in experience. I have to admit, I was a little overawed and star-struck at the start, though!

What was it like as a professional cricketer in the 1950s? What was your journey to a home game?

I used to have to get a bus from Grassmoor to Chesterfield at 7.40am and then get the so-called 'pigeon train' to Derby. It stopped at Clay Cross, Belper, Ambergate and Duffield and it was really slow. It got me to Derby around 9.40am and then I had to get a bus outside the station into Derby town centre and then another that took me to Nottingham Road and the ground.

I used to get there around 10.15am, if it all went to plan. And of course, at the end of the day, you had to do it all again, in reverse! Les Jackson got a car in 1956 and then Cliff Gladwin got one and they used to give me lifts. Les in particular was very good from that point of view.

I had a Lambretta scooter for a while, but it wasn't easy, and probably not very safe, travelling on that. I used to give my wife Jean a lift on it when I went to play snooker and she would sit on the back, holding my cue like Boadicea!

What was Denis Smith like as a coach? I've heard a few stories about him!

He was gruff and you soon knew if you had done something wrong, but his bark was definitely worse than his bite. He was a very good player and senior professional in his time and that was carried through to his coaching role.

You didn't mess Denis around but he was a great help to me. I liked him a lot.

> **Who was the best skipper you played under? In a 20-year career with Derbyshire, you saw a few!**

Guy Willatt, without question. He was a messy bloke in the dressing room and used to shake his gear out of his cricket bag on to the floor and it was all crumpled, stained and creased! But he was a terrific captain and set some wonderful, imaginative fields for everyone. He was a good batsman too.

As players we had total confidence in him and that was a big thing. Cliff wanted to win at everything he did and was never slow to speak out, but he respected Guy Willatt and that said a lot about his captaincy.

Donald Carr was a good skipper too, but sometimes we felt that he thought that if Les and Cliff couldn't bowl teams out, it wasn't going to happen. He could be slow to bowl himself too and that cost us on occasions.

> **Through the 1950s, Derbyshire were a good side but just failed to win a title. What prevented that?**

We were short of a top-class batsman. Arnold Hamer was a fine player, so was Donald, although his availability lessened through the 1950s. John Kelly was a good bat too. Laurie Johnson always looked such a good player, but it took him a long time to score the runs that he should have done.

He had all the shots, but sometimes started playing them too early and got himself out when he should have been cashing in and making runs. Derek Morgan was outstanding at seven and George Dawkes, our wicketkeeper, made runs quickly at eight, but we needed someone who we could really depend on, especially on the uncovered wickets.

Arnold was the best batsman and very good to watch. He was a useful off-spinner too. I remember in 1955 we played Scotland and I took the first nine wickets, then dropped a caught-and-bowled that would have got me all ten.

He shook his head and said to me, 'If you don't want it, I'll have it' – and he did, the next over!

It was a tough school.

> **In that 1955 season you took over 100 wickets. Were there ever any suggestions then or at other times about national selection?**

I was apparently close to selection for an England 'B' tour, but I couldn't go. Working down the mines, I was in a 'reserved occupation' which exempted me from military service. Had I gone to Pakistan, I'd then have been called up and been lost to Derbyshire for some time.

It was funny, whenever we played the RAF at that time, their captain, Alan Shireff, used to come up and ask me when I was going to join up and play with them. They had a strong side in the 1950s, with players like Peter Parfitt and Fred Trueman, but my work in the mines kept me out of their clutches!

Then in 1966 I was bowling really well and was top of the averages for a while in my benefit year. I took 4-9 before lunch against Gloucestershire and then pulled a muscle in my side. Our physio, Sam Weaver, was told to get me fit for the next game, so Colin Cowdrey could have a good look at me, with a view to my playing against the West Indies.

He couldn't manage it and I didn't play. Mind you, I was perhaps lucky, as they had some good batsmen!

> **At the start of the 1960s, the club had lost a lot of good players. Did expectations change?**

Not really. We still had a good attack. Les Jackson was replaced by his namesake Brian and no one enjoyed facing either of them, nor Harold Rhodes. Derek Morgan still got his wickets and I was pretty consistent.

The problem continued to be the batting. We had plenty of good players and in the middle of the decade, David Smith came along to partner Peter Gibbs, who was a lovely bat. Ian Hall was a steady player and once got a hundred in each innings against Kent. Laurie Johnson continued to fascinate and frustrate in equal measure.

We just didn't bat as a team. One player would score runs and the rest largely failed. Consistency remained an issue for us as a batting side throughout my playing career.

Were games well attended in that era?

Oh, yes! We always got bigger crowds at Chesterfield than Derby, but you only got to see players if you went to matches, as there was little cricket on television.

When Les Jackson had his benefit match at Chesterfield against Yorkshire in 1957, there were 10,000 there on each of the first two days and 7,000 on the third. Les won us the game with about ten minutes to go, getting Bob Platt caught at slip by Laurie Johnson and it was fantastic. The crowd was rows deep on the mound towards the bandstand, as far as you could see. I doubt those at the back saw much of the play! Then the tiered seating, that we used to transport between Derby and Chesterfield in lorries, was full to capacity and they were sitting and standing everywhere there was space.

Was that the same seating that was at Chesterfield until relatively recently?

It was. When I was on the ground staff we used to have to put that seating up before every game and if there were nets, we used to put them up each time as well. On a Monday morning we used to put up four nets around the wickets that Walter had cut at Derby. Then we'd brush them and they'd be rolled and cut again before use.

We'd then do chores around the ground and practice ourselves. Finally, between 5.30pm and 7.30pm, we had to bowl at the members who turned up for a 20-minute net.

Presumably Chesterfield was your favourite ground?

I think it was everyone's favourite. The wickets were good, the games were well-attended and we'd some memorable matches. Being local, it was always very special for me.

Someone told me recently that I had taken more wickets at Chesterfield than any other bowler, which is something I am very proud of.

Who were the best players of spin bowling in your career?

One who stands out was Keith Fletcher, but both Doug Insole and Trevor Bailey at Essex made you really work for wickets. All of them played spin well. Peter May was equally at home against pace and spin and loved to dominate. There were two left-handers too – Peter and Dick Richardson at Worcestershire – who played off spin very well. They both took good strides and swept or lapped against the spin. Very hard to bowl against and fine players.

One more for you – Harry Pilling. He was a small player [5ft 3in] and conventional lengths were no use to him. You had to bowl a completely different one, or he would be quick to drive you. If you dropped short he was a terrific cutter and puller and was a very fine servant to Lancashire.

> **You had two fine wicketkeepers in your time at the club. Tell me about George Dawkes and Bob Taylor.**

They were both very fine players. George was a lovely man who gave great service to Derbyshire. He had a good pair of hands and he could hit a ball very hard on his day. He had a great sense of humour too.

I remember one time that we played Yorkshire at Hull and I bowled a ball that pitched on leg and then turned sharply, beating George and going down to the boundary for four byes.

Then we heard a voice from the boundary.

'Hey George. Do'st tha want a brick wall built, lad?'

Bob was simply different class though. From his first game in the senior side, he looked like he belonged. He was another who was recommended to the club by Cliff Gladwin, who could spot a player. It's just a pity that his batting didn't come on as we hoped, as he was a tidy player who might have flourished in a better batting side.

As a wicketkeeper, I've still not seen anyone better.

> **In the 1960s, the one-day game came in. You only played eight one-day games between 1963 and 1971. Why was that?**

There was a feeling at that time that medium-pace bowlers won you one-day matches. There were a few good bowlers of that type around, people like Tom Cartwright and Derek Shackleton, but we were perhaps the only county that relied pretty much exclusively on seam in that type of cricket, at least until Fred Swarbrook came on the scene, who was deemed a better bat.

It was daft. Brian Langford at Somerset was the first and still only bowler whose eight-over spell cost no runs and plenty of counties had similar success with their spin bowlers. Yet we did everything differently.

Would you like to have played more one-day cricket? What would your game plan have been?

Definitely. I would have bowled a full length from around the wicket and aimed at leg and middle. They'd have had to take me on and cleared my long on, or swept me, then my midwicket and deep square leg would come into play and there was a danger of leg before wicket, of course, if they missed.

I'd have just bowled normal flight – no firing it in, just trying to beat them in the flight and hopefully getting them into bother as it turned. You see, most spinners today just roll it. When I started and throughout my career, you used to see spinners really tweak it between their fingers, the purchase affecting the amount of turn, of course. I didn't try to turn every ball – I had the arm ball, as most of us did, which is pretty much what they call the doosra today. But batters knew that I could turn it sharply and sometimes the thought of that was all it needed.

Have any Derbyshire players ever asked your advice on bowling spin?

No, and I find that quite sad. No one seems to ask your opinion now. The only Derbyshire spinner who ever asked me questions and for help was Greg Smith, before he went to Essex. He asked me to show him how I did it and worked on spinning it more himself. Most of the rest just roll it, as I've said.

Even these Derbyshire lads who went to India to spin bowling clinics – I'd have been happy to work with them and give advice and they didn't need to go to the other side of the world to get it.

Did the other players take easily to you becoming county coach in 1971?

Most of them did. Alan Ward didn't, because he thought he knew everything as an England player and we clashed a time or two. But I subscribed to a view that cricketers, by the time they reach county level, don't need too much coaching. I know that's at odds with what's happening at the club now, but the likes of Geoff Miller, Colin Tunnicliffe, Tony Borrington and so on knew their games. They just needed their confidence boosted at times and a little help if they got out of form.

When you retired, you went into the leagues?

I did. I went into the Yorkshire Council League and in my first year after retiring I took 99 wickets at six runs each! I won the bowling prize and played there for some time.

There were a few good players in that league. I recommended John Walters to Derbyshire and he became a useful all-rounder for a few seasons, while I also tried to get the county to sign Steve Oldham. They were too slow and he ended up being a regular for Yorkshire for a number of seasons, before joining Derbyshire towards the end of his career.

I have to ask you these last three questions – who was the best spinner – Muralitharan or Warne? How did they compare to earlier giants?

I'd have to say Warne, because I was never convinced by Muralitharan's action. When I think back to how Harold Rhodes was treated, it makes me quite sad, actually.

Warne was outstanding because he was so accurate and used his head. But there were great leg-spinners in my time, people like Bruce Dooland at Nottinghamshire and Richie Benaud. George Tribe, who bowled left-arm chinamen, was another wonderful bowler. It's all relative, but Warne was undoubtedly one of the game's greats.

And who was the fastest? Les Jackson, Harold Rhodes or Alan Ward?

Oh, Harold, without a doubt. In his prime he could be frighteningly quick and there were few who fancied batting against him when it was a quick track.

Les was quick enough and very awkward. He got it up into people's ribcages and there was none of the protection that they have now, so he was a handful. There was one game at Chesterfield when he was bowling at Colin Cowdrey and it was really going through quickly. I went up to him and told him so and he said that he was trying to see how quick he really could bowl. More than quick enough, was my answer!

Alan was quick but didn't play long enough. If conditions were in his favour he would bend his back and be quick. But not as fast as Harold was in his prime and for nowhere near long enough. There were too many times when he simply didn't fancy it.

And finally, the best Derbyshire bowler?

That's easy. Les Jackson. Even when you consider a lot of very good bowlers over the years, Les was head and shoulders above them all. [Taking] 1,700 wickets at 17 each tells you that.

I'll tell you another couple of things about him. I used to field at forward short leg for Les and you never felt in danger, because he was so accurate. I would stand there and hear the ball 'whistle' through the air on its way down and I was always likely to get a catch, because his natural length was making the batsman play and he got bounce that kept short legs interested.

Then in the mid-1960s, we played a game at Chesterfield against the Rothmans Cavaliers.

I saw that game! It was 1968?

That would be right. Les had been retired for five years and he played in that match and opened the bowling for the only time with his namesake, Brian. He bowled 9-1-19-2. Ted Dexter was batting and he called me over from midwicket, where I was fielding.

'Look at this, Edwin,' he said.

The wicket, at the end to which Les had been bowling, had a solid patch on it, about six inches long and 15 inches wide. Every single ball he'd bowled had hit that perfect length and it was a remarkable example of the seam bowler's craft, from someone who hadn't played a first-class game in five years.

EDWIN SMITH (1951–1971)

He was a great bowler, a wonderful team man and a fine friend. You know, in all the years I played with him, I never heard him swear on a cricket pitch.

Harold Rhodes (1953–1969)

HAROLD RHODES was an outstanding bowler for Derbyshire and almost certainly would have been for England, but for what was effectively a 'witch hunt' against him over a period from the late 1950s onwards.

He had an elbow that hyper-extended. It wasn't bent, like a dart player, as he let the ball go. His elbow actually went past straight, giving perhaps an extra 'whip' to the ball as he let it go in a classical style. His action was as smooth as gossamer, something a thrower could never manage in a million years of trying. He was quick, he was accurate and he jagged the ball around on a helpful wicket as well as any Derbyshire seamer has ever done.

Any bowler who finishes a career with over 1,000 wickets at less than 20 runs each has got to have something special and anyone who saw Harold Rhodes knew that he was just that. He was one of my first cricketing heroes; I wanted to bowl like Harold and keep wicket like Bob Taylor, the stand-out players in the Derbyshire side that I first saw in the late 1960s. Sadly, in trying to play like one of them, I fell well short of the standard of both, but it didn't stop me trying.

I was thrilled when Harold very kindly accepted my request for an interview, something that took me back many years to when I got his autograph at Chesterfield, as he left the field during a game against Yorkshire. I never imagined then that I would get an opportunity to question him on his career and I'd like to think that I handled it better than I did my encounter with him at that time. I'm not even sure I remembered to say 'please' when I asked for his signature, but he was kind enough to give it, something for which a nine-year old boy was very grateful.

If you, like me, were lucky enough to see him bowl, I hope it brings back a few memories. If you are too young and missed out, then believe me when I tell you something.

Harold Rhodes was something very special indeed.

Harold, how did you come to join the Derbyshire staff?

Well, funnily enough – and this didn't make it into the book on my career by John Shawcroft a few years back – I nearly joined Middlesex!

At the point where a decision had to be made on my future, Walter Robins, who was the chairman at Middlesex at the time, offered me terms to go and play at Lord's. This was at the same time that an offer was tabled by Derbyshire and I had to think about it for a while. I'd played for the Club and Ground side and done well, which was where Middlesex had seen me in action.

I decided to show loyalty to my county, where my father had played with distinction over many seasons and I never regretted it. Over the years though, I have wondered if the controversy over my action would have reared its head had I opted to play at Lord's.

In your youth you were a spinner like your father. What made you change?

I actually started out as an off-spinner. One day I was down at the nets and couldn't bowl them, as I'd ripped the skin off my spinning finger and had Friars' Balsam or something similar on it. Cliff Gladwin suggested that I bowl some leggies. I used to bowl leg spin pretty well and could pitch it fine, but I didn't have the googly that was so successful for my father in his career and you really need at the top level.

At that time I used to bat five or six for the Club and Ground and actually made my debut for the county against Oxford University as a spinner, five weeks short of my 17th birthday. Then one day I turned up to play for the Club and Ground side and a trialist fast bowler's car had broken down. Our coach, Denis Smith, asked me if I could bowl some seam to take the shine off the ball.

So I did – and it went well enough for me to decide to bowl quick. Denis thought I had a bit of pace and soon afterwards, chairman Robin Buckston sat me down in his Bentley and said that they wanted to take me on to the staff as a seam bowler. He also said that I should forget about batting and that I would be going in at ten from now on – just above Les Jackson.

How big an influence was your father on your career? Did you see him play regularly?

He encouraged me, which was the most important thing, and his connection with the club enabled me to practice with the ground staff when I was only 12 or 13. He got me playing for the Chaddesden Cricket Club, which was a good standard at that time and there used to be no end of people turned up for nets in the park.

If you were late arriving, you didn't get a bat! I had to walk a mile there and then again back home – I couldn't afford a bike until I was 16.

I've seen a few references to you as 'Dusty' Rhodes, but always thought that nickname was the preserve of your father. Was that the case?

Yes, my father was called 'Dusty' by most people around the circuit for all of his days as a player and umpire, but only, to my recollection, the Yorkshire and Lancashire players used it with reference to me.

You came into a Derbyshire attack led by Gladwin and Jackson. That must have been quite daunting?

Yes, it was, but it was also a huge advantage. It showed me the temperament and the qualities that I needed to succeed and I count myself as very fortunate to learn from two such outstanding professionals and craftsmen. They taught me how important it was, on good wickets, to stop batsmen scoring, by bowling a good line and length. It built pressure and then batsmen made mistakes in trying to keep the scoreboard ticking over.

It still frustrates me when I see bowlers giving away a couple of 'four balls' an over, so the batsmen have only to wait and help themselves. I had a year as first change to Cliff and Les and it was a wonderful education. People took risks against me, because they'd not had a ball they could hit in the first hour or so.

Our scorer, Gilbert Ryde, came up to me at the interval in one of my early games and asked if I wanted to see the scorebook and check my analysis. Being well aware of my place in the scheme of things, I suggested that Cliff and Les should see it first.

'Oh, they know,' he said. They both kept their bowling figures in their heads and at the end of a day were usually only a couple of runs out. I always did the same after that and encouraged any bowlers that I later coached to do the same.

> **How did they help you develop? I presume they had more to do with your development than Denis Smith, who was a batsman?**

It wasn't so much coaching, as assimilating what you saw and heard. At Wellingborough, in my first season, Frank Tyson steamed in for Northamptonshire and bowled a bouncer first ball to John Kelly. It went over his head, on a rock hard track, then over the head of Keith Andrew, who was keeping wicket 20 yards back. It hit the middle of the sight screen on the full – quite extraordinary.

I turned to Cliff, who was sat alongside me on the pavilion balcony. 'Did you see that?' I said.

'Aye,' said Cliff. 'What a waste of a new ball...'

You had to learn from such people, they just knew so much. It was the same around the circuit and I listened to the likes of Brian Statham at Lancashire, who liked a pint at the end of a hard day. 'They miss and I hit' was his motto – and he usually did!

> **Tell me about them as people. How did you find Cliff and Les, on and off the pitch?**

Cliff was short-tempered and could be unbearable at times if he got his dander up. You dreaded dropping a catch off his bowling, as you'd be called all sorts of stuff. He was a wonderful senior professional though and the discipline when he played was first class. That kind of thing is often overlooked in its importance.

He bowled big in-swingers but cultivated a leg-cutter that kept batsmen guessing. He was the opposite of Les, who was really laid-back and just shrugged his shoulders if the ball was dropped.

Les moved it off the seam. Even on flat wickets he got movement and he should have played for England for years. No one liked facing him, but his 'slinging' action had no fans among the purists at Lord's. They preferred to pick blokes who had nice actions but got far fewer wickets and were less rated around the county circuit.

When I made my Test debut, Fred Trueman said that I had done well, because you needed to be at least ten per cent better than anyone else to get a game for England when you played for Derbyshire. That's what counted against Les. He was a wonderful bowler and a lovely man. It was a privilege to be in the same team as him.

For the benefit of younger fans, who in the modern era were they like from a pace perspective?

Les was quick and awkward. He'd have been bowling at top 80s miles per hour. He got remarkable pace and lift from what was a kind of round-arm sling. Batsmen were always getting hit on the hands or inner thigh and his bouncers, such as they were, used to spear in at batsmen's ribs and chest. He wasn't easy to play and I suppose you'd say that he was around the pace of the likes of Anderson and Broad today. When you'd faced Les on a green top you certainly had the bruises to prove it!

Cliff was a good bit slower, maybe bowling around 70mph, but he got late movement and was backed up by some wonderful fielders in the leg trap. They held some amazing catches, as Cliff darted it around. On a helpful track he fancied his chances of getting anyone, either in that leg trap or in the slips, as he moved one away off the seam.

Why didn't Les play more games for England?

Snobbery. That's it in a nutshell. The big-wigs at Lord's didn't like his action and assumed that he wouldn't take wickets at international level because of it, which was stupid. Year in, year out, Les took over a hundred wickets. They said that he only took them on Derbyshire green tops, but the statistics showed that he took as many, if not more, away from home.

Trueman, Tyson and Statham were all fine bowlers throughout the 1950s and the quickest bowlers on the circuit, but they knew that whatever they could do on a county wicket would be replicated by Les. The likelihood was that he'd have done exactly the same in international games.

He should have played many more times for his country, but it was the usual anti-Derbyshire bias.

What was life like for a professional cricketer in the 1950s?

Very different! I started as a junior professional, of course, and we usually travelled to away matches by train. My job at that time was to get the bags to the station – which required two taxis – and then needed two trolleys at the station to get them on to the platform and then on to the train. You needed to keep change handy for tipping porters and then ensure that everything came off the train at the other end. I'm proud to say that I never lost a bag!

When we played in Essex or Sussex, there could be two or three different trains to catch, so you can imagine it was a lively time. We used to play cards on the train and no one ever bothered us, even if we were recognised. To be fair, few people did recognise you at that time, as it pre-dated the current 'celebrity' culture.

There were relatively few cars on the road at that time and only a few old ones among the team, The only time we travelled by car was for the local games at Nottingham, Leicester and Birmingham. We used to get £8 a night expenses for away games, which covered your room and meal. We used to travel home each night, so at the end of the match we were £24 better off and lived like millionaires for a few weeks!

At what point in your development did you realise that you could make it in first-class cricket?

I suppose it was in my first season. I took over 70 wickets at a low cost in that summer and I bowled consistently throughout. At the end of the summer, Cliff announced his retirement and said that I would be an excellent replacement. I couldn't have wished for a greater reference than that, really.

The County Ground was always high on the list of disliked grounds for players at that time. What was it like?

It was just a big open space. There was an old wooden pavilion and a concrete stand – that was it. There might have been an occasional ice cream van and a stall selling refreshments, but there was little more to it. 'Bleak' describes it pretty accurately.

When I first joined the ground staff, one of my jobs was to help put out the forms [benches] and portable tiered seating that went between Derby and Chesterfield. They didn't even give me a pair of gloves for the job. Although you were there to learn your trade on the pitch, sometimes it felt like I had taken out an apprenticeship as a groundsman.

On my first morning at the club, I was welcomed by coach Denis Smith and shown in to the dressing room, where he gestured towards a hook and told me that it was my gear.

It was a boiler suit!

How did you find Denis Smith?

Denis was tough and some people didn't get on with him because they found him uncouth – he told it as he saw it and didn't mince his words. But he knew his cricket and was instrumental in me getting some good quality league cricket for Frickley Colliery in the Yorkshire Council League. It was a high standard and brought my game on a lot when I was 14 or 15.

As a former batsman himself, he had a lot to offer as a coach, but he could bowl decent seam and spin and he kept everyone on their toes. He justified his gruff manner by saying that no one could hold your hand out in the middle – and he was right.

How good was that 1950s side?

It was very good, but we lacked a couple of batsmen of genuine quality. Arnold Hamer was a very fine opening batsman and often gave us good starts, while Donald Carr was a good player whose availability declined as the 1950s progressed. Derek Morgan was a fine player, but he had a lot of bowling to do. Derek also had several appearances for England as 12th man, on account of his fielding, which was absolutely brilliant.

As a side, we were prone to big collapses though and that cost us more than a few winning positions. Surrey were dominant in that decade, but we gave them some good games and with another couple of batsmen – who knows? The attack was as good as any side had, with the possible exception of Surrey.

> **People often talk about the modern era as having great fielders, but that Derbyshire side had a strong reputation in the field?**

It was different in many ways, but there were people with brilliant hands and the likes of Alan Revill, Donald Carr, Arnold Hamer and Derek Morgan dropped very little and held some catches that other sides wouldn't have even considered as chances.

There was no sliding and little diving though – we wouldn't have had the time or money to wash the kit anyway, but we fielded as you did at the time – we used the 'long barrier' and stopped the ball with our feet if it was the best method available.

There was no expectation that the bowlers should throw themselves around, as they were too precious to winning prospects. Both Cliff and Les were good fielders though, especially in the gully, and Les was as good a fielder off his own bowling as I have seen. On numerous occasions he ran batsmen out by moving quickly towards mid-off or mid-on from his follow-through, picking up quickly and throwing down the stumps.

Nearly every side had a specialist (and very good) cover point – both John Kelly and Laurie Johnson were outstanding in that position for us over the years.

> **Who were the biggest characters in the side?**

Cliff was one, for sure! He always had something to say about most subjects, while both George Dawkes, an outstanding wicketkeeper, and Arnold Hamer were usually involved in the fun that we had on a regular basis. They were great days and a lovely bunch of blokes to share a dressing room with.

> **You played in one of our most remarkable fixtures, when the Hampshire game at Burton-on-Trent ended in one day in August 1958. What do you remember about that match?**

It lasted one day and 20 minutes – we'd lost a wicket in the little play possible on the previous day. The most memorable thing for me was that I got my cap at the end of the game.

The Hampshire skipper, Colin Ingleby-Mackenzie, took his team for a brewery tour the day before, so I'm not sure if they were necessarily at their best! It had rained heavily and, with wickets uncovered in those days, it made for a very difficult batting track.

We won because Les and I were considerably quicker than Derek Shackleton and Malcolm Heath on a wicket where the ball moved around a lot and the bounce was erratic. The only bowling change was when Derek Morgan replaced me and cleaned up the tail in their second innings. I was shattered by that stage, mentally as much as physically.

> **As the 1960s dawned, our fortunes gradually declined as top-quality players failed to be replaced. That must have been a difficult time?**

It was. Arnold Hamer retired, Cliff had gone, Donald Carr's availability was an issue and the batsmen who came in simply weren't up to the same standard.

Brian Jackson [no relation to Les] came in and did a terrific job with the new ball for a few seasons, but we struggled because we hadn't enough good players and – of course – money was tight.

It always seemed like we could have done with another 50 runs to play with. Sometimes we got them, but it was a constant battle to take wickets while not conceding runs, setting close fields without giving away runs down to third man.

> **How fast were you at your quickest? Who was faster than you?**

Frank Tyson was frighteningly quick for a few years, as was Fred

Trueman, but I wasn't far off. I was never timed when I was at my fastest, but a rudimentary test conducted by a couple of school masters suggested I was bowling around 94mph in the early 1960s.

The thing was, you couldn't bowl fast all the time. We played so much – I bowled around 700 to 800 overs a season – that you kept yourself back for days when the wicket offered you more help, or for the last day of a game when you were pressing for a win. That's when the accuracy that I mentioned earlier came in – you relied on line and length and occasional quicker balls to keep people guessing.

Walter Goodyear was our groundsman at this time and the accuracy of the likes of Cliff and Les was extraordinary. At the end of the season, he said that he only had to take around a yard of turf out and replace it, as the rest was pretty much pristine. They were remorseless in giving the batsmen nothing to hit and bowling perfect lengths.

It was difficult too, because there was none of this quick drying cement that they use to fill footholds today. Les used to create massive 'bomb craters', as we called them, when he bowled, so you had to make sure that you didn't land your front foot in, or on the edge of one of those, or you could easily turn an ankle.

How fast was a bowler of a later vintage, Alan Ward?

When he came on the scene in the mid-1960s I was in my 30s and he made me look slow, at that stage, in comparison! He was a very quick bowler indeed and there were a few county batsmen who didn't fancy facing him at all.

He never fulfilled that potential though. I don't think he really had the heart for it when he came up against better batsmen who could handle him and when he had the bad days that all bowlers endure. Injuries came along and Alan disappeared far more quickly than he should have done. It was a shame, really.

I was interested to read that you rarely bowled bouncers. Was that to maintain control and avoid giving easy runs away?

Yes, it was. It goes back, I suppose, to seeing Frank Tyson 'waste' the new ball as I mentioned earlier. It was a bonus if it took a wicket, but those who hooked usually saw it as an easy four, while those who didn't just ducked under it and it usually meant that you were wasting your time and energy. I always used to think that bowling a bouncer showed that the batsmen were rattling me, so I didn't bother.

Our batsmen used to get annoyed sometimes, as they wanted me to dish out some of what they had to put up with. I preferred to try and win the match and to do so had to keep runs to the minimum and take wickets as inexpensively as possible.

How did the salary of a professional cricketer relate to an ordinary working man at that time?

When I was capped in 1958 my salary was £600 a year. That was the same as Cliff and Les, as well as all the other capped players. You got no more for experience or good performances. You certainly didn't play county cricket for the lavish lifestyle, but Arnold Hamer told me that it would create memories, and it was all about the people you met and had a beer with at the end of the day.

That's a side of the game that has slowly disappeared and it's a shame. You learned a lot from talking to other players and most of us got on pretty well.

The issues over your bowling action are well known and the general consensus appears to be that you were offered up as a scapegoat at a time when there was a crackdown on obvious offenders around the globe?

Without a doubt. The cricket authorities were clamping down on throwers from around the world, all of them having the same thing in common.

They all had an open-chested action that 'stopped' as they released the ball from a splay-footed stance. They all had a really quick ball, which was the one that was dangerous, of course. People like Charlie Griffith, Ian Meckiff and Geoff Griffin were called and with good reason when you see the photographs of them in action. With West Indians, Australians and South Africans being called, there was seen to be a need for English cricket to be 'cleaning up' its act and I was the fall guy, if you like.

My action was always side-on, what has always been regarded as the 'classic' style, and to throw from that position would have been impossible. Yet I was called to see a film that had been taken of my action from a mid-on position in the stand and I agreed it didn't look good. Similar films of such great bowlers as Harold Larwood and Ray Lindwall did them no favours either and it was the angle, rather than the action, that was the problem.

I asked the people at Lord's to film the man who was regarded as having the best action in the game from the same place, so they filmed Fred Trueman. He looked as if he threw too, which proved my point!

The law at the time I was first no-balled allowed umpires to call bowlers if they felt there was something DIFFERENT about their action and that's why Paul Gibb no-balled me. Yet when George Cochrane, a specialist from Derby Royal Infirmary, proved to them that I had hyper-extension of the elbow – that the arm went past straight – they still didn't clear me. This was in 1961 and it was seven more years before they finally did. It was too little, too late.

In 1965, I was top of the national bowling averages and the media were calling for me to return to the England team. I firmly believe that the people at Lord's got umpire Syd Buller to one side and told him that he needed to help them out of a tricky situation and no-ball me in the South Africa tour match at Chesterfield.

I knew Syd and we got on pretty well before then, but he was never the same afterwards. Ironically, he umpired in my previous Test match, when I bowled 46 overs! He never saw a thing wrong with my action, nor had he at many other county matches at which he had officiated.

It was all very, very strange and immensely frustrating.

Sonny Ramadhin supposedly kept his sleeves buttoned when he bowled to stop people seeing his elbow clearly. Was that never suggested to you as an option?

No it wasn't and I wouldn't have done it, because I was totally convinced of my innocence. There were other spinners whose quest for spin saw their elbow bend more than was allowed though, Tony Lock perhaps being the best known.

It must have been frustrating to spend so much of your career, when your record suggested you should have been an England regular, trying to clear your name?

Yes. It was very stressful for my family too, but as I said earlier, it has always been difficult for Derbyshire players at international level. Even Mike Hendrick and Bob Taylor only got recognition because of Kerry Packer and Les, Cliff and George Pope should have earned greater opportunities.

Did it take you a long time to get over that?

You know, I always listened for my name, every time an England side was announced, hoping that my chance might come. Although the officials at Lord's didn't finally clear my name until 1968, by which time I had slowed down a lot, I was picked for many touring sides. I went around the world as a cricketer, but never with England, which hurt me, as lesser bowlers went in my place.

Even E.W. 'Jim' Swanton of the *Daily Telegraph* picked me for his touring sides. He was listened to at Lord's and was a member of the 'inner circle', but it made no difference.

Your Derbyshire colleague Peter Eyre also came under scrutiny for his action. Did that create a special 'bond' between you?

Peter and I have been good friends for years and still see each other regularly. His case was silly too – he was double-jointed, like Brian Statham of Lancashire, and it was that additional flexibility which gave a false impression when he bowled.

Peter's action was side-on like mine and the pity is that the people running the game – including former England bowler 'Gubby' Allen – appeared to have no idea of the mechanics of bowling. Had they done so, they would have known that we couldn't possibly throw from our positions at the bowling crease when we let the ball go.

Presumably the events produced more than their share of black humour, as such things tend to do?

Oh yes. The Derbyshire lads called me 'Percy' after the TV gardener, Percy Thrower. Around 99 per cent of people in the game knew I bowled within the rules, but there were a few others around who were far less legitimate.

There was a spinner at Somerset, David Doughty, who was widely reckoned to throw in a brief career. In a game against Kent, the umpires decided he should be removed from the attack at the time that Colin Cowdrey came to the crease. He asked why they were taking him off and was told that they thought he was throwing.

'Leave him on,' said Colin. 'He's not throwing very well!'

> **Do you feel you had the support you should have had from the club throughout your career?**

The committee, chairman and secretary were fantastic and very supportive. So too were the players and Derek Morgan, when he took over as captain.

Being honest, I think Donald Carr could have done more. He was my first county captain but never fully came out and supported me, probably because he was torn by his role as assistant secretary of MCC. Even in my benefit brochure, he wrote that cricket 'had to get it right', without making it clear just what that was.

> **What are your memories of the Gillette Cup semi-final against Sussex at Chesterfield in 1969?**

It was wonderful. I've never seen a bigger crowd and the wicket wasn't easy, but our total of 136 seemed way too small to force a win against the best one-day side in the country. They batted a long way down at that time.

When Alan Ward ran in from the Pavilion End – he had taken my preferred end as the quicker bowler at that time – you could have heard a pin drop. I bowled from the Lake End and they couldn't hit a ball. Alan took two early wickets and conceded only 11 runs in eight overs. I bowled seven overs for only four runs and that was an edge to the boundary! Then Fred Rumsey came on and went for only 13 in nine overs – we had built pressure and Peter Eyre profited as they tried to up the scoring rate. They only reached 49 all out – it was quite extraordinary.

As I said to you earlier, if you build pressure, wickets usually come and it worked like a charm for us that day.

What was your favourite ground?

Oh, Chesterfield. I used to love running in from the pavilion end when I was at my peak and found a natural rhythm there. The tracks usually helped seam bowlers too, so that helped.

I also liked The Oval. Surrey had a good side and a nice bunch of blokes you could test yourself against. I always did well there too!

Who were the best batsmen you bowled at in your career?

Peter May was an outstanding batsman in the 1950s and head and shoulders above the rest. Garfield Sobers was another who gave you no margin for error and would hammer you if you over-pitched, dropped short or gave him any width. A marvellous batsman – and of course, he bowled a bit too!

The two South Africans, Graeme Pollock and Barry Richards, were fine players as well. They had so much time to play their shots and on their day could take you apart.

Who would you have as Derbyshire opening bowlers in a fantasy side?

That's a good one! You have to include Les Jackson, because his figures over 15 summers or more were remarkable. No one liked facing him and he bowled so few bad balls that he often got wickets through the surprise element of a half-volley!

I saw Bill Copson, who was briefly Derbyshire coach for a period when Denis Smith was indisposed and he must have been good in his prime. Cliff was obviously a wonderful bowler, but I'd actually plump for Brian Jackson at the other end.

Brian came out of the leagues at the age of 30 and for six summers was a wonderful foil for me, taking 457 wickets at less than 19 runs each. He had a 'windmill' action, but had learned his craft and seldom bowled a bad ball. Whereas I bowled in the early 90s, Brian was perhaps top 80s – quick enough to make people hurry their shots, certainly bruise them and definitely get them out.

He came in from wide on the crease and his natural delivery moved into the batsman, but he could get it to jag away too.

He was a very fine bowler indeed.

Do you watch much modern cricket?

I do, but I'm not really a fan of the 20-over game. Aside from the money, I don't think it does much for the techniques of the game or the players.

I don't think that the overall standards are as high now as they were then. I only played one season of John Player League cricket, so the long format is my preference. I go down to watch Derbyshire a few times every summer and meet up with old friends, but only for championship cricket.

And what do you think of modern seam bowling? Would you like to have played today?

I think modern seam bowlers have a hard job and there is a much greater expectation on them to contribute in the field, as well as with the bat. They don't get the chance to hone their skills and get into a rhythm as we did.

On the other hand, they don't bowl anywhere near the number of overs that we used to do and they don't have to worry about putting their foot down in a pothole, as was a regular occurrence in my time. They can also have a drink when they want. We used to have to wait for the interval and you could count on the fingers of one hand the times when the captains decided they would have a drinks break in a season!

I used to run in, focus on the base of off stump and bowl a very tight line on or outside it, day after day. Nowadays, the bowlers have to mix it up all the time, with slower balls, cutters, yorkers and all sorts of stuff. It is a hard thing to do and it is no surprise when sometimes they get it quite badly wrong.

Keith Mohan (1957–1958)

KEITH MOHAN only played ten first-class matches for Derbyshire so, at first glance, may seem an unusual subject for this book. Born at Glossop in 1935, he was on the staff for several seasons without getting the breaks that he needed to move on to the next level.

Everyone I spoke to who was involved in Derbyshire cricket in the 1950s said to me that I simply had to talk to him. Most of the funny stories from that period seem to have Keith at the epicentre and without exception, the mention of his name brought a smile to people's faces. When I e-mailed him to ask if he would be happy to be involved, a reply in the affirmative came within ten minutes. It impressed me.

Walter Goodyear laughed and shook his head when I mentioned Keith.

'He were a rum 'un,' came the reply. 'Always up to something, always having a laugh, always trying to get one over Walter.'

I wanted to know more about a man whose brief career was at the centre of more tales than others who had played the first-class game for a decade. Keith was not the most talented player in this book, but, as he said to me, he enjoyed his cricket more than many of the others.

He has a ready laugh and an infectious sense of humour. The conversation flowed and there were plenty of chuckles as he recounted his tales of life as a county cricketer 60 years ago. He is a naturally funny man and I have seen stand-up comedians with a worse sense of timing.

One of his contemporaries told me that had he taken the game more seriously, he could have been a very good player. He needed a little more luck too, as you will see, but Keith Mohan was a man who people enjoyed having as a team-mate and friend.

At the end of the day, that has to be worth something.

Keith, tell me how you got started on cricket?

I started playing at the age of 11. I played for the local chapel, Glossop Tabernacle, in the Sunday league. I was never keen on going to church, but if you didn't attend you didn't get picked for the team!

We used to play on a field that belonged to a local farmer and he kept the cows and horses away from the square by putting a fence around it.

There were four-foot posts that were hammered into the ground at intervals to hold the fencing and these went down a foot and were usually protected by plastic covers. We didn't have enough of them though, so sometimes the ball went down these holes. That's how I first made myself indispensable to the team – I had the thinnest arms and was the one who normally had to put my hand down to get the ball out!

When I was 13 I started going along to watch Glossop practice in the nets and was quite happy just throwing the ball back to them. Then they asked me to have a bowl. I bowled off spin and turned it a lot. I had already been asked to go along to play for Old Glossop, but they said, no, you come along and play for the 'big' team. So I started to play for Glossop, which I did for many years. I played my last game of cricket when I was 70.

I took over a hundred wickets between junior and second-team games when I was 13 and they started to pay me.

I got a shilling a week to go and pick up the potted meat and the bread on my way to the game. I must have been one of the youngest professionals ever!

How did you come to Derbyshire's attention?

When I was 15, the Glossop coach was the former Derbyshire stalwart and county coach when they were champions in 1936, Sam Cadman. He used to talk to me all the time about how to set a field and if the second-team captain tried to do it for me, he used to tell him off, saying that I knew more about cricket than he ever would. Of course, he'd told me!

I started playing for Derbyshire schoolboys and appeared for the North of England schools against the South in 1950, largely thanks to Sam's recommendation. He put me in touch with Derbyshire and it went on from there.

You played several second-team games at 17 in 1952?

I went for a trial in 1951 and joined the staff in 1952. But of course, at that time you had to do National Service and I was doing that, based at Catterick, in 1953 and 1954, so it was 1955 before I started playing regular cricket again.

You were on the ground staff and in the second team until 1957, when you made your senior debut. That was a long time coming?

Well, at that time Derbyshire had 11 capped players and so you only really got a game if one of them was injured or ill. They didn't have the money to leave them on the sidelines while they tried out a youngster, so you had to bide your time. Derbyshire didn't have all that many second-team matches either, so it was hard to make an impression. Of course, realistically I just wasn't good enough to force a way into the side.

What was your batting style?

I think I was seen as a bit of a dasher, someone who liked to hit it and was perhaps too impetuous at the start of an innings. I gradually worked my way up the order and ended up opening for Derbyshire, where I tried to be more selective with my shots. I was probably best when I was going for it, because I was told I looked like I was struggling when I started leaving balls and playing defensively!

How did you find life on the ground staff?

Oh, we had some great times! The worst part was on match days, when we had to put out forms [benches] all around the ground and build up the wooden stand. We all hated it and they bought us all overalls so we looked the part. We used to grumble, because we just wanted to play cricket. The stands were all numbered and lettered by Walter Goodyear, so you knew what fitted where, but it was very time-consuming. There were numerous chores that we had to do, even before we got to put on our cricket gear. I think it was Alan Ward who eventually saw it stopped. He said he was there to play cricket and refused to do it.

After we had done our chores and of course, had practised ourselves, we had to bowl at the members. Generally, there were some fairly wealthy ones who tipped well and so we bowled gently at them, as well as a few who were better and just wanted to slog you into the middle distance. At Derby at the time there was a straight mile and I used to toss them up and they'd try to hit me as far as they could. It meant I only bowled one or two to them, so there was method in the madness, but they'd go away and brag to their mates that they'd hit so-and-so who was playing for Derbyshire.

There was one night when the boiler went on fire! Harold Rhodes and I used to stay behind until dusk to practice and we used to fire the boiler up before we went out. When we got back into the dressing room later, it was smouldering around where the metal chimney went through the ceiling.

I ran upstairs to where Will Taylor, the secretary, had his office. I didn't have any clothes on, and all the time the night watchman at the club, a former policeman, Mr Jordan, was running around like Corporal Jones in *Dad's Army* shouting 'Don't panic…there's a fire… don't panic!' – it was quite funny really, looking back.

Harold and I got all the stuff out of there before the fire brigade came along, apart from a couple of bats that belonged to a player who we felt was a little 'snobby'. It was a bit naughty, to be honest, and the bats warped with the heat and the water and were ruined. I remember afterwards I asked the firemen if I could get a lift to the front gate and they told me in no uncertain terms where to go!

The next day it made the local papers that two quick-thinking members of the ground staff had helped the fire service put out a fire and when Harold and I went to get our wages, Will Taylor asked to see us. He had a slow, very pukka way of speaking and said, 'I'm trying to decide whether I should sack you both or not. The pavilion was insured for £5,000 – why didn't you let the bloody thing burn?'

▌I've heard a few tales about Will Taylor. How was he?

He was a lovely man and was secretary for over 50 years, but was very protective of the club's and his own money. Walter Goodyear used to go in and ask him for a rise every week and he would make out he couldn't hear him. Then Walter came out and said, 'I've got what I wanted,' and we would all look at each other and laugh, knowing full well that he hadn't.

I went in to see Mr Taylor one day and he said, 'I say, Keith, do you smoke?' He was taking one out for himself and I said, 'Yes please, Mr Taylor.'

He looked at me and said, 'You don't? Then have a toffee.'

He was a little deaf, you see, and one time confided in me that he had now got a discreet hearing aid. He told me not to tell anyone, but of course, I went straight out and warned them all to be careful what they were saying!

I went in and asked him for my travelling expenses one day and told him that they were £5. He looked at me and said, 'Didn't I take you to the match for a couple of days? I'll give you five shillings.'

Another time I had made a few runs and when he saw me later he said, 'Well batted, John.' I told him my name was Keith and he said he never knew that! He would come up to me occasionally and say, 'Do you know I have a hole in my head?' It was from the Great War, when he was wounded, but he asked me that a few times. He was a lovely man, but quite eccentric.

There was another time when we were playing an away game against Shropshire and we got to lunch at 80/1 and were all out afterwards for 120. They used to serve us Shropshire Stilton, which was soaked in port and was served with a glass of it. The following year Mr Taylor told me to remind the players they had not to partake of either cheese or port until close of play!

Perhaps the funniest of all was when we were playing a game at Newark and had to stop overnight. Mr Taylor was due the next day to pay our wages, so the players all knew that. Now the place we were staying had a parrot and I sat up till around one in the morning, repeating my impersonation of Will Taylor – 'Ahhh yes…let me see now' was something he always said and eventually the parrot had it off perfectly.

When the players came down the next morning, the parrot was behind a curtain and kept saying this. Some of them had perhaps not fully observed the dress code and thought he had arrived early to take a private breakfast. You should have seen their faces!

Many of the stories I have heard about you seem to revolve around Walter Goodyear?

I used to like a laugh. Walter was a wonderful groundsman and a lovely bloke. He used to reckon I was a ladies' man and one time he had a load of paper in his hand and was telling everyone he could find that they were love letters he had retrieved from my cricket bag!

I had quite a journey to Derby on Monday mornings. We only got ten shillings a week for travel expenses and if I went by train that was it gone. So I started to get a bus from Glossop to Manchester and then from there to Derby. It was a long journey and this particular day I arrived late and the nets, which we had to put up, were almost finished. Walter said that I should do my bit and asked me to tighten up a guy rope at the far end.

Well, I must have slackened it off instead and a big gust of wind came and blew five rows of nets over! Walter was calling me for all sorts and gave me a rope, telling me to take it and go behind the stand and hang myself.

Of course, I set off with it with my head down and Walter was shouting after me, 'Come back, I didn't mean it.'

Another time I volunteered to reverse the roller out of the nets and got my gears wrong. I drove straight through the back of them and took them down again!

There was a game against Glamorgan too, where he had finished preparing the wicket and asked me to take a kettle of water and water the area of the stumps.

I went out and did this, but then, knowing Walter would see me as he cycled around the boundary, walked up the wicket with the empty kettle, pretending I was watering it. 'Not the bloody wicket you fool,' he shouted, running from the boundary edge, in a mild state of panic that his pitch preparation was in danger of being ruined!

Mind you, he got his own back. I got back to Glossop one night, shattered after a hard day and having found my cricket bag unusually heavy. When I opened it up, I found that he had put four or five bricks in the bottom of it, underneath my cricket gear!

In the first 11 you made a number of appearances but never quite made the step up?

I think batting everywhere from seven to opening didn't help me, but I was in line to play regularly in 1959, or so I was told, as I had started to work out my game by that stage.

At the start of that season I broke some ribs playing for the second team and they took some time to heal. I also had a bad outbreak of psoriasis, which has troubled me throughout my life and that saw me hospitalised for several weeks. I was told I was being released and then scored 113 and 39 against Yorkshire seconds and 97 against Warwickshire seconds. Denis Smith, the coach, sat in his car with me and told me I was an idiot for not getting another hundred, but he said, 'Don't worry, you will get another chance.' By that time I had a good job (I was an electrical engineer) and a family and it made more sense to stop gambling on what wasn't an especially lucrative career.

Tell me about Denis Smith.

Denis was blunt and could be quite coarse, but he was a good coach. There was one time we had a young quick bowler on trial from one of the universities. He bowled badly, spraying it around and not really impressing. At the end of the day he had four or five gin and tonics before, to our surprise, getting behind the wheel of a sports car and roaring off.

'Don't worry about him,' said Denis, 'if he drives like he bowls he won't hit owt.'

Another time, we were in a hotel for an away game and were sitting down to dinner. The waitress sat the tureen of soup down next to Denis and went through to the kitchen to get a ladle to serve it. When she came back, Denis had his napkin tucked in and was getting stuck in to the soup from the tureen!

> **You finished your short first-class career in 1958 and ironically after a couple of decent efforts as opener. You made 49 against Jack Flavell at Chesterfield, before being lbw to Doug Slade?**

I did and it was a decent effort against a good attack. I did myself no favours though because I was suspended for a couple of matches after that.

I turned up late for a second-team game – a chap from Shropshire named Billy Shilton was supposed to meet me at the station and we missed each other, meaning I missed the train. I ran from the station to the County Ground and Will Taylor gave me a lift to Chesterfield, where the game was being played. We only got there around 20 minutes before the start and I was opening the batting.

My opening partner, Jim Brailsford, was angry when I told him why I was late and we almost came to blows and had to be separated. We walked out to bat that day yards apart and Jim tried to run me out in the first over. He ended up being run out himself, as I was quicker than him and they threw to his end. I knew he was angry with me and I told the opposition that I wasn't going to get out because I didn't want to face him in the pavilion – he was much bigger than me.

So I stayed out there all day and made 144.

The next game I was picked for the first team and was out first ball at Ilkeston, but I was selected to play and open against Middlesex at Chesterfield. Harold Rhodes, who had a car, said he would pick me up in Breadsall, where I lived at that time.

Well, he was running late and thought I would have made my own way. So again, I had to phone Will Taylor and he again gave me a lift to Chesterfield. We got there with 30 minutes to spare, but Donald Carr had already announced the team and David Green took my place. Cliff Gladwin showed another side to his character, seeing how upset I was. He sat with me and consoled me.

Of course, the press got hold of the story and the news went out that I had overslept, which was wrong. But over the next couple of weeks I had 20-odd alarm clocks sent to me in the post. I sold some and gave others away, keeping one for myself.

Cliff was well-known for being a little volatile at times?

There was one occasion when we played Northamptonshire and I dropped a 'dolly' off his bowling. It was their star batsman, Denis Brookes and I caught my foot in a pothole on the outfield. It didn't matter to Cliff and he was cussing and calling me all sorts. At the end of the over Denis Brookes came over to me and said, 'When I get 50, I'm going to give you another catch off Cliff. Make sure you take it.' He did and I did. You wouldn't see that today.

Very few people answered back to Cliff, who was a big man, but I remember Arnold Hamer, who had put on a bit of weight, once at Pontypridd telling him he was going to get a 'bunch of fives' if he didn't shut up moaning. Arnold had let a ball go to the boundary off Cliff, who said, 'Don't you think you would be better in the slips?' He was a mild-mannered man, Arnold, but he'd had enough that day.

It was unusual though, because everyone normally got on so well and considering we spent the best part of the summer in each other's company, the rows were few and far between.

I saw Donald Carr once recall a batsman that the umpire had given out, because we knew he hadn't nicked it. That was the sort of era it was, sportsmanship was important.

Guy Willatt ended the practice of the team coming out of different gates you know. At that time there was a staff gate, another for amateurs and one for professionals. Three different gates and on one occasion we had 13 men walked out on to the pitch! Guy had to 'drop' two players very quickly.

Amateurs used to turn up and expect to play, sometimes even after the team had been announced to the press.

What was it like to bat against Cliff and Les?

They always made you play. You got very few balls to leave but they were quite different. Cliff wasn't fast but he swung it in to you, with a good one that either stayed straight or moved away. Les was much quicker, but always endangering your stumps or your ribcage. He was a wonderful bowler.

You continued to play second-team cricket for the club until 1970. It seems strange, having been deemed surplus to requirements a decade earlier?

Denis Smith asked me to play for the seconds in 1963 and I got an unbeaten 82 against a Warwickshire attack that included future England bowler David Brown and Pakistan all-rounder Khalid 'Billy' Ibadulla. Denis asked me about coming back, but it wasn't worth my while. I was in sales by that stage and I could take a couple of days off here and there for second-team games, but it was really too late for me by that time. I enjoyed it, but I had to be realistic.

I was a professional in the Birmingham area and in Yorkshire for a number of years. I was also cricket professional at St Peter's School in York between 1974 and 2002.

And finally, when you look back on your career – any regrets? Anything you would have done differently?

I would have liked to have got my county cap. It would have been special, but it just wasn't to be.

Peter Eyre
(1959–1972)

THE ARDENT cricket fan can reel off the initials of the good and the great of the game with considerable pride. Learned from scorecards and old editions of *Wisden*, they roll over the tongue like a vintage claret.

P.B.H May; M.J.K Smith; L.E.G Ames; A.P.E Knott – the list is both long and illustrious, with one of its members T.J.P Eyre.

Self-confidence seems to have been a barrier to greater success, but for 14 summers he was a fixture in Derbyshire sides and at times produced some very good performances. As you will see in the following interview, bad luck, especially with health, cost him a lot of cricket over the years and he was perhaps more insecure about his ability and his place in the side as a result.

He admits to worrying a lot, about letting his team-mates down and about not doing himself justice. Had he only realised what his colleagues really thought about him and how highly he was valued, he might have relaxed and been even better.

I remember seeing him in one of my earliest matches and, at a time when hairstyles were creeping down to and past the collar, Peter had none. It was a thing called alopecia, my father told me, something that I could neither spell nor had knowledge of at that time.

Some theories suggest it can be caused by stress or worry, although as something that attacks the auto-immune system it was perhaps just another of the ailments that affected and ultimately curtailed his career.

Edwin Smith told me that if he had a team of Peter Eyres he could take on anyone, because he knew he would always get 100 per cent. At his best, he was a fine bowler with a perhaps unusual method, but he was capable of dismissing the very best batsmen.

He could also hit a ball hard and score runs, often when they were most needed by the team. Every team needs a man who will run in hard all day, uphill and into the wind, allowing the 'names' of the side the glory from the better end. Peter was that selfless individual for over a decade.

Whether he fulfilled the talent that he showed when dominating local schools cricket is a moot point, but you don't hold down a place in county cricket for that length of time by being anything less than a good cricketer.

Plenty of people will attest to Peter being better than that. I'm one of them.

Peter, when I have spoken about you to your contemporaries, the word that recurs is 'unlucky'. Would you say that was a fair assessment of your career?

To some extent, yes. It didn't help me that I lost my hair early, through alopecia. In those days someone with no hair or very short hair was unusual and it actually affected me, from a self-confidence perspective, more than perhaps it should have done.

I also suffered a little when, at the same time that Harold Rhodes's bowling action was being called into question, there were suggestions that mine was under scrutiny. I was called to Lord's and although I was told they had no complaints, I was conscious of it for a long time afterwards.

So what did they think they had seen in your bowling?

I had an unusual action. My arm didn't come all the way round, but I held it out behind me and then brought it over. It was a little like that of Brian Statham, of England and Lancashire. They never queried his bowling!

They decided to change my bowling style and I went down to Trevor Bailey's indoor school in Essex to work on it. To be honest, I never felt as comfortable or natural with it afterwards.

Was the alopecia stress-related?

I think it must have been. I have always been a worrier and I used to worry about things before they happened and things that never did happen. I wore a wig for a while and there's a funny story about a game at Ilkeston, when I didn't attach it properly with the straps and webbing. As I ran in to bowl, my team-mates were all watching the wig bouncing up and down, perhaps rather more than the ball!

After a while I stopped bothering with one and I suppose accepted things a little more.

You were one of many Derbyshire players who came from the High Peak. How did you start playing the game?

I came from a very small hamlet of only half a dozen houses and used to play in our back yard with the only other lad there! We drew some wickets on the wall with chalk and would bat and bowl at each other for hours.

When we got to around 11 or 12, the local farmer let us mow a wicket in the field next to our house. We put wickets at either end and then we would bowl at each other. We didn't run – what we did was make up nine or ten boxes, each with a number from one to six. You scored runs by hitting these boxes and adding your total up.

The only way you could get out was being bowled, or caught and bowled and we played for hours.

I then went to New Mills Grammar School, which was 17 miles away. I had to get to the station at 7.15 in the morning and didn't get home until 5.30 every night.

Did they have a team at the school?

We were lucky to have a games master who was a keen cricketer and there were inter-house matches and various school teams. I did very well and got a lot of wickets and runs, then had a trial with Derbyshire Grammar Schools, which saw me picked and also doing well.

I was spotted by Derbyshire in these games and signed a contract with them at the age of 17.

> **You made your first appearances for the second team in 1956. Cliff Gladwin and Les Jackson were then in their prime. Did you see much of them?**

No, not really. I saw them about, but as a member of the ground staff you didn't really socialise with them. I got to know Cliff when he was captain of the second team after retirement.

> **How was that? He had a bit of a reputation on the field.**

He was actually very supportive and encouraging. As you say, he had a reputation in his playing days for being blunt, but I only ever found him helpful. He had a lot of advice and experience and you needed only to be prepared to listen and learn.

> **Your emergence in the first team came after Cliff retired in 1959. Was there pressure on young seam bowlers at that time, with Les Jackson also nearing the end of his glittering career?**

I made my debut opening the bowling opposite Les at Cambridge and he was such a wonderful bowler. His line and length were always right, he was deceptively quick and he would bowl you 30 overs a day without complaint. He set the standard, that's for sure. I felt more privileged than under pressure and it was a great dressing room to be a part of. I was lucky though, as I got to bowl with Les, Harold Rhodes and Brian Jackson. The first two are better known, but Brian was one of the most underrated bowlers I have seen. He could move it about, hurry batsmen up and get them out. The three of them would have handled modern cricket without doubt, even with the bigger bats today, because they were outstanding players.

> **Les was renowned as being phlegmatic as a bowler, where Cliff was more volatile. What about you?**

I was the same as Les. No one drops catches, or misfields on purpose, so I saw no point in shouting and swearing at people who were my friends and team-mates.

You had two very promising summers in 1960 and 1961, then struggled for four years, barely playing in two of them. That must have been a tough time?

That was around the time of the 'throwing' issue. I had lost a lot of confidence and for a while they played me as a specialist batsman, which I was never good enough to do.

The effect of the filming of my action cannot be overstated. For a number of years afterwards I felt constantly under scrutiny, whether from officials or umpires. I never got called, but it was always on my mind.

So they never told you at Lord's that they were satisfied you bowled legitimately?

When I had been to Lord's with Harold, I went in first and they said, 'We don't know why you are here, we've filmed you.' I had bowled at the Australians in the nets at Derby in 1961 and one of them felt there was something unusual in the way I bowled.

That's all it was though, unusual.

Your best year was 1967, when you had 64 wickets at under 20 runs each. How did it all change that summer? Fitness?

Yes, but I was also given the new ball for a good part of the summer and I think I responded to the fact that they obviously had confidence in me. I did well over the following two seasons as well and that was undoubtedly my peak as a professional cricketer.

Your highest score and best bowling performance came in 1969, a century and eight wickets?

I got 8-65 against Somerset at Chesterfield. On the first day, in helpful conditions, I didn't bowl well. It had rained and there was a humid atmosphere but my line and length wasn't right. I was sick with worry that night, because I knew I should have done better, but the next day it all came right. I got it moving about and everything went to hand and was held.

My century came against Leicestershire, also at Chesterfield and we were in trouble. I went in at number seven against an attack led by internationals Graham McKenzie and Barry Knight, with quality spinners in Jack Birkenshaw and, of course, their captain Ray Illingworth, who was also the England skipper.

We were 74/5 when I went in and I got 102. It was a lovely feeling, walking in to the applause, but I never got back to that level after 1969.

> **And of course, there was that legendary performance in the Gillette Cup semi-final against Sussex at Chesterfield? Tell me about that day.**

It had rained the day before and the ground had been soaked. We got to the ground early and the ground staff worked wonders to get it ready for play.

Derek Morgan won the toss and elected to bat but we could only make 136 on an awkward pitch. Peter Gibbs got 44 and Derek Morgan batted a long time for an unbeaten 26, but that was pretty much it.

The wicket was getting worse though. When Harold Rhodes and Alan Ward started bowling so well at the start of their innings, I had never heard a noise like it on a cricket ground.

The place was packed, row after row of people on the bandstand side and Fred Rumsey kept the pressure on them before Derek tossed the ball to me.

Whenever I bowled, I always knew, after my first over, if it was going to go well. I wasn't consistent, like Harold Rhodes or Brian Jackson, but I'd know quickly if my rhythm and line was right. That day, from the first ball it was just as I wanted it to be. I was pitching middle and off and it was shaping away nicely.

I think they took some risks against me, after being tied down and I ended up with 6/18 in ten overs. We knew we had won when Derek caught Jim Parks at midwicket off my bowling, as he was a fine player and their only batsman to make double figures. Harold only conceded an edged four in his seven overs, that's how accurate we all were, and Alan Ward and Fred Rumsey went for much less than two an over, as we just kept it tight, ball after ball. They were 49 all out in 35 overs – in a one-day match!

After making just 136, did you still think you could win?

Yes, we did. That year we had such a good seam attack that we reckoned we had a chance on a good wicket with 150 against most sides. On one that offered us help – which this one did – we knew we could win it, if we bowled well.

It was great for the crowd though. They were all over the ground at the end, shouting and cheering. The atmosphere was unbelievable, because they were right on the boundary edge, sitting and standing wherever they could find a space.

Author note: *The club yearbook for 1970 records a crowd of 10,500. The current capacity for the same ground is set at 4,999.*

It took us to the final, against Yorkshire at Lord's. The performance and result were an anti-climax?

For some reason, after winning the toss again and agreeing at the team meeting the previous night that we would bat if he did so, Derek opted to bowl.

We didn't bowl as well as previous rounds and maybe the occasion got to some of us. Doug Padgett was given not out after he edged Ian Buxton through to Bob Taylor, we dropped a couple of chances and we didn't bat well. Excited as we were to get to Lord's, we didn't give a good account of ourselves and they won easily.

The last three summers must have been an anti-climax after that and fitness issues again loomed?

Yes. I damaged a cartilage playing football in the winter and was only just recovering from that when I went down with glandular fever. It effectively finished me as a first-class player. You feel so unwell and so lethargic and I struggled with that for quite some time afterwards.

There must have been some characters and funny stories over those years?

Mike Page was always good value from a comedy angle in our dressing room, but we all just got on very well. It was a happy place to play the game.

One of the funniest men on the circuit was Ray East, of Essex. We played them once at Chesterfield and made 300, then it rained. The next day the wicket was spiteful and was bouncing and lifting nastily as we worked our way through them.

Ray walked out for his first ball, backed away and shouted, 'Catch it!' Then he walked off, even though he hadn't hit it!

I must tell you about Brian Jackson too, a long-time friend of mine who enjoyed his cricket and his beer. We used to pair up for trips to away games and I was driving the two of us down to Hastings to play Sussex.

We left Chesterfield and had not gone 20 miles when Brian asked if I fancied stopping for a drink.

We went into a pub and Brian ordered three pints. Of course, I was looking around wondering who the third one was for. By the time the barman had poured the third, he'd drunk the first!

So what happened after you finished with Derbyshire?

I continued to play cricket, mainly for either Hathersage, who I captained for several seasons in the North Derbyshire and South Yorkshire League, or at Knypersley, where I was professional for several summers.

Hathersage won the league five years in a row, though not necessarily because of me!

The social side of the game, which I loved, had gone latterly. We used to go for a couple of pints at the end of a game and when I played my last game of cricket, playing in an emergency after being retired for a couple of seasons, there were four players in the bar after the game and an umpire. It is quite sad, really.

Work-wise I was a builder for many years. When I played I did a range of jobs, including driving coal trucks around the local farms for a few winters, but then I went into a building business with my brother.

It went really well, but he died of a heart attack when he was only 47.

Around 60 per cent of our work was for the National Trust, who I subsequently worked with until 2000.

And what about today?

Well, I've had both my knees done, which has given me a new lease of life and I still keep my hand in now and then with the building firm that my son now runs. My other son is a joiner and I give him a hand if he wants one too. I play a round of golf occasionally, which keeps me active.

I also keep shire horses. I do weddings with them and for 14 years, until 2004, I did weekend rides with them and a cart around Carsington Water in Derbyshire. Since then I've been doing the same thing at Chatsworth House.

It's nice and if I got paid for every pat the horses got and every photograph that people took I would be very well off!

To be fair, though, everything after cricket has been second-best. The nearest I ever got to the feeling after that Gillette Cup semi-final was when I drove a pair of horses around a show ring at Bakewell Show and won, against all the big breweries.

I still live at Brough. I was born there and, after we lived at Castleton for 15 years when I got married in 1961, I got permission to build a bungalow at the back of the row of houses where I was born.

Now, I always tell people I live in my old back garden.

Brian Jackson
(1963–1968)

GIVEN ECB incentives for county clubs to produce their own young cricketers, their financial support of them ending at the age of 26, it is fairly safe to say that we are unlikely to see the likes of Brian Jackson again.

He was 29 when he made his county debut and 30 during that summer, having learned and honed his skills in the tough school of the leagues. Yet over the following six summers, until he decided that he wasn't the bowler that he used to be, Brian was an admirable foil for Harold Rhodes and the pair made as good and hostile a partnership as any in the country.

As I told him in the course of the interview, I never saw him bowl, but those who did remember a bowler of aggressive intent, who ran in hard and with the same sense of purpose from the first ball of the day to the last. Coming in from wide of the crease, he had a 'windmill' action but one that generated steep bounce.

He was good enough too to take 457 wickets over his six summers in the first-class game, at an average of less than 19 runs each. Serious statistics from a bowler who many good judges have told me was up there with the best of them. He wasn't a batsman – his highest effort in 160 innings was 27 – and he was a functional, rather than dynamic fielder. But with a ball in his hand he was as good a seamer as there was in England during the mid-1960s.

In 1965 he took 120 wickets at 12 runs each, as he and Harold Rhodes came first and second in the national bowling averages. His previous two seasons had been steady and he was the county's most successful bowler in 1964, but in 1965, opening batsmen looked to their game against Derbyshire with a degree of trepidation. Runs would be hard to come by and their techniques would be fully examined by two of the best bowlers in the country.

My interview with Brian flew by. He was every bit as engaging as I hoped he would be; the sort of man whose company you would thoroughly enjoy down at the local.

Much more than facing him in his pomp, from 22 yards.

Brian, how did you come to join the Derbyshire staff?

I was a professional in the North Staffordshire and South Cheshire League for Knypersley and Victoria Colliery, between 1959 and 1962. I also played Minor Counties cricket for Cheshire, which was played over two days at that time.

We played against Lancashire, Yorkshire and Warwickshire second XIs, as well as Durham [then a Minor County] and Staffordshire and I had to take time off work to play – this at a time when you only got a fortnight's holiday a year!

Cliff Gladwin had just retired and he was playing as professional at Longton against us. He saw me bowl and passed his favourable comments on to the Derbyshire coach, Denis Smith, who came up to Knypersley to see me the following week.

I had already had offers from Warwickshire and Leicestershire and turned them down, but I was working as a cashier in a factory which was closing, so I decided that I should throw in my lot with Derbyshire and give the first-class game a go at the ripe old age of 29. I signed on for Douglas Carr, the secretary of the time, and joined the county for the start of the 1963 season, although I'd played a few second-team games before then.

Did turning pro make any difference to you financially?

Not really. I was working full-time but playing as a professional at the weekend. The two incomes were about what I made at Derbyshire, but you didn't do it for the money – it was the friendship of the circuit and the fact that you loved playing the game.

Were you always a seamer?

I was and you know, I was never coached by anyone! I guess I was a natural and started playing for the RAF in 1952, when I was doing National Service. We played on wickets of rolled sand with matting stretched over them in the Middle East and they were quick with good bounce. I used to bowl quite quickly and enjoyed it.

Back home, I started playing for my local club in the High Peak League and was top of the bowling averages, I think, in 1955. I played for Whaley Bridge on a Saturday and Buxton on Sundays and they were great days, before I moved on to Knypersley as professional in 1959.

I learned a lot at Bollington Cricket Club between 1956 and 1958. They were in the Lancashire and Cheshire League and I was playing there when first selected for Cheshire. They didn't pay me, but I was picked up, ferried around and generally treated very well in my time there.

How did you find county cricket when you started, compared to the leagues where you made your name?

I never had a problem with it! I don't mean that to sound big-headed but you must remember I had learned my trade in the leagues as a professional. With that came responsibilities and a kind of pressure, but there was no real problem for me. I had a year on the staff with Harold Rhodes and Les Jackson as the first-choice opening bowlers, but I never felt that I had anything to prove and I didn't think that the established county players were better than me. I was confident in my own abilities.

I went straight into the first team in 1963, taking 75 wickets and getting my first XI cap in August of that season. Not bad, considering I left league cricket one Saturday and was playing for Derbyshire on the Wednesday of that week.

The leagues had some fine players too, so it wasn't like facing them for the first time. There was Frank Worrell, Garfield Sobers,

Sonny Ramadhin…I still remember seeing these big placards outside the ground one day – 'Norton CC with Frank Worrell v Knypersley with A.B. Jackson.' It was quite a thrill – I wish I'd kept one or two of them to show the grandchildren.

It must have been daunting following such a legendary bowler as Les, though?

Well, I knew how good he was, of course. It was certainly useful to be able to chat with him and get his thoughts on bowling. He didn't play every game in 1963, but he stressed to me that when the wicket was helpful, as an opening bowler you had to bowl the other side out – there were no excuses. He told me about the strengths of different batsmen and how you had to watch them closely to see how they move their feet.

What about Harold Rhodes?

Harold and I became good friends. When I got into the first team in 1963, Charlie Lee was skipper. Harold and I quickly hit it off as a bowling partnership and as friends. Quite often we would sit in the dressing room and have tea and sandwiches together at breaks, talking about the game, what we'd done right and what we could have done better.

Harold told me that his team-mates used to complain that he didn't bowl enough bouncers, when the opposition quick bowlers were dishing them out frequently?

That's true. I've thought about it over the years and I could and perhaps should have bowled more. I had a high action and I naturally got the ball to bounce, but my biggest asset was movement off the wicket. We were both well aware that as well as taking wickets we had to keep the runs down – bowling bouncers seemed like a waste of energy and runs to Harold and I.

I understand that your father was perhaps your sternest critic?

Oh, he was – and my biggest fan too, of course. When I took 7-21 against Cambridge University at Fenners I was really pleased, but his reaction brought me down to earth. 'They're nowt but school lads, so it doesn't really count.'

He was much more impressed when I took 8-18 against Warwickshire at Coventry in 1966!

For the benefit of modern fans who never saw you bowl, who would you compare yourself to from a pace perspective?

That's a good question! I think the closest would be Graham Onions at Durham. He's a very good bowler and in pace and what he does with the ball he reminds me of myself in my prime.

What was life like for a professional cricketer in the 1960s?

It was very different, less competitive. Of course we wanted to win and we played hard to do so, but there were a lot of convivial evenings in the bar after games, when you could chat to other players from the opposition. That hardly happens now and I think that the game is worse for that.

I remember talking to Brian Statham and asking him where he used to aim when he bowled. I'll never forget his answer – an INCH outside off stump! An inch. That showed how accurate he was and I tried to aim for that level of consistency, because we rarely had a lot of runs to play with.

Those of us that had cars used to take it in turns to drive to away games. We got sixpence a mile expenses for away games, at a time when a gallon of petrol was five shillings. It wasn't a lavish lifestyle but it was a lot of fun.

And of course, I should mention that like most players I had to work from the end of September until the second week of March each winter to pay the bills. I was a cashier in a different factory to the one I'd left to join the county circuit.

At what point in your development did you realise that you could make it in first-class cricket?

From the first ball! Like I said, I knew I could bowl and I was glad to get the chance to prove it to a bigger audience than had seen me at league level.

You had an astonishing season in 1965 with 120-odd wickets in the summer at only 12 runs each. Harold and you came first and second in the averages. Did you ever hear of interest from England selectors?

Not really. You must remember that I was 33 then and that was too old to be starting an international career. I was proud to be selected for the MCC v Surrey, the champion county, in 1966 though. It was played at Lord's and I was very excited – but it rained for nearly the whole game so I didn't get to play much cricket.

The County Ground was always high on the list of disliked grounds for players at that time. What was it like?

It was just a big open space. You must remember it was the old racecourse. There were small saplings that have now grown into sturdy trees and they have acted as a nice windbreak over the ground, but it used to be really windy – and cold. There weren't too many days when you could dispense with sweaters. The facilities were pretty basic too – it was a world apart from today.

I far preferred Chesterfield, which nearly everyone did. At that time we played around six three-day matches at Queens Park every summer and it was always a thrill to play on such a beautiful ground. The wicket was often favourable to bowlers too, so there was a lot to like.

I used to bowl from the Lake End – Harold was quicker and took the Pavilion End. At Derby I was happy with either and we used to rotate, but the old grandstand end was probably where I did most of my bowling.

The side you came into wasn't the strongest. How quickly did you form an opinion on their merits?

The batting was brittle at times and that cost us too many games. But they were a great bunch of lads. Ian Buxton, who passed away far too young, Derek Morgan, Ian Hall and, of course, the incomparable Bob Taylor. Mike Page was a great lad too and a very good cricketer, but we never strung enough good results together to challenge for honours.

BRIAN JACKSON (1963–1968)

| Who were the biggest characters in the side?

I don't know if you'd say any of them were 'characters'. They were just good lads and we all got on really well. There were no stars, no prima donnas, but we'd do anything for each other.

That really hit home when Harold was no-balled by Sid Buller at Chesterfield against the South Africans in 1965. I remain convinced that Sid was put up to it to avoid a tricky situation where Harold otherwise had to be picked for England, but the lads rallied round. It was a horrible, awkward, surreal experience and the crowd came on to the ground pretty much en masse as we went off for tea. Yet the lads kept Harold going and we all knew he didn't throw. It was nonsense, the whole thing and I felt Harold handled it all remarkably well in the circumstances.

| The county won that game?

We did. I bowled 19-2-32-2 in the first innings and 18-5-25-3 in the second. As a reward for the win we all got a bottle of sherry – South African, of course!

| You retired after the 1968 season, with over 450 wickets at less than 19 runs each. You were only 36 and perhaps had more to give?

Maybe, but I felt it was time to go. To be honest, I broke the middle finger on my bowling hand at The Oval in 1966, when I was picking the ball up in the outfield. It bobbled badly and I felt the finger go. I was out for six weeks and it was never quite the same afterwards. The physios of the time did their best, but they didn't have the stuff they have these days and the ball didn't feel the same when it was coming out of my hand after that, though I still took my share of wickets. I also had a few hamstring problems, which didn't help either.

It was my time to go in 1968 and I went back to the leagues and a job with Marston's Brewery for the next 25 years.

| How long did you play on for?

My last full season was as late as 1986, when I was 53 and playing for Buxton. I took 38 wickets at 14 and only went for two an over.

I'm proud of the fact that I still hold the league bowling record for Knypersley too. In 1970 I took 66 wickets at just 7.24 runs each.

The previous league record holder was Garfield Sobers, so not bad company to be in!

What were your favourite grounds outside Derbyshire?

As a professional cricketer, your favourites are the ones on which you do well. I always did well at Edgbaston, so I liked it there! I also enjoyed Lord's, where I bowled from the Pavilion End and usually got wickets.

I never did that well at Old Trafford though, for some reason. Coming from Whaley Bridge I'd have liked to, but it never worked out for me there.

Who were the best batsmen you bowled at in your career? Boycott, presumably?

You know, he was difficult to get out but I don't remember him ever taking us to the cleaners. I recall him getting a fifty once, but I also bowled him once at Chesterfield, which is a nice memory.

Roy Marshall could play, but he was another who didn't always get runs against our attack. Kenny Barrington was a fine player, and of course Colin Cowdrey. Mike Procter, who was a wonderful servant to Gloucestershire, was another very good player. He could bat and bowl so well.

Who would you have as Derbyshire opening bowlers in a fantasy side? Harold put you into his.

That was very kind of him! I'd have to reciprocate because he was such a very fine bowler, as well as being a lovely man. And of course, I couldn't go past Les Jackson as his partner, because they didn't come any better than him. Any side that had to face those two knew they had been in a game.

Do you watch much modern cricket?

I watch quite a lot. I go down to Derby sometimes, as well as Chesterfield. We also go up to Old Trafford and watch a few games in the North Staffordshire League. My son has played the game for a number of years, while my grandson is now playing too.

And what do you think of modern seam bowling? Would you like to have played today?

Oh yes! I am confident that I would have got wickets if I was playing now. We didn't play solely on green wickets in my day, there were times you had to bend your back and work hard for them. They might have cost me a few runs more than they did then, but I would still have got people out. A good ball is a good ball, whenever and wherever it is bowled.

I'd have enjoyed one-day cricket too and the challenges it presents. Mind you, I might have had to up my fielding. I used to get told that I suffered from 'vagrancy' in the field – usually when I was chatting to a spectator.

But don't get the idea that we couldn't and didn't field at that time. Derek Morgan could catch swallows, while Mike Page was brilliant at either slip or short leg. And of course, we had the brilliant Bob Taylor behind the stumps.

What advice would you give to a young seam bowler?

Stick at it. Learn to bowl and get your action right, so that you can put the ball where you want it to go every single time. The only way to do that is to bowl and bowl, then bowl some more. And make sure that you study the batsmen like I used to, just like Les told me. Watch their feet, watch how they make their runs and then come up with something that will counter that.

Bob Taylor MBE (1963–1984)

I HAVE watched Derbyshire cricket for 48 summers now. If I was given the same number more, I don't expect to see a better wicketkeeper than Bob Taylor.

There were times, especially in the dark years of the early 1970s, when there was little else but his glovework to savour, as a Derbyshire supporter. Early retirement of the better batsmen and the best bowlers left a young squad, with experienced recruits not always proving to be sensible signings. A player with England aspirations today would quickly head for pastures new and greater opportunity to impress, but that was generally not the way of things at that time.

Instead, Bob continued to be a shining beacon of quality through many dark days. I still recall sitting in a deckchair at Chesterfield, in one of my early viewing seasons, watching Derbyshire's young attack being mauled by experienced opponents. My Dad turned to me after a ball had gone through to Taylor behind the stumps, late on an idyllic summer day when we had taken another pasting.

'Did you hear that?'

I shook my head, unsure what I was supposed to have heard. Maybe the distant chime of an ice cream van? The first toll of the bell at the local church?

'Exactly.' He smiled and then explained. Even when his team had been under the cosh for several hours, Bob's standards were still high.

You didn't hear the ball when it landed in his gloves, nor did you hear him. He may have been known as 'Chat' for his friendly demeanour, but on a cricket pitch there was nothing remotely demonstrative about him. He just did his job. Very well.

Over the years from 1920 to 1984, Derbyshire had only three wicketkeepers, Harry Elliott, George Dawkes and Bob Taylor. The other two were fine players, but Bob sits atop the county record books like a colossus. His tally of 1,649 first-class victims, and over 2,000 in all cricket, is more than anyone else in the history of the game and likely to remain that way forever, especially as batting is now the preferred dominant skill for the men behind the sticks.

Alan Knott was better with a bat in his hands and was himself an outstanding wicketkeeper, but in Derbyshire we *knew*. It took the Kent man's involvement in Kerry Packer's World Series Cricket for the world to find out that Bob Taylor was as near flawless behind the timbers as a man could expect to be. A mishandled ball was as great a surprise as if one of our more obdurate opening batsmen had gone down the wicket first ball and deposited it over the sight screen. We didn't call him 'Brilliant Bob' for nowt.

I thought the chance to interview him for this book had gone when he suffered a heart attack in July and subsequently underwent bypass surgery. I didn't want to intrude on his recuperation but a chat with Geoff Miller confirmed that he was progressing well, his recommendation that I call much appreciated and quickly acted upon.

Which was how I spent time over a couple of evenings on the phone to a legend, a lifelong hero if you will. He sounded enthusiastic and friendly, just as I expected. He was in very good spirits and I hope that he enjoyed talking about his career as much as I did.

The man is a legend. That's all you can really say about him – and no one will argue.

Bob, you were one of many county cricketers over the years who came out of Staffordshire. How did you come to Derbyshire's attention?

Well, I was playing for Bignall End in the North Staffordshire League and was spotted by Cliff Gladwin, the former Derbyshire bowler, who was playing as a professional for Longton. He suggested to Denis Smith, the club coach, that I might be worth having a look at and it went on from there.

> **You played your first games for the second team in 1960 and took over from George Dawkes in 1961. Did you have much contact with George on the staff?**

I made my debut, on trial, against Lancashire's second team in 1960 and met a few people who were to become team-mates in the years ahead. Edwin Smith was there, who was a very fine off-spinner, but he wasn't able to play because of a broken bone in his wrist. It's funny, my first impression of Edwin was that he must have smoked a lot, because his fingers were stained brown. It was the Friars' Balsam that he used on his spinning finger when the skin tore!

I met George when I joined the staff in 1961 and he was very helpful. He had been first-choice wicketkeeper for many years and I felt sorry for Gerry Wyatt, who had been his deputy since 1950. He only had 11 matches in all that time, such was George's consistency and level of fitness.

George was a fine player – a very solid wicketkeeper and a punishing batsman, once he got going. He broke down in 1961, with a knee injury against Lancashire at Old Trafford and I played for the rest of the season. Then, in 1962, he damaged the same knee in a car accident while travelling from his home in Leicester and it effectively finished his first-class career.

Because I hadn't been born in Derbyshire, the required special registration necessitated a three-year contract, which gave me the stability to prove myself. Nowadays too many are on the scrapheap before they have really started.

> **There are similarities in your early start to a first-class career and Harvey Hosein in the current side?**

There are. I sent him a congratulatory telegram when he beat my record of catches in a match on his county debut, which was a wonderful achievement. I've never met the lad, but he appears to have a lot of potential. Good hands, which you really need.

> **You had a couple of bad accidents in your earlier career and Bob Stephenson, who later went to Hampshire, replaced you for a while?**

I missed a few matches in 1964, when I damaged my ankle playing football. I told the club that I had slipped on an escalator, as I knew I would be in trouble if they knew the truth. It taught me to be more careful with my fitness and to do the right things.

The other time was when I got hit in the eye when facing Tony Lock at Leicester, in 1967. I went to sweep him on a turning wicket and the top edge went into my eye. I was in hospital for six weeks and I was concerned for my career at that time. Bob came in to the side and did a very good job for the rest of the summer.

At the start of the following season, he told me that he had an offer from Hampshire and wasn't sure whether to take it. I told him that if he wanted to stay and fight for the place, that was his prerogative, but I wasn't going to give up. So Bob went down south and had a fine, successful career with them, winning trophies and becoming a key member of a fine side.

> **Yet you got through your entire career as wicketkeeper without breaking a finger?**

I did, although they don't look so clever these days – they are a little twisted! My two index fingers are the worst, because they took the brunt of the impact.

Spectators perhaps think the ball comes straight through, but in fact the ball, through aerodynamics, dips and swerves. If you don't get your hands just right, those two fingers can take a lot of stick and, over time, mine have gone out of shape.

> **You must have taken the ball cleanly over all those years, though?**

They always used to say that I had soft hands; in other words that I took the ball well, my hands 'gave' with the impact and there was little noise when it landed in my gloves.

I far prefer to have been known for that than to have been called 'iron gloves', like a few others over the years!

┃ They called Rodney Marsh that at the start of his career?

That's right, but Rodney was keeping to Jeff Thomson, who for a few summers was bowling as fast as anyone perhaps has ever done. When you get a ball moving and dipping at that pace, unless you are in your best form, there will be balls that you miss or drop. To be fair to him, he became a very good wicketkeeper, at least standing back, which was where he had to do most of his work for that Australian side.

┃ The team you came into was not the strongest, though there were still some good players. Could you compare keeping wicket to Les Jackson, his namesake Brian and Harold Rhodes?

Les was just extraordinary. He used to bowl the ball and the seam would come down straight, every single time. Then, depending what he had done with his fingers, it would cut into or away from the batsman. If they got a nick, the ball still came through with the seam straight. It was astonishing, the total command that he had over a cricket ball.

It was his accuracy too. He would hit a spot, around 12 inches square, all day long, with bad balls coming as a real surprise to all of us.

Harold was another very fine bowler, who did very well to rise above the nonsense over his bowling action. He was quick, there was no doubt about it, although his real express days were behind him when I came into the side. He more often kept the quick ball for the element of surprise.

Brian was a wonderful bowler too. He came into the game late but bowled a consistent line, on or just outside off stump at decent pace. Geoff Boycott calls it the 'corridor of uncertainty' and Brian found that line on a regular basis.

He was a handful. They all were.

┃ How did Harold compare in pace to Alan Ward of a later vintage?

Alan was very fast when he first came into the side. We played Glamorgan at Sophia Gardens in 1968 and he took ten wickets. Alan Jones was one of the best opening batsmen in the country at that time and he was done twice by pace. A few of his team-mates weren't keen to get into line and we thought we had a real world-beater on our hands.

Then the injuries came. He went to the West Indies with 'Jim' Swanton's side and broke down. He was never the same after that, except for occasional performances.

Peter Eyre was another very good bowler. He was very underrated.

> **If you were choosing a fantasy Derbyshire side from those you have kept to over the years, who would you select as your opening bowlers?**

One would have to be Les Jackson, without doubt. The other, probably Harold, who maintained high standards under a lot of pressure. Brian would push them both, as would Ole Mortensen later. 'Stan', as we called him, was very volatile and admitted he 'didn't give a toss' for reputations. He was a very fine bowler though!

> **There were a few summers of struggle, where wins were rare and finances very tight. Was there any point at which you thought of moving to a more fashionable county? Was there ever an offer to do so?**

There were offers, but I was never interested. I saw Derbyshire as 'my' county and I was always happy there. Maybe I could have moved and got greater attention, but I always told myself that if I maintained standards and kept working hard, opportunities at a higher level would come eventually.

> **You got a Test appearance in New Zealand at the end of the 1970/71 tour to Australia. With Alan Knott firmly entrenched as England wicketkeeper, did you ever give up on another international call? After all, you had to wait another six years, until the advent of World Series Cricket.**

I went on a few tours, always well aware that I was number two to Alan, but I kept working and waiting for a chance. At times a few members of the tabloid press would ask questions, hoping that I would run him down or moan. I never did. My role was to train hard and play well in the matches when he was rested, so he was pushed all the way. There can only be one wicketkeeper in the side and Alan was, without doubt, a far better batsman than me.

Did your batting form ever worry you?

No. I always did my best, but the only time I used to worry was if my wicketkeeping standards dropped. That was my main role in the side and the batting was always seen as a bonus.

You took on the Derbyshire captaincy in 1975, but gave it up early in the 1976 season, citing your form as the reason?

That's right. I took it on but said that it was only until it started to affect my family life, or my form. There's so much involved in captaincy. It's not just picking a team and changing the field, but perhaps you have players coming to you with marital problems or the like. Things were building up and it got to the stage when I was getting to the ground and not wanting to play.

There were a few players on the circuit who longed for it to rain so they could play cards all day, but if you want to perform to a high standard, you have to want to play and that disappeared for me. So I told the committee I was stepping down and Eddie Barlow took over.

Eddie transformed Derbyshire, of course. Was that your happiest time at the club?

Yes, without doubt. His three years were wonderful for players and supporters alike. He was a natural leader, hugely self-confident and that rubbed off on everyone else. It was no coincidence that Geoff Miller, Mike Hendrick and I all became established Test players around that time. He made you think about your game and told you your responsibilities. It was all about discipline and self-discipline for Eddie. We were the first team to start running around the boundary before the game and Eddie placed great importance on physical fitness, which knocks on to mental toughness, of course.

You kept to three good off-spinners at Derbyshire – Edwin Smith, Geoff Miller and Venkat. How would you compare the three?

They were all different. Edwin latterly bowled away swingers too often, rather than keeping it as a secret weapon, which it was initially. He was small, didn't get much bounce but was a very good bowler.

Geoff was a more conventional off-spinner and did well for club and country, of course. Venkat was taller and got more bounce than the others. They were all very good bowlers and it was a privilege to 'keep' to all of them.

> **Do you think that Derbyshire would have had a better chance in the 1969 Gillette Cup Final had Edwin played for variation? After all, Don Wilson took three wickets for Yorkshire.**

I have always been a big advocate of spinners bowling in one-day cricket, because the batsmen have to make the running. Against seam, they can use the pace to work it around, but they can't against a good slow bowler. I would have had Edwin in the side, especially at Lord's, when he would have given them problems.

We were all surprised when Derek won the toss and bowled that day though. It went completely against what we had decided at the team meeting the previous night and to this day I don't know why he changed his mind.

> **We lost again at Lord's in 1978. We just never got going with the bat against Kent and, uncharacteristically, both you and Eddie Barlow dropped catches in their reply?**

Sometimes that happens. Eddie was a fine slip fielder and for us both to drop a catch in such a game was unfortunate. I'm not sure it would have made a difference to the result, because we didn't get anywhere near enough runs, but it was a frustration for both of us. Eddie wanted a trophy to finish his stay with the county and we so desperately wanted to win it for him.

The worst I remember was when I had played for MCC against Australia at Lord's and then went back to play for Derbyshire in the John Player League, against Glamorgan at Ilkeston. I dropped their brilliant West Indian, Roy Fredericks, three times in four balls off Ian Buxton! Ian's bowling was away swing to the left-hander and Roy kept edging and I kept dropping them.

I'd switched off – perhaps became a little complacent – and it taught me another lesson.

Did you always prefer to stand up to Ian?

Yes, and Derek Morgan. They wanted me back, but I felt I was in no-man's land, as they weren't quick enough to justify it. So I stood up and put pressure on the batsmen in doing so. It went wrong that day, but generally it was better for them and for the team that I was up at the stumps.

The National Westminster Bank Trophy Final in 1981 against Northamptonshire was more rewarding – and emotional – for you. That was your benefit year and must have helped?

I got the MBE that year too, so it was a good one for me! We won both the semi-final and final on fewer wickets lost and they were incredibly tense affairs. I think Geoff Cook, who was fielding at bat/pad, has nightmares to this day, as he was fielding too deep. For the last ball of the match he should have been up on the edge of the cut strip. The ball hit Colin Tunnicliffe on the thigh and Geoff Miller set off like Usain Bolt from the non-striker's end. He dived for the crease to get home, but he should have been run out easily. Not that it mattered to us, of course. There were a few tears shed that night and after all those years it was a very special moment.

In the semi-final I had been at the non-striker's end for the last ball and Keith Fletcher had all his men around the bat. I told Paul Newman, who was facing, to just run, wherever the ball went.

Norbert Phillip bowled and the ball squirted out into the off side. He ran to pick it up and could have raced me to the stumps and run me out. Instead, for some reason, he turned and threw at the stumps at the non-striker's end, instead of to Brian Hardie, who had gone to them. The ball flew past him and we got home! They weren't happy, I can tell you, but we had won and the celebrations were lengthy.

I understand that you used to modify your Mitre wicketkeeping gloves before use?

That's right. Some players had gloves specially made for them, but

I got mine straight off the shelf. I used to cut the webbing out, then I used to get a scalpel and slit inside the palm of the gloves. I would remove all the filling on the palms with tweezers, so it was just rubber and leather.

It was a different theory to that of Alan Knott. He had his gloves specially made and used two pairs of inners, as well as plasticine in the palm of his hands. He still has hands like a concert pianist, so maybe his theory was better than mine!

My rationale was that, especially when I was standing up, I needed to 'feel' the ball in my hands. Perhaps that makes Alan's standards over the years the more commendable, because with all that padding I don't really know how he could do that.

How long did a pair of wicketkeeping gloves generally last you?

They would last me two or three seasons on average, although the pair that is in the museum at Lord's lasted me five years. Like all wicketkeepers, I didn't like new gloves and liked to get them 'bedded in' as quickly as possible – and make them last if I could.

Who is the best wicketkeeper you have seen and who has been the best since your retirement?

I was a huge fan of both Keith Andrew and Godfrey Evans. I was in the crowd at Old Trafford when Jim Laker got his 19 wickets and watched Godfrey very carefully, but when I turned professional, Keith was the man I really looked up to.

Subsequently, Alan Knott and Ian Healy were wonderful behind the stumps. I talk to Ian a lot and the way he kept to Shane Warne was remarkable. Jack Russell was outstanding too.

More recently, Chris Read and James Foster have been the best on the county circuit. They have combined a high standard behind the stumps with scoring a lot of runs, as well as the captaincy at times. Both have been poorly treated from an England perspective.

I think Jos Buttler needs more experience. He is a fine batsman, but doesn't look a natural behind the stumps. It is perhaps the same as how Alec Stewart became a good wicketkeeper. When he started in the role for England, he wasn't first choice in the role for his county, which had to be wrong.

And since retirement? How have you filled your time?

When I first retired I worked for Mitre Sports and endorsed their cricket products. Since then I have worked for British Cricket Balls for the past 20 years. We supply the cricket balls for Test matches, county games, league cricket, colleges and public schools. I work between January and June.

I used to lead cricket tours too, but I am 74 now and don't want to be travelling all the time. It is good to spend time at home!

Peter Gibbs
(1966–1972)

PETER GIBBS was a very good opening batsman for Derbyshire and subsequently has become known as an even better writer. From 1968 to 1972 he passed 1,000 runs each summer, yet surprised fans by retiring in the latter year, well before reaching his peak and when he was arguably the most reliable batsman in the side. He was a delightful player to watch, especially with his driving through the covers and may well have scored even more heavily in a side with a little more support. He scored more than 10,000 first-class runs and his brief career suggested a player of considerable talent.

His style was that of a man brought up on wickets more firm and true than those of his county. Those at The Parks were conducive to his game, but he adapted his style to suit all surfaces and he formed a fine, but too-short-lived opening pairing with Yorkshireman David Smith. A right and left combination, the club's fortunes in the 1970s may well have been better had they been able to stay in the first-class game. Yet Peter retired at 28, David at 31, when both had plenty left to give. Cricket was not sufficiently lucrative for either and other, long-term opportunities beckoned.

For Peter, that career was in writing. He is perhaps best known as the writer of 52 episodes of *Heartbeat,* as well as episodes of several other TV series, including *The Bill* and *Hetty Wainthropp Investigates,* plus a number of acclaimed plays.

In addition to his ongoing contributions to television, he has been a writer of commercial training films, a sports correspondent for the *Daily Telegraph* and *Sunday Telegraph* and a feature writer for *Wisden*. His debut novel, *Settling the Score*, was published by Methuen and short-listed for the MCC Book of the Year Award.

He is a very talented and engaging man and I was delighted to catch up with him.

You grew up in the Potteries, a rich source of cricket talent for Derbyshire over the years. Where did you play your cricket there?

It was a stroke of fortune to grow up in the Potteries as a cricket-mad kid. The 'five towns' that formed the city of Stoke-on-Trent made for a conurbation with a number of sub-districts within a small radius. Just as the textile towns of Lancashire and Yorkshire boasted thriving cricket leagues, so did the North Staffordshire Potteries. At my state school, pitch preparation was poor. I got an early indication of this when I saw the school roller being pulled by a tractor!

Did you come up against any other county players in that time?

I played for Norton Cricket Club on a ground owned and maintained by the National Coal Board. Boys in the junior section got to play on the excellent pitches used by the senior side the previous weekend. Bob Taylor and David Steele had already progressed to senior level by the time I first played but I did coincide with John Steele, David's brother.

Later, after graduating to the senior Norton side, I played with some of the greatest players the game has ever seen. Before I was out of my teens I played with Frank Worrell, Jim Laker, and Gary Sobers, and against Wes Hall and Sonny Ramadhin. Great days for a star-struck youngster like me but dog-days for the West Indians, who were prevented by the registration rules from plying their trade in England at first-class level at that time.

You made your Staffordshire debut at the age of 16 in 1961. That must have been nerve-wracking?

Yes, I made my debut at the same age as Bob Taylor and David Steele. Again I was lucky to have ex-England and Lancashire player John Ikin as my skipper and mentor. I managed to hang around to help get some first innings points, but truthfully I was well out of my depth for a couple of seasons. At that stage I thought of nothing else but being a first-class cricketer.

> **You then studied at Oxford University, where you gained a 'Blue' in your first year. Was the jump to playing against first-class cricketers noticeable?**

It is hard now to credit the unbelievable privilege I had in playing cricket at Oxford with a schedule of continuous three-day first-class matches throughout the summer term. My tutors were extremely accommodating, just as long as I made up for my absences in the winter.

Needless to say there was a step-change in the standard of cricket when we were confronted by professional opposition. Some people suggest that the counties must have sent second XIs to play at Oxbridge. Not likely, not in my time anyway (1964–66). It was not only a case of early-season practice for the 'pros', but the possibility of padding their averages – and most professionals were paid a match fee, which they were unwilling to forego.

To illustrate the point, in my second game, the Yorkshire line-up included Close, Trueman, Illingworth, Wilson, Sharpe, Hampshire, Ryan, Taylor and Padgett. Perhaps because of my league and Minor Counties experience, I was less overwhelmed than others who were making an even sharper transition from schoolboy cricket.

> **What are your main memories of cricket in The Parks? Presumably better batting wickets than you got in Derbyshire?**

The half-timbered pavilion at The Parks stands as a reminder to those who play there that the place has an illustrious history. Wood panelling inside is inscribed with past 'Blues' teams including the likes of Cowdrey, Nawab of Pataudi, Imran Khan, and M.J.K. Smith.

Something of a comedown then, that my debut appearance is recorded as 'Gibbs, run out 0'.

How did the Derbyshire approach come about?

Though I was still keen to become a fully-fledged county cricketer, after three years at university I was older, wiser and more aware of the pitfalls of committing to a sporting career. I had talked to Mike Smith about joining Warwickshire, against whom I had made a couple of centuries while at Oxford. He was welcoming but realistic. I'd have to be patient – his side was already stuffed with batsmen.

In contrast, Derbyshire's strength was in its bowling. My decision was finally an easy one when Rolls-Royce offered me a graduate apprenticeship with time off in summer to play county cricket. Yes please. Wow!

What was your first impression of the Derbyshire set-up when you joined?

It was just as well my cricket had been first formed by hard-nosed league experience rather than the 'dreaming spires' of Oxford. At Norton I had played with a slag-heap the size of the pyramids in the background, so Derby held no terrors for me, even if it did call its football arena the Baseball Ground and its cricket field the Racecourse.

As many have testified, the County Ground was so exposed in April and May we were paid survival money! The uncovered wickets of that era and the prevailing dampness of the Peak District made it a perfect environment for seam bowlers and favoured the sort of gritty, uncompromising cricket we played. In the season before I joined, Derbyshire had scored over 200 on only nine occasions. They made under 100 in 11 innings, their opponents under 100 in nine, yet the team finished halfway up the championship table.

The pavilion was adapted from the old racecourse buildings. You couldn't view the field of play from the dressing rooms. When you went out to bat you walked past the saddling enclosure and through an alley by the stewards' box.

You had to laugh.

Denis Smith was coach at that time. He had a reputation for straight talking and not molly coddling players.

The Derbyshire team I joined were a great bunch – though our surroundings sometimes made it feel like the equivalent of doing military service, a feeling reinforced by the club coach, our sergeant major. Denis had been a fine player in his time and lived and breathed cricket. He may have frightened some young trialists but to those who got to know him, his bark was much worse than his bite.

> **You made your county debut in 1966 and hit your first century in that season. Do you have particular memories of that innings?**

I played my first game for the county after the 'Varsity' match at the tail end of 1966. The following season started reasonably, but then I got bogged down on a run of wet wickets, got dropped, and spent six weeks in the second XI.

When I returned to the side I scored 90 against Yorkshire and a run of good form, including two centuries, took me to 84 runs shy of a thousand for the season.

My late improvement not only helped to confirm that I was worth my place in the side, it also marked the start of my successful opening partnership with David Smith.

> **From 1968 to 1972 you passed the 1,000-run mark every summer, which was quite a feat in an average batting side. At what point did you feel you had 'arrived' as a county batsman?**

To score a thousand runs in a season was a first-class batsman's benchmark of respectability. Of course it took more innings to achieve it in the era of uncovered pitches, but missing that target would have been a let-down.

The point at which you were thought to have 'arrived' as a county batsman was clearly marked by the award of your county cap. This wasn't just ceremonial, it meant an increase in salary. David Smith, John Harvey, and myself were awarded our senior caps on the same day, before we travelled to play a three-day match at Bath.

It was raining heavily when we got there and we gathered in the bar to celebrate our caps, hoping for a delayed start the next day. In fact the rain kept falling to such an extent that when we got to the ground in the morning, Derek Morgan, our skipper, was casting his fishing rod on to the flooded field from the steps of the pavilion!

I'd love to hear your thoughts on the Derbyshire dressing room at that time. Who were the characters?

From 1968 to 1970 my left-hand right-hand opening partnership with David Smith meant the team were usually given the good starts necessary for success. Alan Ward had stepped in when Brian Jackson retired and together variously with Harold Rhodes, Peter Eyre, and Fred Rumsey our seam attack was still formidable. Playing in such a competitive side was enjoyable, especially when hard-hitting South African, Chris Wilkins, joined the club. His positive style of play was infectious and gave all his team-mates a more confident attitude. In 1970 I scored 1,441 runs at an average of 41. I thought that was to be the launch-pad to a prosperous future but sport has a way of bringing you sharply down to earth.

I've already described the Derbyshire team I joined as a great bunch. As players they were canny, resourceful, and hard to beat. When I joined them from Oxford a certain coolness could have been forgiven but I was absorbed into the squad without any awkwardness. A county cricket team played, travelled and roomed together continuously, like a travelling circus or repertory theatre company. The team was much like a 'family', with all that that implies in terms of friendships, resentments, laughter and tears. Just to complete the picture of a home from home, we had a gas fire in the dressing room at Derby surrounded by a clothes horse!

We had our England 'stars' like Bob Taylor, Harold Rhodes, and Alan Ward but they were given no special treatment in the dressing room. The banter could come from any quarter but would probably revolve around Mike Page. The subject matter would not surprise anyone – birds, booze, horses, pay, travel expenses, inadequate catering, ignorant pressmen, committee incompetence – everyone had an opinion and expressed it. Some players were placid, others hot-headed. Some were chaotically untidy, others fastidious to a fault.

No names, no pack drill!

| **Were you ever aware of being under consideration for higher honours?**

As an opening batsman in the 1960s and early 70s, I was very aware of the many fine openers around the country. Boycott, Luckhurst, Milburn, Prideaux, Edrich, Amiss, Russell, Sharpe, Barber, Jones, Green, Pullar – the list was a lengthy and illustrious one.

Even in my best year, higher honours were well out of reach. However, I was selected to play for England under-25s in 1968 – sadly it coincided with my wedding day!

The Derbyshire coach nearly swallowed his pipe when I told him I had turned the selectors down, in favour of a walk up the aisle.

| **A couple of other names for you – Harold Rhodes, whose career was blighted by the throwing controversy. Did that hang over the club to some extent?**

At Oxford there had been a persistent lack of penetration in the pace bowling department so it was a joy to join a side with genuine menace. Rhodes, Jackson [Brian], and Ward were class acts. As an opening batsman it was nice to know your opposite numbers were getting worked over the same as you. At the time it was felt Harold was the most notable victim of MCC's drive to eradicate throwing in the vain hope that other countries would follow suit. Harold had a hyper-extended elbow – it went past straight – which from certain angles could make the joint look bent.

As further proof, he rightly claimed that nobody with such a side-on, close to the stumps action such as his could throw the ball. Yet his international career was fatally damaged, while that of Charlie Griffith continued.

| **Alan Ward? When he first burst on to the scene he shook up a fair few opposition batsmen with his raw pace. What was said about him on the circuit at that time?**

Alan had an impressively high classical action which generated great pace and bounce. For a short time, batsmen around the country must have considered other ways to make a living, but lanky in frame and long in the ligaments, Alan needed luck to stay physically fit. When

E.W. Swanton spotted his potential, he included him in a friendly tour to the West Indies.

Unprepared for the bone-jarring pitches he encountered, Alan came back with a back injury and though he subsequently played for England, his fitness remained compromised. It is a great pity that perhaps now so few people will have heard of him, because he was the real deal and wonderful to watch, from the safety of the boundary rope.

> **I thought Ian Buxton did a good job when he took over the captaincy from Derek Morgan in 1970, but things tailed off badly thereafter. Why was that?**

Instead of building on the success of 1970, the club complacently assumed past form was a guide to the future and the 1971 squad was allowed to diminish in experience and quality. In particular our bowling attack fell apart. Harold Rhodes had left in 1969 and Peter Eyre and Alan Ward were both beset by injuries. Although the batting remained solid, David Smith had retired, a blow for me personally because my subsequent partners all proved to be right-handers. Derbyshire finished at the foot of the championship, having drawn 19 out of 24 matches, winning only once.

Still nothing was done to strengthen the squad, so we experienced an even worse season in 1972, again winning only one game and finishing emphatically bottom of the table. This time only Chris Wilkins and I scraped to a thousand runs. Previously I had not felt under undue pressure to perform as 'a leading batsman' but our collective failure forced me back into a shell that I thought I had escaped from years before.

In an uncompetitive team it felt as though we were playing with our backs to the wall from the outset of each game and I had neither the skill, experience, or capacity to help young players who were being drafted into a struggling side.

> **I was surprised by a review of your novel in a local newspaper that referred to you as a 'dour' opening batsman. My memory suggests you were more aggressive than many of your contemporaries. Which would you say was the more accurate?**

It was during this period that one particular reporter put the knife into me for batting in an ultra-defensive manner and he never let it rest. So perhaps the 'dour' accusation stuck with some people. In my earliest days at Norton, I had learned to ignore the understandable impatience of spectators who wanted to see the back of me and the entrance of Sobers. In that way I developed the sort of obduracy I needed in first-class cricket when the pitch was wet and slow, when my timing went AWOL, or when a particular bowler was tying me down.

Yet there were other days 'in the sun' when things went right and the runs seemed to come easily. Then I like to think it was as much a pleasure for the spectator as it was for me. But generally you hoped to play the type of innings needed by the team at any particular stage of the game.

> **You retired from the first-class game in 1972 when you were only 28. At what point that year did you decide that you'd had enough?**

I decided to retire when arguably the best years of a batsman's career lay ahead. However, during the demoralising 1971 and 1972 seasons, I felt my batting had gone backwards and looking ahead I couldn't see things improving. Chris Wilkins had decided to leave and the only bright spot was the emergence of Mike Hendrick. In 1973, the county avoided its third consecutive wooden spoon by just one point but there were other considerations. Ian Buxton and I had started a sports business in 1970, which had become more and more time-consuming. Disappointing though it was, it seemed the right decision for me and for my family.

In those days it was considered an impertinence to announce your retirement before the committee had had a chance to sack you. In 1972 I scored 1,119 first-class runs, Chris Wilkins 1,033, the next highest, 787. In Sunday League, Chris made 409, me 402, next highest, 241 runs. In an effort to stay connected to the club I offered to play one-day and second-team cricket. This was rejected on the grounds that I wasn't a limited-overs player, yet I was the first Derbyshire player to make a thousand Sunday League runs.

And that was it. Two other counties approached me on hearing the news, but by then I had mentally switched off from the game and was opening a new chapter.

> **Your post-cricket career has been a great success, with successful plays for radio and for theatre. Was that always where you saw your writing career going?**

I had enjoyed writing sketches while at school and carried on producing scripts for college 'smokers' at university – even submitting doomed sitcoms to the BBC.

So writing stories was a hobby that became a living. My big break came when David Puttnam produced *Arthur's Hallowed Ground*, a film about a cricket groundsman, inspired it is said, (I couldn't possibly comment) on Walter Goodyear, the legendary curator at Derby. Other cricket-based dramas followed – *Benefit of the Doubt* about two first-class umpires, and *Taking Us Up To Lunch* about the *TMS* commentary team.

Apart from these projects, I created four six-part series for BBC and ITV besides a number of part-series credits such as *The Bill* and *Hetty Wainthropp*. As an established writer I then got sucked into several development projects that were never produced. When I spoke to Peter Tinniswood (he of *Tales from a Long Room* fame) about my experience in 'development hell', he said I should talk to the *Heartbeat* producer.

> **You became the main scriptwriter for *Heartbeat*, writing over 50 episodes. How did that come about?**

As most viewers know, *Heartbeat* is a family show made to fit an eight o'clock Sunday slot, so writers knew what was and wasn't acceptable. It had a year-round production schedule to which a writer would contribute scripts (four to five per year in my case) based on his or her own stories. After my frustrations with development projects it was a relief to know that my scripts would regularly see the light of day. The nature of the show meant it didn't take itself too seriously and it was great to work again within a team environment.

I took guard and set myself to score 50.

> **And so on to your debut novel – *Settling the Score*. How did it come about?**

My novel took me on and off 18 months to write and had been simmering for some years. Cricket has a wealth of literature but very little of it in fictional form and I was warned by people in the publishing business that sport and fiction do not mix. I thought this was strange. If novels can be created out of the most mundane material why not out of something as unpredictable and exciting as sport? Certainly reading a book and watching a match take place are two different experiences, but in turning pages aren't we similarly present, as a story unfolds to an unknown conclusion? True, the writer manipulates events, but for reasons of litigation or taste, fiction can get where cameras and reporters can't – sometimes to the truth.

What it comes down to, in my view, is authenticity. If we watch a crime or legal drama, it helps credibility that most of us aren't detectives or judges. But when it comes to sport, EVERYBODY is an expert – enough of one, at least, to spot a fake. Note that in the three cricket-based dramas I mentioned earlier, none of them had players in action. The thought of actors pretending to be professional cricketers fills me full of horror, as the viewer would not believe it. But nobody who reads *Settling the Score* could doubt that it is written by someone who has been there and therefore believes those characters could indeed exist.

> **The action is fast-paced and there is great characterisation. Some of them seemed to be based on people – at Derbyshire and elsewhere – that I remembered. Is it safe to say that these are composites, or are some of them based on specific people?**

When people ask me for advice on writing, the ability to create believable characters is the first requirement. Excluding a biopic, a real life character very rarely provides all the elements needed to serve the writer's story. That's why it is genuinely the case that people in a drama or a novel are made up. True, KC, the senior pro in my book, might be seen as an amalgam of Les Jackson (brilliant bowler overlooked by England selectors), Cliff Gladwin (hard as nails, rough-tongued), and Fred Trueman (anti-authoritarian, sentimental). KC is all of them and none, and that applies throughout my fictional teams.

Of course, I can't stop people trying to muscle in on the act. Some old colleagues may well be offended that they haven't been selected for my book. Even in shows with an all-male cast, my mother used to swear I had included her in the action. In a way, genetically, I had.

> **The 1960s were the first time that footballers became real social 'animals'. Was cricket the same at that time, bearing in mind the nightclub scene in the book?**

Sportsmen changed their off-the-field behaviour in the 1960s, but only along with everyone else. George Best was, I suppose, the most prominent sportsman who was characterised by the media as a playboy footballer. Fit young adults in sports teams were likely to have busier 'social' lives than most.

However, those who played professional cricket six or seven days a week could not drink or go clubbing to excess without affecting their performance on the field. There were plenty of distractions, but many players shunned the nightlife, if only to preserve finances. Others burnt the candle at both ends and shortened their careers.

You made your choice.

> **The book looks at personal enmities and rivalries in some detail. Was that commonplace in the era in which you played?**

If a hectic social life did affect a player's performance, the first people to tell him would likely be his team-mates, who had to take up the slack. A dropped catch through lack of concentration, a stupid run-out, or a brainless slog would qualify for criticism within the dressing room and perhaps long-term suspicion of a player's commitment to the job. Rivalry between players was present, but also veiled.

Teams tended to be more unchanging in that era, so if you lost your place you were probably out for a while. Naturally you were self-interested in how your replacement was faring. Bowlers might compete for choice of ends, but I never recall it being a big issue. So, generally in my time we were a pretty co-operative combine. In a fiction, of course, such harmony would have the reader nodding off to sleep.

As my old opening partner, David Smith, said after reading the book, if all the matches had been like that, our careers would have been a hell of a lot shorter!

Finally, what next for Peter Gibbs?

Another book probably, but not about cricket. It could be about a scriptwriter of a popular Sunday evening TV drama – so it will be the same mixture of sex and violence…

Tony Borrington (1971–1980)

THE REALITY of Tony Borrington's career is somewhat different to the perception of it from some followers of the game.

Read critiques of his career and such words as 'dour', 'dogged' and 'stubborn' appear. Yet such terminology ignores the fact that, at the time of his retirement from the first-class game in 1981, he had scored over 1,000 more one-day runs than any other Derbyshire player.

Indeed, in his early career Tony was quite a dasher, more likely than most in the Derbyshire batting line-up to ensure that the scorer used his different coloured pens. He had all the shots around the wicket and could be good entertainment value in a side that wasn't always known for such things when batting.

Indeed, he was the second man to score a limited-overs century for Derbyshire, being beaten to the draw by his long-time friend and opening partner Alan 'Bud' Hill. Even now, if such a question came up in a quiz, the chances are the casual Derbyshire fan wouldn't know the answer – and quite possibly may not believe it once they heard.

Later, as he admitted to me in the course of our chat, when he became a professional cricketer the status could weigh heavy on his shoulders. That was when some of the attritional innings, for which Derbyshire batsmen have been better known over the years, were played. On wickets that more often than not favoured the county's seam bowlers, the onus was on the batsman who did get in to sell his wicket dearly. 'Giving it away' was a crime, when too many players struggled to get in at all on green wickets where the ball zipped around off a length at great pace.

That is the other side of the story, because Tony opened the batting, more often than not, in a period when almost every county had a fast bowler. Most of them came from the four corners of the globe, as the English county game became the place to forge your career, hone your skills and make your reputation.

The stories about facing them came thick and fast as we chatted at the 3aaa County Ground during a tough evening session for Derbyshire. As one might expect from a man who spent his subsequent career as a well-respected teacher and headmaster, Tony is engaging and articulate company, in demand on the after-dinner circuit and at cricket society meetings.

Tony, you were born in Spondon – how quickly did you come to Derbyshire's attention?

Well, I had played age-group cricket for England from under-15 level and when I was in sixth form was selected for the same England under-19 side as Bob Woolmer. The following year I was captain of the England Schools Cricket Association at Winchester and scored 92 against the visiting schools side from South Africa. I think I was the first Derbyshire player at that level.

Were you keeping wicket as well at that time?

I never kept wicket! When I made the Derbyshire first team, Bob Taylor needed a game off and I said that I would do it, as it got me into the side and I kept wicket in my batting pads. There is a picture of me taking a catch off Alan Ward, against the Indian touring side, which looked very impressive but sadly was taken just before an even better dive and roll for full effect.

Bob gave me some basic coaching and told me how I should lean in towards the stumps when I took the ball down the leg side, which was all well and good, until I kept on another occasion against Oxford University.

What happened there?

It was when Eddie Barlow was captain. Bob needed a rest and Alan Hill told Eddie that I had kept before, so I got the role against Oxford University. All went well, until the closing stages of the match. Geoff Miller bowled a ball down the leg side to Richard Savage that he went to sweep. The trouble was he followed through and I had 'leaned in' so far that he clubbed me on the side of the head with his bat, knocking my cap off in the process.

The lads were laughing at first, but then I collapsed to the floor and blood started spurting everywhere. I was rushed to the John Radcliffe hospital in Oxford.

The club yearbook said that you received a nasty wound 'that required several stitches'.

They shaved half of my head and inserted 18! This was on a Friday and I was allowed out of hospital and spoke to Eddie Barlow. I asked if, rather than going home, I could go down to London with the team – we were playing Surrey at The Oval on the Sunday.

'Of course you can,' said Eddie. 'You're playing.' The doctor had assured him it was only a surface wound and we put on 69 for the third wicket, while I sported the prototype of cricket's first Mohican haircut!

I kept a hat on the whole time we were in London.

You first played for the club second team in 1965, but it wasn't until 1971 that you made your first-team debut – that was a long apprenticeship?

I was at Loughborough University from 1967 to 1971 and Derbyshire were quite happy with the arrangement. You must remember that at that time, senior players in county sides were only replaced when they retired. Only if you were exceptional were you going to force your way into a side before the age of 21 or 22 and young players all knew their place.

A lot of senior players retired around that time and it left an opening that, coincidentally, arose at the time that I had finished university.

> **In that game you opened and top-scored with 70 against a fine attack, led by John Lever and Keith Boyce. What do you remember of it?**

I was at home with tonsillitis, feeling pretty rough and in my bed when there was a knock on the door. My mother came and told me that Denis Smith, the Derbyshire coach, was looking for me.

I went downstairs and he told me that Peter Gibbs had broken a finger and that I had to get myself down to Ilford to play. I told him that I had tonsillitis and he said, 'Tha' doesn't bat with tha' tonsils, lad – get thi'sen down there.'

So I got a train down to London, another to Ilford, then a taxi to the hotel. I got there around half past ten at night and Ian Buxton, the captain, met me. He told me that nobody would share with me, because of my illness, so I ended up in a room with Mike Carey, the local journalist, who I kept awake all night.

We fielded first and bowled them out for 173, then we batted and I was 38 not out overnight. I could hardly stand up at the end of the day and thankfully it rained on the second day, which I spent in bed.

By the time the third day came around, I felt a little better and eventually made 70, which at that time was only three runs short of Frank Sugg's record for a Derbyshire player on debut, which had been made in 1884.

> **You became a regular player in 1973 and did quite well for a player lacking experience, then rarely featured in 1974 and 1975. Why was that?**

In 1973, both Alan Hill and I were given a decent opportunity, but we finished the season with averages of around 20 from 700 runs. We knew that we needed to kick on and Bob Taylor took me to one side and said that I needed to go and play abroad.

John Jameson was a close friend of his and was not returning to a coaching role in Rhodesia, now Zimbabwe. I went out and coached alongside Robin Jackman, Mike Procter and Brian Davison and it went really well.

When I got back home for the 1974 season, we had signed Lawrence Rowe as overseas player, but his paperwork hadn't come through. I played the first Benson and Hedges Cup match against Nottinghamshire at Trent Bridge in his place. I made 81 against Garfield Sobers, then held a full-length, diving catch to get him out from Geoff Miller's bowling, earning the man of the match award.

I was then dropped. I spoke to Brian Bolus, the captain, and he said that they had to play Lawrence Rowe, but my reply was simple – why at my expense? Brian said that he was going with senior players, which was his prerogative, but after a good winter and that start, it affected me more than I realised.

I played a handful of championship games and volunteered to keep wicket against the Indian tourists, telling Brian I had kept wicket before, when I hadn't. I caught Eknath Solkar off Alan Ward's bowling and was thrilled with a newspaper report that said, 'Borrington kept wicket most efficiently.'

At the end of the summer, I was so disheartened at the lack of opportunity that I told them I was leaving. So I went into teaching, taking the job of head of PE at Grace Dieu Manor School in Leicestershire.

I didn't hold a grudge against Brian Bolus. As I got older, I understood his dilemma and sympathised, because senior players, whether in form or not, were expected to be in the first team at that time.

Did you play any cricket in that year?

I signed to play for Cresswell in the Bassetlaw League and it went really well. I got three hundreds in the first month of the season. When news of my scores reached Derbyshire, who were carrying a very small staff that year, I was asked to play a few Sunday League games. Phil Russell was a big supporter of mine, while Harold Rhodes, although retired from first-class cricket, was still playing one-day games, was a club legend and was equally supportive.

My first game back was against Middlesex at Chesterfield. We won by five wickets and I made 50 before being run out. I got 61 against Somerset, with Ian Botham in the opposition, then made 73 as we beat Surrey, again at Chesterfield. I recall hitting Geoff Arnold, an England bowler, for several sixes that day!

I was playing only for expenses, but at the end of the summer, Phil Russell sat down with me and asked if I would consider coming back on to the staff the following year. I told them that to make it worth my while I would need at least a two-year deal, so they offered me three.

The school was great. They gave me the summers off to play cricket, on condition that I went back to teach in the winter. It meant I couldn't go overseas again, but gave me long-term job security.

It turned out to be the best three years of my career, in many ways.

That was down to the arrival of Eddie Barlow? What did he do?

He made it clear that he rated me. I played almost every game in his three years at the club. You must remember that professional sportsmen are fragile and they need to feel that they are rated and wanted. Going back to when I was dropped after a man of the match performance, the effect of that was to make me wonder if I was actually good enough to play at that level.

Eddie de-mystified the game. He wasn't into analysis or statistics, it was all about one man with a bat and another with a ball. I remember before we played Sussex, who had England legends John Snow and Tony Greig in their side, he told us to play the ball, not the reputation. It was the same when we played Gloucestershire – we were a little in awe of Mike Procter, but Eddie said, 'He doesn't like quick stuff himself. Watch what happens when I bounce him.' No one had ever done that before.

He did the same to Wayne Daniel at Lord's, against Middlesex. He bounced Wayne, who didn't like it at all, while Alan Hill was jumping up and down at third man, excitedly shouting, 'Give him another!' Then he got his pads on and went out to face Wayne with the new ball, not remotely bothered.

Eddie used to tell Alan Hill and myself that we thought too much about the game. He would hold up the bat and ball, then ask which was the widest. See the ball, hit the ball: that was Eddie's way.

We had a team of largely young local lads who all thought the world of him. He made average players into good ones and made good ones into internationals. That's how he did things. Yet it was so important that Eddie, who also coached us, crossed the line on to the pitch with us too. He led by example and expected you all to follow, which we did without question, as we trusted him, implicitly.

That was an era when almost every county had an express fast bowler. Who did you think were the fastest?

That's an interesting question and hard to answer. The England quicks, the likes of John Snow and Bob Willis, didn't always bowl fast in county cricket. The overseas players, whose livelihoods depended on it of course, were rarely coasting. The likes of Joel Garner, Michael Holding, Colin Croft and Malcolm Marshall were always running in hard. So too did Garfield Sobers, who was quicker than he perhaps looked and could be very 'slippy' with his lithe, classical action.

Alan Hill and I have often talked about this and the ones who were consistently the quickest, who you knew would always be giving it everything, were Mike Procter and Wayne Daniel. Imran [Khan] could be quick as well, but there were plenty who could bowl a really quick ball.

I had my skull fractured by Clive Rice at Trent Bridge, where he and Richard Hadlee had so much success. I'd just come off three days at Abbeydale Park in Sheffield, where I scored 137 and 61 against Yorkshire and was on the pitch for all three days, then fielded all day against Nottinghamshire, whose innings ended after the statutory 100 overs at that time, leaving us half an hour before the close.

I told Eddie I was shattered and asked for a night watchman, but he said no. John Wright went early and Clive's first ball to me was a really good bouncer, which I evaded. I thought his next one would be pitched up, but halfway through his run-up, the little man in my head said, 'It's another short one,' and I ducked again. It wasn't especially short, but I ducked into it and it hit me on the back of the head.

This was before helmets, of course, and Alan Hill said to me afterwards that it was scary, seeing blood coming out of my ears. I told him he should have tried it from my angle – I was in hospital for three or four days! I wasn't long back from that when we played Kent. As I walked in to bat, Bob Woolmer told me to get my hands up early, as Kevin Jarvis was going to try out my confidence. I got them up fine – but he broke my wrist!

Walter Goodyear – the doyen of groundsmen at work on the County Ground turf

Edwin Smith – One of only seven men to take a thousand wickets for the county and an England spinner in many subsequent eras

Harold Rhodes – cruelly treated by the cricket establishment and a wonderful, genuinely fast bowler, applies a splint to his elbow to prove he bowled with a straight arm

Keith Mohan – a talented batsman, at the centre of many of the funny stories of his era

Peter Eyre – an unlucky cricketer, who starred in the legendary Gillette Cup semi-final against Sussex in 1969

Brian Jackson – learned
his skills in the leagues
and made up a feared
new ball pairing with
Harold Rhodes

Bob Taylor MBE –
has there ever been a
better wicketkeeper?

Peter Gibbs – graceful opening batsman turned successful writer

*Tony Borrington
– an underrated
batsman who
adapted well to the
greater needs of the
team*

*Alan Hill – the
journeyman
professional, who
always sold his
wicket dearly*

Colin Tunnicliffe – a perfect foil for Mike Hendrick who played a pivotal role in the county's first trophy in 45 summers

Geoff Miller OBE – one of the county's finest all-rounders who reached the pinnacle of the English game

John Wright OBE – stoic and skilful, one of the finest of overseas stars who became a highly-regarded international coach

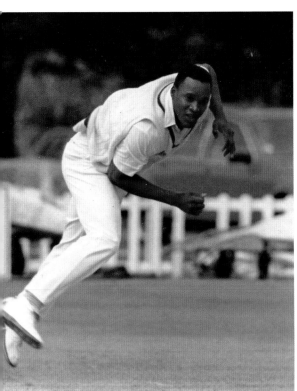

Devon Malcolm – serious pace and an awesome sight when the rhythm was right

Kevin Dean – king of the swingers. Many worse bowlers have earned international selection

Graeme Welch – one of the county's most popular players and now Elite Cricket Performance Director at the club

James Pipe – a combative and appreciated cricketer and now highly-regarded lead physiotherapist at the club

Wayne Madsen – a graceful batsman and consummate professional who leads by example, on and off the field

Chris Grant – the club chairman has overseen a successful period of development, on and off the field

This was only three weeks before the Benson and Hedges Cup Final and my arm wasn't completely right for the game. I had a painkilling injection, so I could play, but as it happened, I nicked one early.

It was a dangerous game and kept you on your toes.

For a batsman with a reputation for being dour, you were perhaps surprisingly effective in the one-day game?

You know, it's funny. When I retired, I had scored a thousand more one-day runs than any other Derbyshire batsman. I was the leading scorer in both the Sunday League and the Benson and Hedges Cup and won four man of the match awards. I had also made more appearances in one-day cricket than anyone else at that time.

I remember batting in, I think 1973 and I made 80-odd in 25 overs, before Chris Wilkins ran me out. When I started, you must remember I was straight out of the leagues and was unafraid to hit the ball. Later, when the responsibility of being a professional, capped cricketer took over, I valued my wicket more.

I got my cap in the interval of a game against Lancashire and I remember David Lloyd congratulating me, but warning me that runs would now be expected as a matter of course. The cap effectively doubled my salary, but with that came a necessity to do well on a regular basis. That's when I tightened up my game.

I remember Bob Willis referring to me as dour in a television commentary when Paul, my son, was playing. He seems to have overlooked the 78 I got off him and the Warwickshire attack in the Benson and Hedges Cup semi-final of 1978.

Mind you, Eddie Barlow had asked for a slow pitch to negate Bob and their quick bowlers. He bowled a bouncer in the first over, which bounced like a tennis ball and ballooned through to the wicketkeeper!

The departure of Eddie in 1978 saw a tailing off in your first-class career and you played your last match in 1980. Coincidence?

We had some experienced players come in around that time, people like Barry Wood, David Steele and John Hampshire. My place was no longer secure and, when I snapped my Achilles tendon in 1980, I was already thinking about life outside the game.

I played a few one-day games in 1981, but then that was it.

You then went into teaching and ended up head teacher of a private school. Were pupils there aware of your sporting career?

They were, yes. That sort of thing is valued in the private sector and it gives you a certain standing when you have a teaching qualification too.

I went back to Grace Dieu Manor as head of PE, eventually became deputy head and finally head teacher. My first speech day as head, I got Mike Brearley to come and give a speech. The chairman of the Board of Governors told me that Mike was his cricketing hero and I was determined to get him along.

I'd been retired for 15 years by this point and had no idea how to get his number. I called Mike Gatting and he said he couldn't help, because no one got Mike Brearley's number. I pleaded desperation, so Gatt relented and gave it to me, but told me not to tell Mike it was him.

When I called Mike, he asked where I had got his number and then said, 'Anthony, why on earth would I want to drive to Loughborough to talk to a thousand parents, teachers and pupils in a marquee?'

I said, 'Well, Mike, you owe me. I never made a run against you in my career, you won the championship and we didn't beat you many times over the years.' Then he laughed and said he'd do it!

His speech was brilliant and people still talk about it. I used to take players like Devon Malcolm, John Morris and David Gower to the school to talk and coach. They were good times and I had many happy years there.

You retained links with Derbyshire and for a number of years were a committee member, the link with the playing staff. How did you find that role?

Don Amott, when he was chairman, asked me to take it on. Paul, my son, was at that stage playing age-group cricket and I told Don that I was happy to do it, but only until the point, if it happened, that Paul became a first-team player and my position was then compromised.

Did you feel that way when he made the first team?

It is an impossible role to be on the committee when your son is in line for first-team selection.

I told Chris Grant, when he took over as chairman, that I wanted to stand down and he asked me to keep doing it until he had a replacement in place.

So I did, until Kevin Dean took over.

Which was the hardest – the nerves of watching your son bat, or of facing Sylvester Clarke on a fast wicket?

It is a different kind of difficulty. You control what happens when you are batting, for better or worse. Your feet, hands and eyes are in coordination and you have to stay alert to get runs and to avoid injury, of course.

I got nervous watching Paul, but I never let the nerves get to the point where I couldn't enjoy watching him. I had many wonderful days watching him bat – for England under-16s in South Africa, at Lord's, at The Oval – they are great and lasting memories that I will carry with me always.

Do you have any regrets from your career in the first-class game?

None whatsoever. I played with and against some fantastic cricketers, some of the best the world has seen.

I may not have set the world on fire, but I played with and against plenty who did!

At all times I gave it my best and you can't do any more. You can't carry grudges or regrets, because if you go into professional sport, the one certainty is that it will end at some point.

As a professional cricketer, you play on the best grounds and it should be a privilege to travel the world playing the game that you love.

What about funny stories from the circuit? Characters within the Derbyshire staff?

There were always plenty of stories with Alan Hill and I. Since we were both qualified school teachers, the rest of the lads would have a go at us from time to time.

I remember we opened the batting against Yorkshire one time and Tony Nicholson, their very fine opening bowler, said, 'Here they come, nick and block.' Alan was block, I was nick. He turned round to moan at his captain, 'Don't tell me I have to bowl at these two.'

First ball, I edged down to third man. 'Good on you nick. I suppose you will be blocking the next five then?' he said, turning to 'Bud' Hill. And he did, which set him off again. 'Who pays to watch these two?' It was good fun.

Bud and I had a lot of laughs. One time down in London, we were preparing to face Sylvester Clarke in the nets and getting our hands up in front of our chest and face for the short stuff he would be bowling the next day for Surrey.

That night, we were in our hotel room, drinking cocoa in our pyjamas, when Bud asked if I fancied one last practice.

'How are we going to do that?' I asked. He gave me a coat hanger from the wardrobe and rolled up the wrapper from his chocolate bar. For the next half-hour, we threw this wrapper at each other's faces and tried to fend it off with the coat hanger.

'How do you feel?' I asked him eventually.

'Great,' he replied. 'As long as Sylvester Clarke bowls at me with the rolled-up silver paper from a Kit-Kat, I'll be fine!'

I remember when we played Nottinghamshire at Ilkeston in 1973, Garfield Sobers was their captain and made a brilliant century. He then bowled a lively spell with the new ball when it was our turn to bat, then later, when the shine went off it, he came on to bowl his wrist spin. It prompted Bud to ask if he was likely to be making the tea later, as he seemed to be doing everything else!

In another game, Peter Lever bowled a bouncer at Bud for Lancashire at Old Trafford. It flew through and Keith Goodwin, keeping wicket, took the ball, leaping above his head and there was a huge appeal from all the Lancashire fielders, as there was a definite noise. The umpire gave it not out. Then we saw Bud peering down at the ground, crouching as he walked. I wondered what was wrong and thought one of his contact lenses had dropped out, so I walked down the wicket to see him.

He looked at me and shaking his head, said, 'You know what, Borrers? He's knocked the bobble off me cap...'

Alan Hill
(1972–1986)

ALAN HILL was a cricketer's cricketer, one perhaps best appreciated by the aficionados of the game, as well as his team-mates.

Not for him the flamboyant 20-ball fifty, that has made others of a more recent vintage wealthy beyond their dreams. Alan was more about the century duly completed just before the end of the day. An innings compiled at a steady 20, 30, 40 runs per session, as he built – no, crafted – an innings and ensured that his own side's total would give the bowlers something to work with.

In style, he was very much a man of the area of his birth. Rough hewn, like the High Peak itself and with nothing especially fancy, he followed in a tradition of obduracy that had been observed by most Derbyshire openers over the years. There were a few more flamboyant types, Arnold Hamer and Kim Barnett the most obvious, but others valued their wicket and lost it with the reluctance of a miser handing over a shilling to a charity box. Thus, Alan followed such names as Harry Storer, Albert Alderman, Charlie Elliott and Ian Hall into the Derbyshire cricketing pantheon. His record was better than all of them.

I watched him many times and I saw myself in him. He was so much better, of course, but as an opening batsman of similar, dare I say attritional style, I empathised with Alan. While others around me were, perhaps on occasion, wanting him to go early so that we could all enjoy the latest edition of the Wright and Kirsten show, I always enjoyed his battles with fast and seam bowling of a standard that had never been seen before in county cricket and never will again.

Alan opened the Derbyshire batting against county sides where almost every team had a lightning quick overseas fast bowler. Sussex had the silky smooth Imran Khan AND the strapping Garth Le Roux to keep you hopping around at either end. There was no respite in such games, nowhere to hide. Only the brave survived.

There were the silky quicks, like Michael Holding, Malcolm Marshall, Dennis Lillee and Richard Hadlee; the powerful ones, like Wayne Daniel, Mike Procter and Andy Roberts; the quick and sometimes erratic ones, like Greg Armstrong, Jeff Thomson and Colin Croft. Plus the downright nasty ones, like Sylvester Clarke. You needed to be alert, have a sound technique and be brave to tackle these bowlers. You had to be a good player to make consistent runs against them at the top of the order.

Alan Hill was just that. He scored over 12,000 runs at an average of 31, with 18 centuries and 65 fifties. He also had four one-day centuries and a good number of half-centuries, to destroy the myth that he was a one-trick pony. He was the Derbyshire Boycott and we loved him for that. Let's face it, there are many worse names to be compared to.

He retired in 1986 at the age of just 36, having just scored 1,400 runs in his most prolific season of many. Of course I was going to ask him about that, but I had plenty of other questions in my head.

He was expecting one about the catch at Lord's in 1981, and about the century he scored in South Africa without a single boundary, one of only two occasions that has ever been done at first-class level. But I hope a few of the others were different and gave him cause to think.

He was patient, friendly and accommodating as we sat by the tea room at Derby, talking while we watched wickets fall like the flakes of an early winter snow shower. I could see why his reputation as a coach is high and his insight into the mind of a professional cricketer was fascinating, as were his comments on the first-class game in what he rightly called the 'golden age' of county cricket.

It is hard to argue. He played while I watched the most liberal scattering of the world's greatest cricketers that the county game has ever known, or ever will know. You can watch the IPL now and see some of the world's best compacted into a 20-over thrash. You could watch it then and see the greatest of batsmen craft centuries of sublime skill, while the finest of bowlers tried alternately to knock their heads off or get them out with bowling of rare cunning and technique. If you survived, there were plenty of quality spin bowlers out there too, so relaxation having seen off the new ball wasn't an option. It lasted all summer long.

Alan Hill played with and against these players and more than held his own.

Alan, you were from the High Peak in Buxworth – tell me about your early life.

I grew up in a cricket-mad family. My father loved his football, but he liked cricket too. He was a decent player and represented the Royal Navy, as well as being a good batsman for Buxworth over many seasons. He was the only rating to get into the navy side – the rest were all officers, so it was quite an achievement.

He gave me my competitive edge. He didn't like losing, though if it happened he took it with good grace, but he instilled in me the belief that you win if you can, but if you can't, stop the opposition from doing so, as there is honour in a draw. That got me through my professional career and I think it is a worthwhile attitude for any cricketer to have.

When did you get started on cricket?

Our house looked out on to the cricket and football field in the village and I spent 90 per cent of my free time on that as a youngster. I spent hours outside with my older brother Bernard, who was on the Derbyshire staff for a year and also played professional football for Liverpool. The bulk of our practice was bowling and batting to one another, for hour after hour.

Modern ideas are that to be an elite cricketer you should have practised for around ten thousand hours – well, Bernard and I did that, on the road outside the house, using a sledge as a wicket and moving it if a car came up the road. We would be out every night after school, using a tennis ball and learning to play straight, as otherwise you were out quickly or lost time chasing it.

The great Garfield Sobers said that it was the best way to learn, as you need to play off the back foot and you don't get hurt – key factors for a budding player.

You started playing for Derbyshire juniors in 1965. How did that come about?

It is quite an outpost in the Peak – our house was 45 miles from Derby and 18 from Old Trafford. I came down for a school trial and got picked up from there. Denis Smith was the coach and I had my trial under his very watchful eye. Bernard had been here, which helped, but I progressed to play for the county colts, initially under the captaincy of Tony Borrington.

He was a year older than me and I took over from him as skipper when he became too old for the age group.

What was life like for a budding young cricketer then, compared to today?

The place was much different. The County Ground was pretty ramshackle, but we had some good lads who just wanted to play the game. The facilities were largely peripheral to us and, although it bred some humour in the dressing room, we knew our place in the scheme of things and it gave us a good grounding in the game. It is better now, because youngsters are more readily accepted and they can be assimilated into the team more easily. But it toughened you up.

Denis Smith was a gruff old coach, but his bark was worse than his bite. He could be blunt, but he had played the game and knew all of its pitfalls. If you had a bad day he would empathise with you, as long as he could see that you were putting the effort in.

Denis taught me things, long before the days of videos and statistical analysis and I still use them when I coach. If you study top professional cricketers, perhaps the most important thing is balance. When I wasn't playing well, I started to fall over to the off side and got out leg before wicket.

He came up to me in the nets during such a trot and said, in his broad Derbyshire accent, 'Ey up…when tha' walks down street, what position is tha' head in?' I was baffled, but showed him.

'Exactly,' he said. 'Now try doin' it with tha' head to one side.'

I couldn't do it and it showed perfectly where I was going wrong. He also taught me that when you drive the ball and drag your back foot to do so, you should drag on your big toe. It keeps your shoulders and hips side on and a few players tend to get opened up by not doing that. It's the same for bowlers – if they're balanced at release, they will generally bowl good lines, while those who arch away tend to over-compensate and are more erratic.

Did you always open the batting?

Yes. Occasionally I would drop down to three and if I was out of form I dropped down the order, but by and large I opened throughout my career.

You joined the Derbyshire staff in 1970. Was that a big moment, or did you see it as just the start of things?

No, it was a starting point. You have to work your way up the ladder. I remember when I got my cap and we were playing Lancashire, little Harry Pilling came up to me and said well done, then told me I'd done the easy bit!

It had taken me seven or eight years, but Harry said that the hardest thing was to stay there, having reached the standard. David Steele used to say that it didn't matter how many runs you scored the previous summer, you started a new one with nought against your name. The really good players achieve consistency, whereas the mere mortals have to endure the bad trots.

Your first-team debut came in 1972. How did that come about?

It was towards the end of the season and at that time coaches are starting to give chances to young players, aware of others that are leaving and wanting to see who might be able to step up. I had been in and around the second team for three years by that stage, so I had a good grounding.

A lot of young players now are impatient and wanting to play the first-class game early, perhaps when they're not always ready for it. I felt I was ready and, in an era when batsmen had to face some seriously talented players, especially from overseas, you really had to be to survive.

> **You faced Somerset at Chesterfield, against the wily Tom Cartwright and the lively Hallam Moseley. Quite a step up?**

Cartwright was a master of moving the ball off the seam. They perhaps wouldn't look at him now, because he was a very gentle medium pace, but he zipped it around all day. I remember facing him one time at Weston-super-Mare and I must have played three or four balls an over with my front pad.

It was a real education, as at his pace you had to move it in the air and off the seam, as well as bowling a 'forward' length.

> **You then faced Bob Willis at Edgbaston against Warwickshire, before going on to Blackpool, where you made your first senior fifty at Stanley Park. That would have been special against a decent attack?**

My memory of that Warwickshire game is fielding at fine leg for Alan Ward. Their great West Indian batsman, Rohan Kanhai, got a quick bouncer from him and picked it up so quickly that, instead of top edging to me, he hit it over mid-on, one bounce for four. It was an extraordinary shot but, as I saw subsequently on several occasions, far from unusual for him. He was a fine player.

That first fifty was on an uncovered wicket, which was a little lively. It was very satisfying, but I still had much to prove.

> **I think it's fair to say that it wasn't a great Derbyshire side at that time. How did you find it, coming into a struggling side?**

We struggled at times, as there were some good sides around. We had some good players, like Peter Gibbs and Mike Page, but we never seemed to fire as a team.

Mike was a wonderful player, especially of spin, and I learned so much watching him play it with soft hands and quick feet. He loved

139

the social side of the game and perhaps suffered from being seen to not take it as seriously as he might have done. He didn't smash spin all over the place, but I remember seeing him make two 90s against Ray Illingworth and Jack Birkenshaw at Leicester and he looked on a different level to the rest of us.

He was also a brilliant fielder at short leg and held many catches off Brian Jackson and Harold Rhodes there. He did get hit badly once and that shook him for a while. There were no helmets and pads at that stage, of course.

He was great in the dressing room. He was playing a second-team game one day and had been having a bit of banter with Lancashire's wicketkeeper, Keith Goodwin, who he knew very well.

During the tea interval, Mike persuaded our seam bowler, Michael Glenn, to bowl a tomato to Keith, first ball after tea.

Michael bowled a full toss and Keith hit it, bang in the middle of the bat and was showered in tomato seeds as we all broke up, laughing! I think he got hauled before the committee, but that was the sort of man that he was.

A really lovely guy and a very talented cricketer.

Chris Wilkins was coming to the end of his stint as our first overseas player. How did you find him?

He was one of the hardest hitters of a cricket ball I have ever seen. Only Clive Lloyd matched him and if you were batting in the indoor school at Derby, where there wasn't much room as the bowlers waited to bowl their next ball, you never turned your back on him.

He was a talented all-round player. He could bowl useful seam, kept wicket pretty well and was a fine all-round sportsman.

He had an amazing eye and he made the first switch-hit that I ever saw.

It was in his last season and he was batting in the nets against David Wilde. He was a pretty lively left-armer and Chris switched round and absolutely hammered this ball. We all stood there with our mouths open, just wondering at how good an eye you must have to do something like that.

> **Then of course Lawrence Rowe came in for a summer, having put England to the sword for the West Indies. There must have been great expectations on his arrival that never came to fruition?**

Well, he came off the back of scoring 302 against England that winter and expectations were high. In his first game at Derby, against Sussex, he made 94 in the second innings and batted with his red West Indian tracksuit underneath his whites – he was so cold!

He was a very cool, laid-back West Indian and oozed calm and class whenever he batted, but he found the county grind very difficult. Various ailments and illnesses didn't help, but we never saw the best of Lawrence at Derbyshire. Michael Holding will tell you he was among the best batsmen he ever saw, so it is hard to argue with that.

> **Your own style was usually described as 'dour' or 'attritional'. Was that always your style or were you conscious of a need to stay in there and minimise risks?**

It goes back to my upbringing in the Peak District really. We played on uncovered wickets and you could never play forward with confidence, because the ball 'stopped' on you. I think that was a factor, but I was told that one of my roles was to see the shine off the new ball and ensure that the side made a solid start, so that meant that I tried to stay there as long as I could.

I wasn't blessed with great self-confidence either, and the demons took over when I had a bad trot. If I was batting well, I went out confident that I could make runs against anyone, but there were times when I would wonder where the next run was coming from, especially against the many fine opening bowlers of that era.

> **Your career seemed to kick on in 1975 with the arrival of Eddie Barlow. What did he do to improve your game?**

Eddie was a terrific bloke. On the surface he was supremely confident, yet he must have had his demons. He was 36 when he came to Derbyshire and past his best as a batsman. There were times that he struggled for runs, but you would never have known it. He was very shrewd, always positive, good fun. We thought the world of him and it was good to be able to bring him back to some player events towards the end of his life. He was never happier than in the company of cricketers, having a laugh and a beer.

He used to take us to a pub at Darley Abbey after training sessions. They call it bonding now, but Eddie started that at Derbyshire and he pulled us together, both on and off the field. His bowling won us a lot of games and he really was a fabulous player.

There was one game when we were playing Middlesex and Tony Borrington had been injured in the first innings. Wayne Daniel was seriously quick and we were all panicking a bit, wondering who was going to open against him with me.

'Calm down lads,' said Eddie. 'I'm going in.' He did well too and it was just typical of him to lead from the front.

He used to take me into the nets and just get me to hit the ball. 'See the ball, hit the ball' was his maxim.

So was it Eddie who helped with the winter in South Africa?

I think he might have, behind the scenes, but I never knew. I got a phone call asking me to go over and play club cricket, as well as for Orange Free State and I did pretty well. I would have liked to go back, but I had just met my future wife and she had a secure job in nursing. It wasn't to be, but it is one of the regrets of my career that I never went back.

I suppose the dour reputation was cemented by making a century with no boundary for Orange Free State in the winter of 1976/77. What do you remember of that innings?

We'd been hammered in the previous game by Northern Transvaal in Pretoria and we were playing against Griqualand West in Bloemfontein, our nearest neighbours, though around a hundred miles away.

We bowled them out for 59 and Geoff Arnold, who was coaching at the time, came to me and told me to go out and get my head down. I did that and we ended up winning the game. I had no idea when I came in that I hadn't reached the fence and my excuse was that the mower had broken! The grass was very long in parts and some of them would have gone for four easily on a shorter outfield. I got a slow hundred and a team-mate got a quick one – so you could say that the end result made it all worthwhile.

> **Despite your reputation, you were the first Derbyshire batsman to make a John Player League century. That must be a source of pride?**

That was at Buxton and was the best I ever played. If you're going to have one special innings, you want it to be on your home 'turf' and I was really pleased with that one. I was feeling confident, despite a poor pitch and I made 120 out of around 200. I was out in the 32nd over, so I could have gone on further, but everything felt right that day, against a good Northamptonshire attack.

I searched for that innings for the rest of my career, but never felt that fluent again. My hands, eyes and feet were all in synch that day and I loved every minute I was out there.

I did get 150 in the NatWest Trophy against Cornwall and that felt good, but it wasn't a first-class attack, of course.

> **I've chatted many times with Tony Borrington, who said that as an opener you played in an era with the quickest bowlers the game has ever known. So who were the quickest?**

The quickest weren't necessarily the best. It depends on the wickets you play on and The Oval at that time was fast and bouncy. The quickest ball I ever faced was there against Sylvester Clarke. He bowled me a bouncer and Jack Richards, 30 yards back, could only fingertip it 'over the bar' for four byes. It was seriously quick.

Chesterfield was fast then too and I remember facing Australia there and Len Pascoe was very quick. Malcolm Marshall was always lively at Portsmouth, but of course, he could do it all.

> **And the best?**

Malcolm Marshall and Richard Hadlee. Richard dissected your technique and was a wonderful bowler, though he bowled on some very 'sporting', green wickets at Trent Bridge that were specifically prepared for him and Clive Rice.

Overall I would say Malcolm shaded it, as he was a fine bowler and competitor who took wickets all over the world, even on the sub-continent. That was often a bowler's graveyard, but Malcolm adapted his style to suit conditions. He was a delightful man too, unless you were 22 yards away from him when he had a cricket ball in his hand.

He never said much to you on the field. He didn't need to. When you can bowl at 90 miles an hour, the ball does all your talking. It was funny, you'd see opposition batsmen offering to carry his bag from the car before a game, hoping that he would then go easy on them! They did the same with Michael Holding here at Derbyshire and we asked him if it made a difference.

'Oh no,' he said in his deep Jamaican voice. 'They will still get it.'

The other thing Michael used to say was, 'If you want to drive, go buy a car.'

I have to ask you about Lord's 1981 and that game against Northamptonshire. Tell me about that.

It was an amazing day wasn't it, between two of the less fashionable counties! Lord's was bursting at the seams, unlike for recent finals when it was barely half full. I found that quite sad.

The thing I always remember was that we had to play the next day, despite all the nervous energy that went into a last-ball finish. Things come flashing back at times, like watching Jim Griffiths running in to bowl that last ball from the dressing room window. Bob Taylor, who had played for England, had his head in his hands and couldn't watch. Neither could a good few others. Some of the guys stayed up, others – including me – went to bed because we were mentally shattered and had to drive to Hove the next morning!

We didn't get back to Derby after the Sunday game until 1.30am on the Monday, with the wives and girlfriends in tow. We were all very aware that but for that one ball, it could have been an eminently forgettable weekend.

It was an emotional time. Bob Taylor had played for us for 20 years and never tasted success. The Duke of Devonshire was in tears, so too was Gerald Mortimer of the *Derby Telegraph*. They knew what we had been through as a club and how much it meant to us all.

144

And what about that catch?

The way Richard Williams shaped to hit it, I thought he was hitting it towards midwicket and I set off in that direction, not having sighted the ball against the crowd.

Then I heard Barry Wood, who knew my brother and thought we were facially alike, shout, 'BERNARD!' I realised at that point it was coming my way and then I saw the ball just to my left and dived for it. Thankfully, I held on and, as I have told people ever since, it's amazing what you can do with your eyes closed.

I didn't bat very well though and got out to one of the worst shots I ever played. Mind you, that brought together John Wright and Peter Kirsten and they were much better players than me.

I've heard stories that despite the success, that wasn't always a harmonious dressing room?

No, that's been exaggerated. Barry Wood was a black and white cricketer and he told it very frankly. But he was super-committed and a very fine player. He expected people to follow his lead and sometimes, when he called a spade a shovel, it didn't go down too well. But that wasn't a bad dressing room – certainly not compared to what you hear of dressing rooms of a later vintage. Woody had a sense of humour and there was a lot of banter. There were times he might have put things differently, but you couldn't fault his commitment and ability.

In the early 1980s you were Mr Consistency. You reeled off 1,300 runs plus in 1983 and 1984 and in 1986 had your record aggregate of 1,438 runs at 42 – and then retired at the age of 36. That always struck me as premature. What happened?

Well, I was 36 and had a draining benefit year. If I'm honest, I hadn't planned my future away from the game as well as I might have and had an opportunity to stay in it. I'd qualified as a teacher, but hadn't decided between that and coaching, so when the chance came to take up a coaching role with Derbyshire I thought about it, long and hard. My knees had been giving me problems and I felt the aches and pains more at the end of the day.

I reckoned that the opportunity may not have been there again, so I took it. I had played for 17 years and I felt that physically, I was done. The expectations were considerable and for me, irrespective of how well I had been doing, I had to keep scoring a thousand runs a season and I wasn't sure I could keep doing that against really top bowlers. At 36, your eyes aren't as sharp as in your prime either, nor are your reflexes, so it would have been an increasing challenge.

Whenever people talk about the current side, depending on their age, they refer to us needing either a Steve Stubbings or an Alan Hill. That must be a source of pride?

It is. I did my best and I never went out to give any less than a hundred per cent. Perhaps people recognised that and I've always been grateful for their kind words and support.

As must be a first-class average over 30 in a tough era?

Yes, especially on some of the wickets that we played on and against the bowlers I've mentioned. Places like Chesterfield, Trent Bridge and The Oval – and there were many others – you knew that your first two hours of batting would be very hard work. If you could get through that, you could go on to decent scores, but it needed a willingness to graft in that opening session.

That opened my eyes to batting really. I regard the best batsmen as those who score runs when the conditions are against them, not the flat-track bullies who boost their average with 200 on a shirt front.

I spoke with Peter Willey recently and we agreed that it was a golden era. I envy – but don't begrudge – players today with their year-round contracts, but I wouldn't have swapped the time that I played for anything. I faced some of the greatest bowlers of all time – people like Richard Hadlee, Malcolm Marshall, Imran Khan, Andy Roberts and so many more. You had to be at your best to survive and yes, I am proud to have finished as I did.

Who was the best batsman you saw?

Oh, Garfield Sobers. He was unbelievable and just had so much time. He allowed the ball to come on to him, which made that time, but was a fantastic player. If he played now he'd be a multi-millionaire, as he had it all. He bowled pretty quick left arm, or could slow down and swing it; he bowled orthodox left-arm spin and could switch to bowl chinamen; he was a terrific fielder...he was genuinely the complete cricketer and would probably have been a decent wicketkeeper too!

At any one discipline he was outstanding, but he was a top-drawer performer in them all. A remarkable, extraordinary cricketer.

Majid Khan was a fine player too and a character. I remember him coming to Derby one time and being surprisingly scratchy when he batted. When he was out, he asked for the groundsman and requested a saw. Keep in mind that this was a time when you had to pay for your equipment, and we all sat incredulous, watching him saw this bat in half. All the time muttering, 'This bat is a piece of shit.'

I'd have loved to have seen Walter Hammond at Gloucestershire. He carried them for years and scored thousands of runs at a time when the game had evolved sufficiently for his scores and records to be taken seriously. He played pace and spin with equal ability and must have been a remarkable player.

He once told his team-mates that Tom Goddard, who took thousands of wickets for them with his off spin, hadn't bowled especially well in a game and that it was just poor batting that got him wickets. He proceeded to go out and bat against him in a turning net, using just the edge of his bat – and Goddard didn't get past him once.

That takes a serious eye and major talent.

Who was the best batsman you played with? I assume either John Wright or Peter Kirsten?

They were top lads. I didn't see it, as I wasn't playing, but John made 96 against the West Indians at Chesterfield when they had a strong pace attack and a fast track to bowl on. David Steele said it was the best innings he ever saw, which was quite an accolade, but it illustrates what I mean about good players. Wrighty got bigger scores, but against lesser attacks and in more favourable conditions. That one would have been special for him.

I saw John fairly recently in New Zealand, after going to see some Ashes cricket. He's still doing well and looking good. Peter was a more fluent player, but there were plenty who thought that on all pitches and against all attacks, John maybe had the edge.

He used to lead sing-songs on buses and play his guitar – he had a kind of residency at a local pub for a while, I think. He has deservedly made a lot of money from the game, but he is exactly the same as he ever was.

Kirsy was a good lad too, a top cricketer. He was a brilliant fielder and on his day he was unstoppable. David Steele used to call him 'The Don', which is a pretty good accolade.

A couple of bowlers of real talent retired prematurely in your era: Alan Ward and Fred Swarbrook?

It was a shame. Fred was a really good cricketer and a gritty player. I once saw Mike Procter give him a really tough time when he came out as night watchman. He was peppering him with really fast, short deliveries into his body, but Fred stood his ground and he didn't get him out.

He was a fine bowler. He was taking a good number of wickets for Derbyshire every season and then came back one year and simply couldn't pitch the ball. It was a great shame for Fred as it brought about the end of his first-class career.

He's still living and coaching in South Africa and Fred is a super lad.

Alan is living on the Gold Coast in Australia with his wife, Helen. It's a lovely part of the world to live! He met her when he toured with England in 1970 and although they moved to this country, I think they went back to Australia around ten years ago.

It was a great shame what happened to him. He was one of the fastest bowlers in the country, possibly the world at one point. Certainly Majid Khan reckoned that he was, and he was a good judge. When I saw him at 18 he was a fantastic sight, like Concorde taking off. He had this long approach, with his body leaning forward, then he would arch back and unleash this missile at the batsman.

But he wasn't a confident guy and used to get really nervous before he bowled. Can you imagine, bowling at that pace at batsmen who themselves were nervous at facing his thunderbolts? It was a shame that he didn't have that self-confidence, because he was seriously quick.

Who were the characters of your era? Always involved in funny incidents?

Well, I've mentioned Mike Page and Colin Tunnicliffe was a great personality. He would come in every day with a smile on his face and there were always jokes and stories flying around the dressing room.

The camaraderie of that time is something that I remember fondly and Colin and I remain good friends after all these years. He's a lovely lad. It's the great thing about the game and I always tell young players that if they play it the right way they will get so much from it.

Things were said on the field – it's a man's game after all – but we didn't get hugely personal and you gave it and took it in equal measure. It was competitive stuff and you had to be prepared for it.

I was batting against Yorkshire at Chesterfield once and their opening bowler, the late Tony Nicholson, stood halfway down the wicket, arms akimbo, as he stared at me, having beaten my outside edge once more without success. He shook his head and said, 'I tell thee what Hilly. If tha' were battin' on my front lawn, ah'd draw the bloody curtains.' Now that is proper, humorous sledging!

You became a first-class umpire on retirement but only for a couple of seasons. Why was that?

I wasn't decisive enough. It didn't work out for me and I will admit that. My talents were better suited to coaching and the pressure of umpiring is considerable, especially now, with instant replays and referrals.

Did getting sacked by Derbyshire as a coach change your opinion of the club?

No. It changed my opinion of some of those involved, but this is and always will be my club. I'm down at the ground regularly and if I can't get here I follow the scores closely.

It's given me some heartache over the years, but it's given me many wonderful memories too.

As a coach, what is the X factor that separates a very good club cricketer from one capable of the next step?

Desire. Once your ability has got to a certain level, you will get opportunity at second-XI or first-team level. Then you need to work at your game and be prepared to keep doing so. You can always learn something and as soon as you think you have cracked it, that's generally when the game will come back to bite you.

If you are prepared to do the hard graft and have the requisite talent, you can make it. But you can't do it without both of those attributes.

You have seen some good local lads emerge to the Derbyshire squad in the past couple of seasons from your role in Staffordshire?

Yes, players like Alex Hughes, Ben Cotton and Tom Taylor have worked hard to get to this stage in their careers and they now need to step it up to make the next level. I'm always wary of making predictions, because a lot of things can go wrong, but if they maintain the desire and keep listening to the right people and working on their games, they have every chance of success.

Colin Tunnicliffe (1973–1983)

COLIN TUNNICLIFFE is a prime example of what is known in cricket as the journeyman professional.

The county's long line of seam bowlers has plenty who were more naturally talented, whose talents brought them higher honours and whose career record ended with several hundred more wickets. Yet Colin's story is one of triumph over adversity, one that saw him establish himself as a solid, reliable county cricketer, after first being released by the county as 'not good enough'.

From 1977 to 1983 he proved a fine foil for Mike Hendrick, offering a different angle with his left-arm fast-medium that kept the batsmen playing and made them work for their runs. In that time he conceded under three runs an over, important for a county where runs have seldom been easy to come by. Having said that, in Colin's time the county enjoyed the services of two of its most consistent batsmen, in South African Peter Kirsten and New Zealander John Wright.

His run-up was not a thing of beauty, like that of Michael Holding, nor was it a spectacle, such as that of Alan Ward. His unprepossessing run to the crease suggested the ordinary, yet he was perhaps all the more effective for that.

Perhaps he wasn't as revered by supporters as others of his kind, but his team-mates held him in the highest regard. Stoic, dependable and reliable are the words trotted out when his name is mentioned.

While every team benefits from a star or two, they seldom do well if the rest don't fulfil their assigned roles. For seven summers, Colin carried his out perfectly.

Mention his name to supporters and the first thing they will mention will be Lord's in 1981, the National Westminster Bank Trophy Final against Northamptonshire, in which he played a pivotal role in the Derbyshire success.

It was typical of the man, doing what was required when it was most needed and with the minimum of fuss. I spent time with him at Derbyshire's 3aaa County Ground, watching cricket as we talked, and was taken with his ready smile, friendly manner and regular laugh. I was left with the understanding that he would have been a good and popular team-mate, as well as a player who would always give his best.

You wouldn't find anyone to dispute the latter.

Colin, can you tell me about your upbringing and how you got into cricket?

Well, I never played until I was at secondary school. I went to Rykneld Secondary Modern and we had an English teacher who had been brought up in India and was really into hockey and cricket. I was around 11 or 12 and we had no grass, so we used to play on concrete initially, using one of the old composition balls.

When I was 13, I used to cycle down to Darley Park and there would be around eight games going on there at that time. I used to go down there and watch, but sometimes teams were short and they would ask me if I wanted to field for them.

Then one of my uncles got wind of the fact I was interested in the game and I started to play for Derby St Michael's, where I got an opportunity to bowl. I always bowled seam, but I was like a matchstick at 13 – it's hard to believe, looking at me now – and I wasn't especially quick. As I filled out, I got a bit quicker and started to get a few wickets.

What brought you to Derbyshire's attention?

It was when I started to play for International Combustion, who were in the Nottinghamshire and Derbyshire Border League at that time.

I was taking a few wickets and getting some runs and came to the attention of the county coach, Denis Smith.

The best young players in the county used to come down to the nets on a Friday afternoon and were given a bus token to get down here and back home. We would practice between 1pm and 2.30pm and I suppose we felt quite important. I first met Fred Swarbrook at that time, who was quite a schoolboy prodigy, though there were other good players who, for one reason or another, didn't make it. I was offered a one-year contract at the end of a prolific club season.

That was when Edwin Smith was coach?

Yes, he took over from Denis in 1971. At that time, the coach's remit was different to now, as they only worked with young players, the assumption being that if you made county standard you could look after your own game. It was all very formal – you bowled when asked to do so and if you were lucky, as a bowler you might get a bat at the end of the session.

Did you still have to do all the menial 'handyman' tasks at that stage, or had things changed?

Oh yes, you could always tell a member of the ground staff as we all had burrs on our knuckles and splinters in our hands! The tiered seating that we were expected to erect before every home game was a nightmare. Sometimes the bolts would be seized up and we would spend hours on it. The club transported it around the county, so it wasn't just at Derby that we used it.

I had six seasons on the ground staff and was then released. The secretary of the time, Major Douglas Carr, called me in and told me, 'The committee feel you have not fulfilled your potential.' I had a right go at him, which was a shame, as it wasn't his fault. I told him that was the problem, the committee only felt, they didn't think. It was a tough time, but things happen for a reason.

So what happened then?

I went back to the leagues playing for Langley Mill and worked hard, before eventually getting my call in May 1973. I played a couple of second-team games and was then told to travel with the first team to play Essex at Chelmsford.

I went down with Mike Hendrick in his Saab and I didn't expect to play, let alone open the bowling. Doing so against the likes of Bruce Francis, Keith Fletcher and Keith Boyce was an experience and I ended up with none for 81.

I was surprised, to be honest, as there was no chat with the skipper, Brian Bolus, about the field I wanted, or anything like that. I just ran in and bowled.

In 1974 and 1976 you took only one first-class wicket and didn't play in 1975 at all. Tell me about those years.

I suppose I thought my chance had gone. I had worked from school as a manufacturing optician and cricket became a recreation. By 1976, Eddie Barlow had taken over as Derbyshire skipper and he invited me to play against Oxford University. My manager was away at the time and I told Eddie there may be a problem. His response was blunt, 'Do you want to play first-class cricket or don't you?'

So I phoned the owner, Roger Boyden, on his holiday and he told me to go away and play, then pay back the time at weekends or whenever I could. It was a very generous thing to do and although I didn't tear up any trees, I was offered a contract for the following two years.

Indeed, Roger even said that if it didn't work out there would be a job for me after those two years, which was a wonderful gesture and speaks volumes of the man. It took a lot of pressure out of the decision and I have always been grateful to him.

Was there a coach or player responsible for your improvement, or was it a case of knowing your game by that stage?

Eddie Barlow, without question. As a captain and coach he was years ahead of his time. We were the first to warm up by running around the ground and other teams used to take the mickey out of us for that.

We were a fairly young team and we would sit listening to Eddie talking about cricket and cricketers for hours. He simplified coaching and was a great man-manager. He had such an aura and we loved the guy. If we had only had him five years earlier, who knows what might have happened?

What was so special about him?

When he took the captaincy, he invited all the players round to his house to talk about what we were doing wrong and how we could improve. Some of the senior players were less impressed by his demand for better physical fitness, but they were soon moved on. There wasn't an opt-out clause with Eddie.

We were all given winter fitness regimes and when he returned in the spring you were expected to have met your fitness target. We had three-mile runs around the outfield, shuttle runs in the old indoor school, running sessions around the touchline of Burton Albion's old ground. If we weren't the best side, there were few fitter ones! Mike Hendrick said that if someone in the other team hit the ball a mile, we would be the best team in the country at fetching it back.

It was the same in the field. We couldn't all be like Peter Kirsten and John Wright, but Eddie expected 100 per cent effort from everyone and woe betide you if you waved one past.

He was very fair though. I remember one day, a junior player copped some flak from a senior one in the field. Eddie said nothing but at the end of the day, when we were sitting in the dressing room discussing what had happened that day, he asked the senior player why he had done that, but not subsequently shouted at another senior player for the same thing. It made a point and the younger lads respected him all the more for it.

Eddie first came up with the concept of the 'pinch hitter' as it is now known. He said to us that while 30/0 from ten overs was a good start in a one-day game, it was only three an over. Why should the best batsmen, which they usually were, then expect the lesser lights to score seven or eight an over off the last ten?

He got me to open in a couple of games, one of them against Leicestershire. Alan Ward was playing for them by this stage and his face was a picture when he saw me walking out to open! I told him I had been sent in to slog him and he laughed, but then I hit back over his head for four, first ball.

Eddie would take on anyone. We played Middlesex in one match and Wayne Daniel, who was seriously quick, gave Eddie a lot of bouncers when he batted at number four. When they batted, I took the ninth wicket and Wayne came in to bat.

Straight away, Eddie took me off and came on himself. He nearly took Wayne's head off with a bouncer and we soon got him out. It was obvious that Wayne was really angry as we came off, but Eddie's response was typical – he went out to open the batting against him, seeing him off in the process.

He was as tough as they come. A wonderful man.

Phil Russell was well-regarded as a coach too?

Phil took over as coach and was very smart. If you batted in the nets and hit one well, you might say, 'That's six,' but Phil would walk down the wicket and say, 'Actually, you would have been caught in the deep there and been heading back to the pavilion.'

He made us think about the game and would stand with a clip board and tell the bowlers that he wanted the next 18 balls bowled as yorkers, or similar. He was big on self-discipline, working on your game until its skills became second nature.

It must have helped having Bob Taylor behind the stumps?

Oh yes. He was fantastic. He was glad to pass the captaincy over to Eddie, as it affected his game a little, but he was such a good wicketkeeper. I remember in my third season he held a blinding catch in the opening game and he got up and said, 'It's good to see I've still got it.'

The rest of us were standing there looking at one another thinking, 'You're never going to lose that talent.' He didn't, either.

Your real breakthrough game was against Middlesex at Ilkeston in 1977, when you had an extraordinary all-round match?

Yeah, that is a special memory. There was a bit of competition for the tenth wicket between Mike Hendrick and I. He already had five and I'd never done that at that stage, but he ended up getting Allan Jones out to finish with six and I ended with 4-22. We were 218/8 when I went in, but Harry Cartwright and I decided we would play a few shots and I started hitting Phil Edmonds further and further. I think they thought I would be out any time, but we added 120 for the ninth wicket and then Hendo and I hit at everything before he was out. I ended up with an unbeaten 82, by some distance my personal best.

Again, it was down to Eddie. He had stressed that we all had a job to do with the bat and I started to be seen as a player who could score quickly, if not always consistently.

> **You were steady in the following years, taking three or four wickets several times, but your best haul wasn't until 1980, when you took 7-36 against Essex, at Queens Park?**

It was wonderful to take my career-best figures against a very good team. What many people would not realise is that in the previous match against Northamptonshire I took six wickets. David Steele caught my fifth wicket one-handed at slip, something he continually reminds me about.

> **For all your successes in the longer game, you will always be associated with the one-day game and, of course, the NatWest win of 1981. Before we chat about the final, the semi-final was a gripping affair?**

It certainly was, played over two days, because of rain. To bowl out that Essex side for just 149 was excellent work, with all the seamers conceding only 20-odd runs in their 12 overs.

Having said that, we wouldn't have got close, except for a terrific innings by Kim Barnett. He made 59, by a distance the highest score of the match, but it came down to our needing a single off the last ball.

To this day, I don't know why Norbert Phillip threw at the stumps, when he could have walked up with the ball and removed the bails, or even thrown to the man behind them. Pressure, I suppose, but we didn't care and we ended up celebrating very well. As we were doing so, we could hear the Essex team next door having a right go at each other. There was no false ceiling in the old dressing rooms and it must have been tough for them.

We went to Burton-on-Trent to play a match in aid of Bob Taylor's benefit that evening and it is safe to say that a few of us were probably in no condition to play a game of cricket!

That game was perhaps when Kim Barnett first announced his talent to a wide audience?

It was his first fifty in one-day cricket and came at the right time. Of course, he went on to become one of the county's greatest-ever batsmen.

Then the final of course. What are your memories of the day, even the night before it?

We went down the day before on a coach and had a team meeting. At that meeting we agreed that everyone should keep their usual evening and morning habits – no compulsory team breakfast, for example, so the players were as relaxed as they could be.

We won the toss and reckoned it would move about early on, as it so often does at that time of year, so Mike Hendrick and I decided to pitch it up. I went for 20 in my first two overs! Geoff Cook and Wayne Larkins were a good opening pair and Cooky went on to make a hundred. I always tell him when I see him that I got him on to that winter's tour of India!

We fielded well. Geoff Miller took a great catch on the boundary to dismiss Larkins when he and Cooky had added 99 and Alan Hill an even better one to get rid of Richard Williams. There were three run-outs too, including Allan Lamb who could have put them out of sight. As it was, they made 235/9 and we had reckoned before the start that anything from 230 to 260 was within our range.

We made a good start before 'Bud' Hill was out, then Wright and Kirsten did what they did so often and took us to 163/1, before both went quickly. We started to panic a bit then and wickets started to fall. I had been told to go in ahead of David Steele, but when the next wicket went down he was out of his seat and out there before I could move. Then he was coming back quickly, clean bowled for nought!

I went in to partner Geoff Miller and we needed 23 from 17 balls.

I hit a couple of fours off Sarfraz, one square and one back over his head, to leave us needing seven off the last over.

What were you saying to each other at that point?

If I had to do it again I would have gone for it, because knocking it into gaps for one was Bob Taylor's game and he was in next. But Geoff said we should just knock it around for singles, aware that six would win it for us because we had lost fewer wickets.

Of course, we ended up needing one off the last ball, just like the semi-final. Jim Griffiths bowled a good ball, it hit me on the pads, but Geoff was legging it down the wicket and just got there before the short leg! People have said to me subsequently that Geoff set off before the ball was bowled, but if you watch the footage, he didn't.

And then the party started?

It had started when we got back to the dressing room! One bloke tried to grab my bat as we were running off, but I managed to hold on to it and it wasn't a day for hitting him!

We got our trophies and medals presented and it was all a little surreal from there. I walked back to our hotel, which was on the corner of Lord's, around quarter past nine. I was with Dallas Moir, who had the trophy because he was huge (6ft 8in) and no one of sane mind would have bothered him. We had a nice reception at the hotel and watched the highlights on TV, then went to bed.

I was rooming with John Wright and we went to bed around 1.30am. We had a game the next day down at Hove, which is hard to believe now. We sat in our room drinking tea and we were both still buzzing, so we decided to go out again!

John still made top score the next day. That's the sort of player that he was.

John Wright and Peter Kirsten are club legends, of course.

They were great. Lovely blokes, top cricketers. A lot of overseas players got bored and of course, there were long days spent waiting on the rain stopping at times. Yet they sustained a level of performance. Eddie had been instrumental in both coming over – at one time we had Peter, Garth Le Roux and Allan Lamb playing for our second team – all of them young lads, over from Western Province.

Who was the best batsman you bowled at in your career?

It has to be two unrelated men of the same name. Viv and Barry Richards.

Viv loved to dominate from the first ball and we used to say, 'Don't wake him up,' because if you kept it low profile, maybe the concentration might not be there in a county match. If you got him annoyed, or he had a point to prove, he was almost impossible to bowl to.

You could set a six-three field and he would keep working the ball into the side with the least fielders, just to show that he could handle you. You could always tell when Viv was 'into it', because he used to tap the top of his bat handle against the palm of his gloved hand. When we saw that, it was time to worry!

I remember getting Viv out twice in a day at Taunton, which was special. The fact that one was caught at long on didn't matter, they all look the same in the scorebook.

Barry was different. With him it was all timing. I watched him 'knocking up' at Basingstoke one day and from gentle taps back to the bowler, the ball was rattling the advertising boards. We used to try and bore him out; put the field back and wait for him to get fed up.

There was one match where Fred Swarbrook bowled him just after lunch, when he had scored freely before it. We all agreed he had walked past it and later found out that he wanted to watch the tennis from Wimbledon!

I've never seen a batsman who made it look so effortless and easy.

Surprisingly you only had two more seasons after that final, finishing in 1983 when you were only 32. How did that happen?

I'd worked for the club over the winter months, going round the local pubs in an Allegro that was provided as part of a 12-month contract, selling raffle tickets and doing what I could to raise funds. Then Roger Pearman, the club secretary at the time, suggested I did it full-time, getting companies involved in the club, sponsoring advertising boards and the like.

I played a few one-day games in my last season, but that was it. I didn't think it right that I should effectively 'pick and choose' matches, when there were lads on the staff full-time who could have played.

The club wouldn't give me a benefit – I think they thought I would use my contacts for personal gain, rather than theirs. It wasn't very nice, really, but they gave me a one-day game at Heanor in recognition of services. I was upset at the time, but life is too short to be bitter about things.

Once I played that game, I never played another game of cricket. There was a chance of a move to Glamorgan but we had young children at school and it was never an option for me. It was time to put away the gear and get on with the rest of my life.

And after that?

I had five years at Derbyshire as commercial manager and then moved to Derby County, where I did a similar role for 14 years. When I tell people I have had 30 years in sport they're amazed. I haven't done a day's 'work' in my life. I was being paid for what was effectively my hobby, as I have always been a massive Derby County fan.

It also coincided with a successful period for the Rams, when Arthur Cox was manager. They were very happy days.

Finally, over the course of your career, there must have been some characters, some funny stories?

Oh yes, there were. Ray East of Essex was one and it was at Burton-on-Trent that he was fielding at third man at either end. After doing this for a few overs, he borrowed a bike off a spectator and started using that!

There was a lot of daft humour went on though, especially when we were on away trips. There was one time that we were in Bath and had no Sunday game, so were wandering around and enjoying the scenery. David Steele bought a bag of Thornton's Continentals and wouldn't give one to anybody, so after a while, John Wright grabbed the bag and quickly shoved them all in his mouth, eating furiously while running away from Steeley! It might sound daft now, but we had a lot of laughs over that sort of thing.

It was a great dressing room to be in and I loved every minute of it.

Geoff Miller OBE (1973–1990)

CRITICS, EH?

Mention the name of Geoff Miller to the average cricket fan, or read critiques of his career and you will be met with the negatives. He never bowled sides out; he took years before he scored a century; he never became established in the England side. Such is human nature, a reluctance to celebrate what someone has and contributes to a side and rather focus on what they are perceived to be unable to do.

Geoff Miller took 'just' 60 Test wickets, but he made a major contribution to an Ashes win in Australia, which is a decent claim to fame for any cricketer. He 'only' scored 1,200 Test runs, but helped to both win and save matches for his country, something to which the vast majority can only aspire, or consign to their night-time sleeping fantasies.

In the county game he scored 12,000 runs at just under 27 and took nearly 900 wickets at under 28. There are plenty of all-rounders who would die happy with such statistics and truth be told, only Leslie Townsend, a similar, though more bucolic cricketer between the wars, has exceeded the returns of Miller as a spin-bowling all-rounder in the county colours.

There were just two centuries in his career, but over 70 times he passed the 50 mark, something I was keen to talk about. He looked composed, even classical at the crease and I still recall cricket legend

Jim Laker waxing lyrical about his batting in a televised Sunday game many years ago, when Sunday afternoon television on BBC2 was all about cricket (and all the better for it).

Indeed, at times we were stunned when he was dismissed, so easy did he make it look and at his best he lost little in comparison to the likes of Peter Kirsten and John Wright, two of the finest batsmen to wear the county badge. He had so much time, coupled with the elegance of the best and while he was no Ian Botham, watching him bat had plenty for the aesthete.

As a spinner he had 39 five-wicket hauls and seven times took ten wickets in a match, something the Derbyshire fans would be happy to 'settle' for today. He was a very safe slip fielder but took catches with aplomb anywhere. Many will recall the nonchalant, running boundary catch in the 1981 National Westminster Bank Final, one that arguably changed the game when Northamptonshire were running away with it.

He skippered the side for three seasons and was certainly appreciated by his own, as much for his friendly persona as for his ability with bat and ball. An acclaimed and busy public speaker, I wasn't sure if he would be happy to chat with me, yet his response was both immediate and positive. It took us a few attempts to get together, but we finally sat in one of the executive boxes at Derby, watching the game unfold on one of the closing days of the 2015 season. He was warm and friendly, happy to answer all of my questions and talk about a life that, by his own admission, has gone way beyond that he dared to dream of in his boyhood back in Chesterfield.

Geoff, 34 Test matches, 25 one-day internationals and ultimately England's national selector during a period when we won the Ashes three successive times. Not bad, for a lad from Chesterfield Grammar School.

Absolutely! I left school with a very poor academic record, but if you had offered me a career of playing cricket, talking about it and selecting the England national side, I would have settled for that. You know, it all stems from January 1959, when I heard a noise downstairs and went to see what it was. I found my Dad making the fire and he had the radio on. When I asked him what he was listening to, he said it was the Ashes, the pinnacle of cricket. I remember that Fred Trueman was bowling to Norman O'Neill and Dad told me that it was what sport was all about.

He went on to say that perhaps one day, he would be able to listen to me on the radio, playing in the same fixture. It got me thinking that maybe a career as a sportsman would be a good thing, though unfortunately it was to the detriment of my 'proper' schooling.

He lived to hear me do that, though, which was great.

When you first attended nets with Derbyshire, was an international career ever something you thought or dreamed of?

Well, I played with England Schools in India and in the West Indies, which gave me an indication of what life might be like if I worked hard enough at my game. I did pretty well at that level, but I knew there was a lot of work to make the next step.

In other interviews for this book, Edwin Smith, who was county coach in your early years at the club, told me that he had to convince his namesake and predecessor Denis to sign you up. Apparently Denis wasn't sure about you.

I never knew that. I guess I owe Edwin more than I even realised! I know when I first went to the nets at Derby, Mike Page was a great help to me, telling me what the game was all about and what I had to be prepared to do and to sacrifice to make it to the top.

Mind you, at my first net session, Edwin asked me if I would like to bat first or last. With the naivety and perhaps cockiness of youth, I said I would bat first, little realising that I was merely the 'net gauger' to judge how it would play. Then I discovered I was batting against Alan Ward, Harold Rhodes, Mike Hendrick and Fred Rumsey. On a green wicket, that was a baptism of fire, I can tell you!

How important was having Edwin, a fine off-spinner himself, as an early mentor?

Oh, it was very important, as was having Venkat on the staff, who we signed as our overseas player. Both were very good, very different bowlers, but my place in the side was initially blocked by Venkat. I was an off-spinning all-rounder, but he was a better, more experienced bowler and they often opted to play an extra batsman, leaving me kicking my heels.

Both Edwin and Venkat helped me, but in those days we used to have a drink in the bar after a game. I remember one time, during a game at Lord's, I spent the best part of a couple of hours one evening chatting to Fred Titmus. I had bowled a few overs that day and Mike Page asked him to have a word with me. I sat listening to him and you couldn't help but pick things up from such players. I had a few sessions with Ray Illingworth over the years too and it is priceless to talk to such knowledgeable players, but especially to LISTEN.

> **I recently read a book by John Barclay, who wrote that you were one of the characters of the England Schools side that toured India, very confident in your abilities, compared to his own insecurities. Did you always back your own ability?**

No, I think he has that wrong. It might have seemed that way, because he was Eton-educated and I was Chesterfield Grammar School, but I was quite insecure in my early days. John and I always got on like a house on fire and still do, but I was never confident, certainly not cocky. I never played in a side in which I was the best player and was always well aware of that.

I think that goes back to Denis Smith, as you say, being unsure about me. I had ability, but I always had to give 100 per cent and if I dipped below that, perhaps I could look a more ordinary player, certainly in my earlier days.

> **What are your memories of those early days?**

Not the quality of the facilities! We used to change in the old jockey quarters that were very basic and practice was in the old indoor school, which was a wartime Nissen hut with the facilities being somewhat spartan. I remember when Lawrence Rowe arrived from the West Indies, he was batting in there. Now Lawrence whistled as he batted and we were all watching him closely, as he had just scored 302 against England in Barbados. Yet he never played a shot in anger throughout his net, content to simply keep the bowlers out. Edwin Smith said to a couple of us, 'Is he any good, this fella? He hasn't got any shots.'

A couple of days later, we played Sussex in the first game of the season and it was freezing. Lawrence had about six layers on and was facing John Snow. The ground at that time was open, with no boundary boards and off John's first ball, Lawrence rocked back and smacked it past point's right hand for four. The ball was last seen disappearing towards Nottingham Road and Mike Hendrick leaned across to me and said, 'I reckon he has got a shot or two, don't you?'

He was a fine player, but very unlucky. A cricketer with an allergy to grass…

> **Your early career saw you partnering Fred Swarbrook as Derbyshire's attack, perhaps for the first time in decades, was stronger in spin than seam, with the honourable exception of Mike Hendrick.**

That's right. Fred and I bowled well together and he was a terrific lad, as well as being a very 'gutsy' cricketer. We struggled for home-produced seamers for a while, to be honest.

> **What happened with Fred was such a shame. He was a good cricketer – what did they do to try and help him?**

Everything really. Fred got what they called the 'yips' and it was very sad. He could go into the nets and pitch every ball on the spot, yet when he got out into the middle, he simply lost it and was bowling long hops and full tosses.

It got to the point where he said he didn't want to bowl any more. He said that there was no point bowling in the nets, as he was never going to bowl in the middle and he tried to focus on his batting. It was so sad, as he had learned his trade and got to the stage where he could have taken 50 wickets or more every summer.

> **Your own career was very successful and you always looked so organised and correct when batting. Yet it took you 380 innings before you finally made a first-class century. Did it become a mental block?**

It got to the stage where I was disappointed I hadn't done it, but I had never been a figures man. I got a few 90s and twice I got there for England, yet never got a hundred. I look back now and think 'two more runs' but at the time I had done my part for the team.

I should have got more hundreds, beyond doubt. Why didn't I convert them? Perhaps it was my concentration, maybe I wasn't as fit as I could have been, but it certainly wasn't for the want of trying!

You had two very prolific wicket-taking seasons in 1976 and 1977, then only once reached similar heights afterwards, in 1984. Was there a reason for this – different wickets, a change in technique?

Eddie Barlow. That's the simple answer. To some extent I was going through the motions and Eddie came along at just the right time. I was lucky in my career, because when I first started playing cricket as a kid, a little chap in our cul-de-sac taught me the basics, but was shrewd enough to realise when I needed more than he could offer, so he directed me to Chesterfield Cricket Club.

When I got there, the late Jim Brailsford, who played a few games for Derbyshire, was my mentor and I used to chat to him when I made the county game. He told me that if I had aspirations of international cricket, I had to speak to someone who had been there and done it.

Eddie was that man and taught me what top-level cricket is all about. He put me up the batting order, but said I would only stay there on merit. He also gave me more overs, but said that I had to justify that by bowling with control and by taking wickets. He gave me responsibility and stood me alongside him at slip, where he taught me how to catch in that position.

Over and above all that, he lived in Chesterfield and we travelled together a lot. He would ask me questions about the day's play and I had to have an answer. He would ask me about things that happened and what I would have done as captain – he saw things in me that boosted my confidence and made me think much more about the game.

But Eddie transformed the whole club. Not just the players, but the members, committee, administrators – he taught everyone how we all had to pull together to succeed. It was much the same as the effect that Brian Close had on Somerset and Ian Botham.

So was he the best skipper you played under?

I couldn't split Eddie and Mike Brearley. Eddie would go into and out of the trenches with you and you'd do anything for him. Mike was an equally astute man-manager and read the game so well. They were different but were outstanding leaders of men.

After Eddie left, did the dressing room remain harmonious? I've heard some stories about strong words being exchanged and that Barry Wood, who came in as skipper, could be quite abrasive?

Barry had his own ideas on how things should be done, but it didn't change anything. There were strong characters, but they could play cricket. It is a necessity to enjoy each other's company in a dressing room, as you are with each other for six months at a time. It was your duty to make it work – we bounced things off each other and had a lot of laughs along the way. David Steele could be wonderful fun, Mike Hendrick was a funny guy, Woody was game for a laugh too – and gave us security at the top of the order as a very good opening batsman.

Moving on to England, what are your favourite memories of your international career?

Oh, there are so many! It was a fine side and we had some very good batsmen, along with excellent bowlers and, of course, Ian Botham.

It was great to bowl in tandem, as two off-spinners, with John Emburey. He was a better bowler than me, but I was a better batsman and it was a side that could do well, whatever the conditions. Captained by Mike Brearley, of course, and with two of my county colleagues, Mike Hendrick and Bob Taylor, often in the team alongside me.

I have to say I was spoiled, having Bob as both my county and international wicketkeeper. If the batsman made a mistake, you never for a minute thought he would miss it and his work rarely dropped from the very highest standard.

Mind you, I got 60 Test wickets and none of them was stumped!

Boxing Day Test, 1982?

It's funny, because I played 34 Tests for England and I say to people that the only thing I am remembered for is a catch, which was a rebound anyway!

The series in Australia when we beat them 5-1 was my favourite memory. It was the only time when I felt I was sure of a place in the side and I responded with both runs and wickets. Quite often I would be in the nets while Mike Brearley was tossing up and he would either nod or shake his head to me as he came back.

When I became selector, I always aimed for consistency of selection, as it gave people the confidence to express themselves.

I've read that you were possibly the last player to field at slip in a Test match with a whoopee cushion up your jumper?

I've read that as well and it's not true! I did have one up my jumper once, but it was at the Scarborough Festival.

We played Lancashire in the final of the Tilcon Trophy, having beaten Yorkshire on the Thursday. We had the Friday off and went down to a joke shop in the town, where we bought a load of stuff. I remember filling the collar of umpire Jack van Geloven's umpire's coat and his shirt with itching powder and there was a lot of daft stuff went on.

Anyway, when Clive Lloyd was batting in the final, I squeezed this thing under my arm as the bowler was about to bowl and Clive stepped away. I did it another couple of times when Steve O'Shaughnessy was batting and he said that he wasn't going to bat with that going on, so I stopped.

It shows how stories grow arms and legs, though!

You were captain between 1979 and 1981. Do you remember them as happy years?

It was tough. I knew the game, but it's not just about on the field as skipper, you have people coming up to you with personal issues. I was 27 when I was given the captaincy and maybe not ready for the 'other' stuff. I think if I had been given the job three years later I would have made a better fist of it, as I would have been older and wiser. Yet you don't turn down the offer of the county captaincy and it was flattering to be asked.

I captained some very good players though: John Wright, Peter Kirsten, Hendrick, Taylor – they were great people to work with.

Lord's 1981. The date is engraved on the hearts of Derbyshire supporters. What are your recollections of that day?

It's funny, because I didn't have a great season that year, yet ended up in the middle with a pivotal role at the finish. The game fluctuated all day and it came down to the final over, as you know, with Colin Tunnicliffe and I at the crease.

Now I don't think that Northamptonshire realised, until the last two or three balls, that we had only to equal their score to win, having lost fewer wickets. We had won in that manner in the semi-final against Essex and we knew we would win if we equalled their score again.

Before that last ball, I told Colin to get a bat, or something, on it because I would be coming. I knew I was going to the danger end and the field was, of course, close-set. Jim Griffiths actually bowled a really good last over and I made sure I didn't leave the crease at the non-striker's end until he was about to release the ball, then just ran… and dived!

It was the quickest 22 yards I ever covered! For me, though, the special thing was that two Derbyshire-born players were at the crease when Derbyshire won a trophy for the first time since 1936.

That side broke up fairly quickly thereafter. What happened?

I'm not sure. Such a win should have been a catalyst, but there were a lot of uneasy players on the staff. Perhaps it was the salary structure, which wasn't great, but you're right, the side fell apart too quickly.

I should have been one of them, because Jack Bond and Clive Lloyd came to see me, with a view to moving to Lancashire. Our chief executive, Roger Pearman, said they didn't want me to leave and they sorted the money side for me.

That was in 1981 and in 1995, when my Dad died, my Mum told me that his one disappointment in my cricketing career was that I didn't go to Lancashire. I was really surprised and she told me that he had been born in Lancashire, in Horwich, when my grandfather worked on the railways between there, Derby and Crewe. I asked my Mum why he didn't say something at the time and she said that he didn't want to interfere. All those years, I had no idea about that.

In 1987 you left to go and play for Essex. What caused that departure?

Well, I was going to retire, but when Essex played at Derby that summer, there was a break for rain and I went for a run. Graham Gooch asked if he could join me and, as we ran, he asked about my intentions for the following season.

I was planning to retire and go into the sports business that I ran with Chesterfield footballer Ernie Moss, but Graham told me that David Acfield was retiring and they would like me to go and replace him. He called me again a week later and I agreed to go and join them. To be honest, I had reached the point where I needed a new challenge, but I thought that would be setting up sports shops with Ernie in different places.

It didn't really work out. Essex won trophies before I went and again afterwards, but nothing in my three seasons at the club.

Do you think that your subsequent role with the English Cricket Board would have happened without moving and perhaps becoming better known down south?

Yes, I think it would. All I have ever tried to do in my career is the best I could and to help other people when I was able to do so along the way. I always tried to be honest, but not create problems and I like to think that was noticed by other people. I always felt I had something to offer when my playing career ended and when David Graveney approached me in 2000 to become one of the selectors, I jumped at the chance. It was a great honour.

I had got to know a lot of people over the course of my career. People like Alec Bedser, Doug Insole and Peter May I knew quite well and I think it was down to playing for England and being 'known' accordingly.

> **Then of course, you got the post of national selector in 2008, overseeing a period of real dominance by England. Was it a case of the right players coming along at the right time, or was consistency of selection key?**

It had been set up by Duncan Fletcher and Nasser Hussain, with a new regime in the changing room and the various combinations since that time had built on the groundwork of creating a good environment and making sound judgements and decisions.

We got a bunch of players together who bought into it. Some had been a part of things before and hadn't immediately succeeded. We sat them down and explained how we thought they could contribute and help to create something special. They were good players and there was good management and it gradually became clear that we were more respected by opponents than previously, which was gratifying.

That helped and the players started to realise that they were a good side and produced a sequence of results that backed up such assertions. There was no deficiency – we could bat, we had good seamers, a quality spinner, an outstanding wicketkeeper/batsman – that's how we won games and Test series.

> **Did occasional media complaints about South Africans in the England side ever get to you?**

No, not at all. They did everything required of them to qualify to play and I made sure that each and every one of them was passionate about playing for England. We did that with the others, of course, but I wanted to be sure that when they pulled on that sweater and cap, they were fully committed and prepared to do whatever was required.

> **You were awarded the OBE in 2013, for services to cricket. A nice day out at the Palace?**

It was! We had a lovely family day down there and I received the award from Prince Charles. He congratulated me and asked if I'd had a lot of stick about the winter results for England. I had to point out that I had stood down at the end of the previous summer!

We had a nice chat and I was very impressed with how he had something to say to everyone, irrespective of their background. With over a hundred people there, that was something that has stayed with me.

You accepted the role of president at Derbyshire in 2014. A source of pride?

Yes, it was another great honour, especially when you look at the names of people who have held the post previously.

I did insist, when Chris Grant offered me the role, that it was that of a figurehead only, not in any way a 'working' capacity. If people have asked my advice I have been happy to offer it, but I didn't want to impose on them in any way.

And the future for the club?

It's tough at the moment, because they have a lot of very young players some way from maturity and still learning the game. They need time, but it is important that you have experience of the right kind alongside them, so their learning curve doesn't see the results going too heavily against you. It is when you allow other counties to overtake you, that you start to have problems.

The young players need to learn together but the ultimate thing will always be results and getting enough ticks in the 'win' column. Every good team has players who can get them into winning positions, with bat or ball, then others who will get them over the line.

To use a popular and very accurate phrase – 'team work makes the dream work'.

John Wright OBE (1977–1988)

IF ONE were to sit down and come up with the names of the truly great batsmen that have played for Derbyshire, the chances are that John Wright would make the top four alongside Dean Jones, Peter Kirsten and Mohammad Azharuddin, with Chris Rogers and Michael Di Venuto bubbling just underneath them. If, however, you were to choose one player who, irrespective of the state of the wicket and who was bowling, would get his head down and graft, I cannot think of any that I would place ahead of Wright.

For all that he had a fine array of shots and, like all good left-handers, was immensely strong off his legs and especially through mid-on, the thing that I most remember him for was his 'leave'. He was a fine judge of the ball to let go and had an unerring ability, on a humid morning when the ball was swinging around, to play only what he had to. The 'oohs' and 'aahs' of myriad county seamers must have been music to his ears and if it bothered him at all he never showed it. Instead, he just leaned on his bat, chewed his gum and smiled.

That was another thing about John Wright. He smiled a lot and seemed to appreciate that being paid for playing cricket, while undoubtedly not easy against the array of quick bowlers in his era, was something that a lot of us cherished. He was one of the more genial players on the circuit and hugely popular with cricket fans around the county.

From 1977 to 1988, he was a model of consistency, his second-wicket partnership with Peter Kirsten for several seasons giving the county the greatest solidity they have ever had in batting. Thinking back to them batting together will always bring a wistful smile to the face of those of a certain age. When they were in full swing, which was often, there appeared little that the opposition could do to stop them. The peak came in 1982. In that golden summer, Wright scored 1,830 championship runs at 56, with seven centuries and five fifties. Kirsten scored 1,941 runs at just under 65, with eight centuries and six fifties. That year, when commitments kept me away from matches, I would listen for the cricket scores on the radio and in my mind's eye Derbyshire always seemed to be something like 230/1, with both going like trains. They seldom failed and for two Derbyshire players to be within touching distance of 4,000 runs between them, even now, seems extraordinary.

He was a very good player and it was a privilege to have seen John Wright. A chance to interview him was an ambition but appeared slim, since we live on different continents. I am indebted to Vic Brownett, one-time Derbyshire chairman and a long-time friend of the player, for putting me in touch with him last summer.

Several e-mails later, over as many months, we found a mutually agreeable time for a chat over Skype, where John proved as entertaining as I had been assured he was and the time simply flew by. He laughs easily and seemed to find it as much fun as I did, as he told me his story.

John, you started your county career at Kent?

I did. One of their players, who later played for Derbyshire, was James Graham-Brown and he played for my club in Christchurch and invited me to go over and play in England in 1976. I stayed with him and his parents in Sevenoaks and Bob Woolmer used to pick us up and take us to pre-season nets. It was a hot, dry summer and Kent had a fantastic side.

I played my first game against the Royal Air Force at Uxbridge and made a hundred, in a side that included Chris Tavare, Paul Downton and Graham Dilley. I continued to score runs and I was offered a contract on £5 a day to play for the seconds for the season. But it was made clear to me that, with Asif Iqbal, Bernard Julien and John Shepherd as overseas players, there was no chance of me getting engaged in that capacity.

To be fair, I had only played five first-class games back home at that point, but I got my second-team cap and probably learned more in that year, playing all the time, than in any other year of my playing career.

I watched a lot of cricket that year too and remember seeing Barry Richards make a couple of superb centuries. For a kid from rural New Zealand, it was a huge eye-opener. I had just finished university back home and at 21 was really trying to figure out what to do with my life.

So how did the move to Derbyshire come about?

Well, I looked around and the only two counties without their full complement of overseas players were Somerset and Derbyshire. Somerset were talking to a bloke named Viv Richards, so that was a non-starter!

I wrote to Derbyshire and got a letter back from the secretary, David Harrison, to say that they were only looking for players with international experience. Then Kent played Derbyshire in the John Player League and I understand that Brian Luckhurst, Derek Underwood and Mike Denness had a word with Eddie Barlow and Bob Taylor, saying I might be worth a look.

Soon afterwards, I got another letter from David Harrison, asking me to go and play a couple of games on trial. Colin Page, his equivalent at Kent, told me that all I had to do was go up there and hold a bat, then they would sign me! It gave me confidence and I got on a train to Derby – it was the first time I had been north of London – feeling pretty good.

I had quite a walk from the railway station to The Pennine Hotel, where I had fish for dinner and ended up getting food poisoning, but the next day, feeling rough, I got a cab to Heanor, where I was playing for Derbyshire against Nottinghamshire. I remember getting there before anyone and chatting to an elderly chap in a flat cap, who was bemoaning the influence of overseas players in county cricket!

I opened the batting with Harry Cartwright against a decent attack on a really small ground and made an unbeaten 159 from a team score of 264. I then stayed with Ashley Harvey-Walker for the weekend and played a charity match up at Chatsworth, where I scored a few runs and hit some big sixes in front of the Derbyshire players, including Eddie Barlow.

Eddie came to see me when I played another match against Northamptonshire and I again got runs, then was offered my first contract. It was huge, coming at a time when the only Kiwis in the county game were Glenn Turner and John Parker at Worcestershire and Geoff Howarth at Surrey. I went home with a contract for half my fare over, plus £1,800.

I didn't care. I'd have played for nothing, I was so excited. I was and remain so grateful for the opportunity and even now, I look back and the best years of my cricket life were at Derbyshire. I loved the area, the members, the supporters – the whole place was fantastic.

You maintained a level of performance over the years that is of great credit to you. How hard was that to do, the county 'grind' being well documented?

Well, in my first season I had played a couple of months and we went down to play Sussex, where I felt shattered and got out early. I told Eddie Barlow that I would have loved a break and a day at the races and got one of the biggest bollockings of my life!

He told me in no uncertain terms that I was a professional now and had to set a standard EVERY day.

He was right and I couldn't have asked for a better captain as a young cricketer. I looked to Bob Taylor, who was one of the most professional cricketers I ever played with and his preparation for matches and his attitude were always first rate.

He would never let me, or Peter Kirsten, or anyone, stand in the covers with our hands in our pockets, even on a cold day.

David Steele was another, as was Alan Hill. They always gave 100 per cent and I tried to learn from that. I was never going to be one of the big names, but in giving my best I tried to match them. I used to compete with Peter Kirsten, a far better batsman than me, but I wanted to score as many runs as he did. He was brilliant, but I wanted to match him every step of the way.

It was a privilege though, something thousands of people would love to do. I was travelling around England, staying in nice hotels, having a beer at the end of the day and playing cricket for a living. I loved every single minute of it and learned so much.

Just talking to other players helped me to handle the mental side and, once you have the technique, that is the biggest barrier to success.

So it was a good 'finishing school' then?

Undoubtedly. It was no surprise that of the two great sides in the past 40 years, most of the players involved made their reputations and refined their techniques in the county game. Clive Lloyd's West Indian side were all over here, working on their game, as were the likes of Hayden, Langer, the Waughs and so on of the top Australian side.

You learned your craft by playing all the time and it was priceless experience.

Your nickname over your career was 'Shake', a reference to your method of unpacking your cricket gear I think? Who coined that?

I can't remember, to be honest, but the truth is I was never very good with an iron! It came about because of my habit of taking what appeared to be my cleanest and best shirt from my cricket 'coffin' and giving it a shake before putting it on.

With my shoulder-length hair, crumpled gear and guitar, I was never likely to be confused with Geoff Boycott!

I was told you were a pretty good musician and had a pub residency at one time?

[Laughs] No! I used to play my guitar to relax and I would lead a sing-song when we travelled on the bus at times. I have always loved music and used to sing in the choir at boarding school. Perhaps there was a time or two where I sang a song for people on request, right enough.

We used to go to a pub called The Woodlark, where there were a lot of lovely people and I played a song or two occasionally. I became very good friends with Alan Fox, a Derbyshire supporter who was a regular there and he and his wife made the best chips in Derby! One year, at the end of the season, a group of regulars, including me, went on a trip to the Algarve, which was memorable for many reasons.

I used to play football for the pub team and I was useless. It was all very irreverent and a great way to unwind, get away from cricket and not take myself too seriously. At the end of a day's play, we would go in for a couple of drinks and Norman, the landlord, who became a very good friend, would say to me, 'So how many did you make today, you useless bugger?'

So you were a football fan?

Yeah, I used to go to the Baseball Ground to watch Derby, but also went to Nottingham and supported Brian Clough's side, Nottingham Forest. They were a fine side and Clough, of course, was a legend.

Did you meet him?

I did. I had a black tie benefit dinner and I was keen to get him along, as the biggest sporting name in the East Midlands. He would rarely answer the phone and I ended up driving to his house to ask if he would come along.

I rang the doorbell and I could see him in his kitchen, peeling potatoes. I knocked on the door for what seemed like an eternity, until he eventually came to answer it. Then he apologised, saying that he thought I was the postman!

I was surprised when he recognised me and invited me in, then sat me down and came back with a bottle of wine and a couple of glasses. We had a long chat and he agreed to come to the dinner with his sons, which was really appreciated. He liked his cricket, as well as football.

I learned a lot from watching, reading about and talking to Brian Clough. He was a quite remarkable man, by any standards.

Back to Derbyshire – was it a happy dressing room in your time?

Oh yes! We had a lot of fun, with some great characters. Results-wise we were up and down, but there were some great blokes in there, probably the best I ever knew.

Colin Tunnicliffe was out there on his own as the ringleader and funniest guy, but then you added in David Steele. Barry Wood came from Lancashire, there was Geoff Miller and Mike Hendrick, John Walters – 'The Welder' we called him – Freddie Swarbrook… they were a great bunch of lads and every day there would be something that cracked us up.

There was one Sunday game when Mike Hendrick arrived late and Barry Wood was getting anxious, to say the least. When he arrived and was asked where he had been, he dead-panned back, 'Church, Woody.' Barry believed him, too!

Another time, David Steele blocked an over when we were a handful of runs short of another bonus point and Woody was furious. When Steeley came back in he said, 'Sorry skip, I could feel a big one coming on.' He already had a hundred!

Perhaps the funniest was one time when David and Geoff Miller were batting together. Geoff was in the 80s and looking set for his first hundred, when David came in to bat. Somehow, there was a mix-up and they were both stranded in mid-wicket, before both started running for the same end, which Steeley won by diving for the crease!

Well, Geoff was furious and as I remember it, he bundled up Steeley's gear, took his cricket coffin and emptied it in the courtyard outside the old jockey quarters, where we changed. Meanwhile, some enterprising person had hung a noose from a beam in the dressing room, where we all sat, eagerly awaiting what was about to happen when David came in for lunch soon afterwards.

Nothing was said for a little while and we all sat with our heads down while Steeley finished a cup of tea and a cigarette. Then he got up and went over to where Geoff was sat and said, 'I'm sorry, I don't know what came over me.' Then he paused before saying, 'Do you fancy a dozen eggs?'

You can imagine, we collapsed with laughter!

We all look back on those times now and still laugh about the wonderful times we shared.

David Steele seems to have been quite a character?

Oh, he was, but was also the consummate professional. We used to bat together and talk about stuff like the length of the sprigs [spikes] we should be wearing, real 'anorak' stuff that other people might not have worried about.

You were quite a theorist and I have been told you glued your batting gloves to a bat handle to ensure your hands were in the right position. Is that true?

Oh yes! It was against Hampshire at Derby and I got a hundred in the first innings and 60-odd in the second. My gloves were glued to the handle and my hands felt great, though I couldn't swap hands when I was running, so had the turning circle of the *Queen Mary*!

That came from a chat with Steeley, who would keep talking to you to make you concentrate. He would say 'Shit shot' if I lost concentration and had a waft at one. I asked him about my grip and he told me that the way I was batting I should simply stick the bat up my arse.

Barry Wood was similar though. He used to warm up in hobnail boots and had this bat that seemed to weigh about 5lb. We thought it was made of mahogany and he used to try and annoy the opposition when he batted. He had a missing front tooth and he would take out the false one before he batted and grin down the wicket at the quick bowlers, holding his pose as if to show them how easy he was finding it.

I'd go down the wicket and tell him to stop, as it just made them bowl quicker.

You played some great innings, but is there one that stands out for you?

I made 96 against the West Indies at Chesterfield on a lightning-fast track which was probably my best. Barry Wood got hit on the hand and had to retire early and I got hit on the helmet three times. I remember getting to 13 and it felt like I had made a hundred.

David Steele got hit in the groin by Andy Roberts and crawled towards square leg on all fours, waiting on the pain easing. When he got up, he asked Andy if he could perhaps go easy, as he only had a couple of years left in the game. Andy apologised but said he was playing for his place in the side, so we were bombarded by a very lively attack.

I was annoyed to cut one to gully and miss out on a hundred, but it was a real test of technique and of bravery. They are the ones that mean something and batting through the innings against Clive Rice and Richard Hadlee on another occasion stands out, both outstanding seam bowlers, of course.

Best of all, perhaps, were the many times that I batted with Peter Kirsten, who was not just a fantastic player but also a great mate. We shared wonderful times together, on and off the pitch and it was such a shame that he didn't enjoy a long and successful international career. Along with Martin Crowe, he was the best player I ever batted with.

We batted well together, as he was right-handed and initially went back, whereas I was left-handed, tall and liked to get on to the front foot. So we kept bowlers thinking and reaped the benefits when they didn't get it right. I was sad when he decided to move on and that changed my career, really. Derbyshire opted to engage first Michael Holding, then Ian Bishop and I became a part-time player who got a game when they needed a rest.

The county were good to me in keeping me on and could easily have let me go, but they were respectful of what I had done and I played on in a part-time role for several seasons.

Of course, other counties were pleased to see me in the side. I remember Vic Marks coming up to me at Taunton and saying that, which was nice, before he ruined it by adding, 'It means Michael isn't playing!'

In that era, almost every county had one, sometimes two fast bowlers. Assuming a quick wicket and conditions that helped them, who were the most challenging?

Without doubt, Sylvester Clarke. He was very tough. Joel Garner and Malcolm Marshall were fine bowlers too, but the wickets they played on weren't always as quick as The Oval. Yet they would always give their best, as did Wayne Daniel. Andy Roberts at his meanest was fast and it was never a picnic facing Garth Le Roux and Imran Khan at Hove, Rice and Hadlee at Trent Bridge or Wayne Daniel and Vincent Van der Bijl at Lord's.

They were all fine bowlers and for a player wanting to get into Test cricket, it was a means of competing against the best.

I have to ask you about Lord's, 1981.

It was a hard day. They posted a decent total that could have been more but for some fine fielding and 'Bud' Hill held a great catch, as did Geoff Miller. Then Peter Kirsten and I shared a big stand before we were both out in quick succession.

I was really annoyed, because the ball should have gone into the stand, but we overcame a collapse for Geoff Miller and Colin Tunnicliffe, two local lads, to take us home. It meant a lot to the players, but I know how much it meant to the supporters and how long they had waited to win a trophy. Peter and I were desperate to win a trophy for them and we did.

Then the celebrations started?

I honestly can't remember. It was a time in your life when you can largely handle such things, but we partied well that night.

I remember feeling less than my best in the following day's Sunday game, but I managed to get top score, so I can't have been too bad!

What were the highlights of your international career?

I was lucky to play for my country in an era when we had a good side and beat England for the first time. I still have a picture taken when I played against Bob Taylor, Geoff Miller and Mike Hendrick in the England side, which was very special.

I remember feathering one through to Bob Taylor early in my debut innings but being given not out, something that impressed none of them. When I got back to Derbyshire the following spring, there was a big bag of Walkers crisps hanging on my peg!

We never lost a home series in the 1980s and won both in England and Australia, so it was a special time.

| **You played in a fine New Zealand side. Who would win a notional match between that side and the current one?**

It is very difficult to compare eras in sport and this would be the same. In any team that has been successful, you have a core group of outstanding players who stand up to pressure.

It was that way with my New Zealand side and, if you look at the Derbyshire one I played for, there were five or six players of proven international quality. Throw in some fine, nuggety professionals like Colin Tunnicliffe, Alan Hill and Fred Swarbrook and you will always have a good side.

Colin was a very skilled but underrated bowler and 'Bud' Hill a real battler. Sylvester Clarke always reckoned him to be one of the hardest players to get out, which is no faint praise.

To answer your question, the modern side would have hammered us in T20 and perhaps in the one-day game, but over the longer format I think it would have been quite close.

| **You have coached at various levels and, of course, in India and New Zealand on the international stage. Which was hardest?**

The pressures at international level are the hardest. I was the first non-Indian coach of their national side, so I knew that once the results went against us I could be facing the chop at any time. It went with the territory and I knew what to expect when I took the job.

Then again it is the same in the Indian Premier League and you cannot expect a long spell as a county coach without delivering results. The main difference is that at county level you are working with players who have a wider spectrum of ability and attitude. That creates different challenges and the things that I learned in my spell as coach at Kent taught me so much that I was able to use later.

You cannot be as ruthless at county level as in international cricket, where if someone is not delivering you bring in someone else. At county level, you need to be patient and wait for players to realise what they are capable of.

Now there are two divisions in England, it is much more competitive. In my time, you hoped to be top and didn't want to be bottom, but jockeyed for positions within that. Now, there are titles to win and teams aiming to be promoted while others fight relegation. It adds to the pressure, without doubt.

Coaching is a combination of teaching and man-management, trying to get your 11 players to work as a team and be the best they can be.

> **You once said that the biggest challenge in coaching the likes of Dravid and Tendulkar was counting the practice balls were all back afterwards. What do you say to such players?**

There is less technical emphasis, for sure. You need to help them to realise their importance to, and role in, the team and how they can help less gifted team-mates to realise their ambitions. They are the best of the best and so the role is more 'hands off'.

If they appreciate their environment, their importance to the team and to results, then you can do well. It is all about professionalism again, helping the team to improve and then, as a consequence, results should follow.

It is also important to have a clear game plan that everyone understands, then you leave them to get on with following it in their own style. For example, players like Virender Sehwag, Sachin Tendulkar and Rahul Dravid were all very different in their approach to batting, but they all knew that if we could bat for five sessions we could then control and dominate a match.

> **I understand that you played a part in Martin Guptill first coming to Derbyshire?**

I did. I am in touch with the people at Derbyshire from time to time and encouraged both Martin and Hamish Rutherford to give the county scene a whirl. I cannot stress enough to them what a great opportunity they have.

Derbyshire is a great place to live and the people are wonderful. I made friends 40 years ago who are still friends today and I recommend it as a mutually beneficial association. New Zealanders normally give good value on and off the field and I would love to retain my links with a wonderful county that gave me a fulfilling career.

Neil Broom is another talented Kiwi who is heading for Derbyshire and is a fine batsman who likes to hit the ball. If you can get five or six proven players in the side, as we had way back when, then young ones can come into it and feel less pressurised.

Finally, what does the future hold for John Wright?

Well, I have a scouting role for Mumbai and watch a lot of domestic Indian cricket, so when the IPL auction comes around we know who can do a job among the young players. I work with Ricky Ponting on this and it is a lot of fun.

Of course, in doing this I am closer to England and fully expect to be back there this summer, watching my favourite county and meeting old friends.

I live in Christchurch, New Zealand now, but a good part of me still regards and will always regard Derbyshire as home.

Devon Malcolm (1984–1997)

THERE ARE few sights in cricket to match that of a genuine quick bowler, in the groove, red ball in hand and on his way in to the crease.

Derbyshire supporters were spoiled in the 1980s and 1990s, with Michael Holding, Ian Bishop and Devon Malcolm providing wonderful aesthetic value and no little skill in the county colours. The opening batsmen of the circuit would have checked their health insurance and ensured that every available piece of protective equipment was packed before their game against Derbyshire, because they knew the ball was going to fly.

Devon was quick. Seriously quick. Yes, he could be erratic. Especially in his early days, when his eyesight wasn't as well-corrected as it was latterly, he could make the life of the wicketkeeper equally difficult. Balls would fly down the leg side, or wide of off stump, people would shake their heads and the negative comments would come.

They said he couldn't field, overlooking the fact that when he got the ball in his hand he had a throw that homed in on the stumps like an Exocet missile. There was never a feeling of a catch to him being deemed a formality, but he held his fair share. Nor was he a batsman, being a confirmed number 11 for most of his days, though when he got his eye in, he could hit it a long way.

Yet he managed over 1,000 first-class wickets and enjoyed a career of almost 20 years, at the end of which he was still as quick as most in the country. He rarely broke down, a tribute to a healthy and active youth that he explained to me, as well as looking after himself properly over the course of that career.

His reputation was confirmed in the eyes of the cricket public with his wonderful 9-57 against the South Africans at The Oval in 1994. It was a spell of fast bowling that raised him to the status of legend, though in Derbyshire he had already attained that, over many years of exemplary service.

For anyone who watched the county over those years, that long, rhythmic run-up, with a bob of the head as he got into his stride as if to confirm all was well, will live with them always. Then the gather, the coiling of the 'spring' before the ball was released, sometimes too fast for the human eye both on the boundary and in the middle.

He has made a great success of his career since retirement too and, as a busy man, took some pinning down for an interview. Yet when it happened, it was worth it. He is very friendly, with a regular laugh that confirms why he was such a popular team-mate.

Some of his stories surprised me, but then Devon made a habit of that over the years.

Devon, you were born in Jamaica, what are your memories of cricket there?

Well, I came over to the UK in my teens, so my early years were spent playing cricket on an island that was obsessed with the game. Anywhere there was space you would see children and adults setting up a game of cricket. It didn't always have a conventional cricket ball, but we would use a tennis ball and even a coconut at times!

Did you always try to bowl fast?

I spent a lot of time listening to cricket on the radio and so you build a picture in your mind of what the commentators say. Our hero in Jamaica was Michael Holding and I had this image of him running in from the boundary and bowling at the speed of light!

I tried to do the same and, of course, by the time I got to the crease I was knackered! The speed of my run-up was greater than that of the ball that I bowled in the early days.

Later, when I was 12 or 13, my friends were amazed how quickly I could bowl the ball, but I had naturally strong arms, legs and back which helped.

So you were always powerfully built?

Yeah. You should understand that we walked almost everywhere and from the age of six, when I started school, we walked three miles to school and the same back home again. Of course, there were days when I was maybe late, at which point I had to run that distance, to avoid punishment, which built up the muscles and fitness still further!

So what brought you over to the UK?

Well, my Dad came over in the 1960s and worked in Sheffield, trying to get the money together for the family. Sadly, my mother died when I was six and then my sister and I were brought up by our grandmother. I moved to Sheffield to join my father when I was 16, but I didn't play cricket for a while, as all my friends were big football fans.

Did you get into football?

You know, my Dad sent over a Sheffield United shirt from time to time when I was in Jamaica, so I used to go around wearing them, quite likely being the only person on the island who was wearing one! I took it with me when I moved to the UK and probably still have it. So I always looked out for their results but I was never a fan as such, going to games.

You ended up playing for Sheffield United in the Yorkshire League, where you made quite a name for yourself?

It all happened very quickly. I was at Richmond College and in March, 1984 I was selected to play for a Yorkshire League select XI against Yorkshire County Cricket Club at Castleford, in a pre-season match. One of my team-mates was Bruce Roberts, who subsequently became a team-mate at Derbyshire for several seasons.

It was a soft pitch, so even then I knew that I had to pitch the ball up. In my first over I clean bowled Martyn Moxon with a yorker of pace, then in my third I knocked Geoff Boycott's middle stump out of the ground with another one! That was really something, because he never gave his wicket away.

I took two wickets and had a clear caught behind turned down, for what would have been a third as we beat Yorkshire for the first time. This was on a Friday and the next day the *Yorkshire Post* had a picture of me bowling Boycott, his bat still only halfway down as his stump went cartwheeling. It was underneath a headline that read 'Yorks Devon creamed' – a clever play on words that has stayed with me!

So was that what brought you to Derbyshire's attention?

Yes. Phil Russell, the Derbyshire coach at the time, was a passionate Derbyshire man and his biggest thing professionally was not losing to Yorkshire. When he saw someone who had come from nowhere to beat them, he wanted to know more.

He actually got in touch on the Sunday and invited me for a trial on the Monday! I told him that I couldn't, as I had college and my Dad would kill me if I missed it. He insisted and said that you only get limited opportunities in sport and to get the train to Derby, where someone would pick me up.

After a little soul-searching, I decided to skip the lecture and go down and when I walked into the changing room, the first people I saw were Bob Taylor and Geoff Miller. My eyes were wide, as I had never met a first-class cricketer before and here were two international players changing alongside me.

I bowled at a good pace to Kim Barnett and had him hopping around a little, then at the end of the session, Phil Russell and Kim took me to the club offices and said that they would like to offer me a one-year contract and told me how much I would be paid. All I could say was that I didn't need to be paid to play cricket, but Phil told me that I was going to be a professional cricketer and would be paid accordingly.

He also sowed a positive seed in my head. He said that while I didn't always bowl with control, he could help me with that and, at my pace, I could easily go on to play international cricket by the time I was 26. To hear someone say that, so early in my career, was very special.

So I became a first-class cricketer over the course of a weekend. I was a student on the Friday and a professional cricketer on the Monday!

People were always quick to point out what you couldn't do in your career – your fielding and batting were often criticised. Did that criticism ever get to you?

I always look for positives in my life. Gerald Mortimer, a writer in the *Derby Telegraph*, once described me as 'a Ferrari without a steering wheel'. I took the positive element of that, the comparison with a great car, when the guys told me about it in the dressing room. After all, a Ferrari has a great engine and great wheels and I said to them, 'That's fine, I just need to get the steering wheel now.'

With my attacking bowling style and the pace I bowled, especially on small outgrounds with fast outfields, the runs could mount from snicks and edges through and over the slips. It was a trade-off, with what I brought to the attack.

There was one time, when I bowled at Heanor, I was almost edged for six! Of course, there were some good batsmen around too, who could take any bowler apart.

There is little margin for error when you bowl at that pace.

Your eyesight was often cited as the cause of your problems. How bad was it in your early years in the county game?

When I started my career I wore glasses and they worked well for me in club cricket. My problem was that I used to sweat a lot and bowl longer spells in the first-class game, which was when they became a hindrance. The guys in the dressing room used to say that I needed windscreen wipers and I struggled to keep them clear and dry. On cold days they would mist up as I sweated, and of course, when there was a little drizzle it was another problem, even with the peak of my cap pulled down.

So I changed to contact lenses, but it took me a year to get used to them. My eyes used to get really sore and I had a problem putting them in. John Morris used to be amused watching my efforts, as my eye used to close in a reflex reaction as my finger approached it! So much so that by the time I got the second one in place, the first one was really sore!

When laser surgery became available, I opted for that and I had my most prolific year in the county game in my penultimate season, playing for Leicestershire.

I was short-sighted, but it wasn't as bad as some people tried to make out. Perhaps the hardest part was running to take a catch, especially in the early days, but I managed to hold on to a few.

You were a confirmed number 11 with the bat...?

Yeah, but that was one of those things about the era. I didn't really get to practise my batting that much and adopted the philosophy, most of the time, of going out to entertain when I batted. People used to find my batting enjoyable and comical, but I really was trying!

If I middled it, the ball travelled and I did get a couple of first-class fifties. Nowadays, when everyone is expected to contribute, there is a need for all cricketers to be three-dimensional and I think I would have had more time working on my batting in the nets than I had then. A few balls from part-time bowlers in the nets didn't prepare me for facing the likes of Allan Donald or Curtly Ambrose.

If I connected, it was usually six or four, but it wasn't always in my arc!

You played the first-class game for almost 20 years, which is extraordinary for a genuine fast bowler. Was a lot of that down to Kim Barnett's 'rotation policy' in your early years?

Kim was a pioneer in something that is now accepted in the first-class game. He used to tell me to take a game off, put my feet up and be ready for the next match.

We had a lot of good seamers and he would rest me, to save me for matches where he knew he needed me or where the wicket would suit me well.

That I was able to bowl quickly to the age of 40 was very much down to Kim's policy, as well as the natural fitness that I mentioned earlier. Nor should my late start in the game be discounted, as my body was fully developed by the time I was playing regular cricket.

You played alongside some fine bowlers in that era. If you were to pick two opening bowlers for a Derbyshire side in that time, who would you choose?

Ole Mortensen for one. He was aggressive, accurate, had all the skills and was a great team man. For the other, I will avoid the obvious options of Michael Holding and Ian Bishop and opt for Paul Newman.

He was unlucky with injury but at one stage looked set for an England career. He had good pace, got bounce and made me realise, as a young cricketer, what I had to do to get a regular place. I saw what Paul could do with a cricket ball and aimed to be as good as him.

There were plenty of good bowlers at that time, but those two were both good on a sustained basis.

Who was the biggest influence on you as a bowler?

Michael Holding. As a youngster in Jamaica he was my idol, then I ended up in the same team as him at Derbyshire. He never took me to the nets, but he would sit down in the dressing room next to me and talk about bowling and what I had been doing right or wrong.

I remember one time at Old Trafford, he took me to one side and said, 'Dev, I can't bowl as quick as you man. You are so fast.' Imagine, hearing that from the great Michael Holding! It made me go out feeling ten feet tall.

He would always find something positive to say to me, relate my bad days to some that he had in his career and generally helped me to handle the mental side of being a fast bowler.

I also admired Richard Hadlee, how he bowled and what he could do with a cricket ball.

It was an era of a strong Derbyshire side, yet one that didn't get the success that it perhaps should have done. Why was that?

As you know, cricket is a team game but also an individual one. We had people who just wanted to do their 'thing' and not necessarily be part of a team. If we had managed to pull together more often, we would have done better.

There were a lot of talented cricketers, but as a small county with perhaps lower expectations than most, maybe some felt that middle of the table in a 17-county championship was a pretty good season.

We needed someone to lift the bar, set individual targets and lay down expectations. Dean Jones and Les Stillman came in and did that, but perhaps the desire to 'coast' and unwillingness to be taken out of their comfort zone was too strong for some.

Having said that, some very talented individuals at times produced spectacular performances. Just not often enough for sustained success.

Under Dean and Les we came close to winning the County Championship in 1996. What did they do that year?

One of the first things that Les Stillman did as coach was to tell us that he could show us how to be a better team, one that achieved more than a group of individuals had managed to do the season before.

I remember talking to Les early on and he told me that he wanted Derbyshire to become the Manchester United of county cricket. By that he wanted young, hungry players in the side and he told me that senior players would have to produce displays that earned them a place in the 11 and the respect of those younger ones.

It sowed the positive seeds I mentioned earlier. They saw the talent and said that we just needed to find an extra ten per cent each – and play as a team – to enjoy greater success. For one season, in a strong dressing room that perhaps had too many individuals, as opposed to team men, we managed to do that.

Yet it all went sour the following year and the side quickly fell apart. What happened?

Dean was a great competitor and wanted to win. He told us that he might say and do things to get the best out of us on a cricket pitch but to wait until we got off the pitch to tell him about it. He could be abrasive, even offensive at times, but that year we largely overlooked it.

The problem was that Kim Barnett should have been looked after and managed better. After a number of years as captain he was simply pushed to one side. He should have been given a role in the team, which didn't happen and it must have been tough for him to have no involvement in the decision-making.

Senior players such as Kim and I were pushed hard, as they wanted an international intensity to our cricket. That went fairly well for the first year but the cracks started to appear, as some didn't enjoy the comments and the expectations placed upon them.

The grumblings in the team started in the middle of that summer and the dressing room split into factions, which was counter-productive, even though we got to the end of it and nearly won the championship.

I'll tell you a story about that year. We played Middlesex and Kim Barnett had the nastiest laceration on his knee that I have ever seen. He could barely put his pads on, or run, but he felt so threatened for his place in the side that he insisted on playing. That was wrong and I said so. Even now when I think of it, it makes me cringe. It was poor management. He should have been told to get it sorted and stitched and that he would be back in the side a fortnight later, or whenever.

> **Your Derbyshire career ended in a bit of controversy, with team-mates accused of conspiring to hinder your benefit year. Were things that bad?**

Well, I mentioned the factions in the dressing room and things got really awkward. I was away, playing with England at Lord's and I took a phone call, asking if I would put my name to a petition to get rid of Dean and Les.

I refused to do it. I felt that, like new management at any club in any sport, they had the right to do things their way, even if I didn't necessarily agree with their methods at times. I wanted to play cricket, not get involved in internal politics, and said so. Besides, if I had an issue about anything, I preferred to deal with it face-to-face, not by signing a piece of paper.

Anyway, when I got back to Derby, I went to train at Breadsall Priory and saw Kim, who completely blanked me in the car park. I asked him what it was about and only then realised the depth of feeling in the dressing room, which had escaped me when I was focused on my job for England.

It was suggested that not signing the petition may have a detrimental impact on my benefit, to which I replied that I would sooner cancel it than do something that was against my principles. It did have an effect on some of my functions, but at least I was able to hold my head high.

I don't look back on it as one of the favourite times of my career, but nor do I bear a grudge. Every time I was up for a contract renewal at Derbyshire, I always said that if Kim was going to be captain I was happy to sign. We had a lot of good times together and that was the only 'blip' in the relationship.

Was that why you left Derbyshire?

No, not at all. When a player has a benefit, there is normally a trade-off. The past performances that warrant the award often suffer, with the many distractions that are going on for that year.

I made it clear to the Derbyshire committee that I loved playing for the county and over the years I had turned down a number of offers to go and play elsewhere. When I was playing with England and tiring, I would think of my supporters and friends in the county and renew my efforts just for them. When I took a wicket, I would tell myself it was one for Derbyshire. In short, I wanted to finish my career for the county.

That benefit year, I had my best season in terms of wickets and I asked the committee about a new deal. I was told that the accepted way of things was that a player retired after a benefit and they weren't going to offer one! The irony was that as soon as I announced I was leaving, every other county got in touch to offer me a contract. It is hard to believe, but true. I played on for another six years and in my penultimate season I was the second-highest wicket-taker in the country. It proved that I still had things to offer.

Going back a little, I have to ask you about the Benson and Hedges Cup Final win at Lord's in 1993. What are your memories of that day?

There was a bit of animosity after the championship match before the game, in which there had been accusations of ball-tampering.

It worked well from our perspective, because it gave us an even greater competitive edge that might otherwise not have been there. We always felt that the so-called big clubs looked down on us with disdain, so that added to it.

It all came down to the last over, which had looked likely from the middle of the Lancashire innings. Frankie Griffith had to bowl it at Neil Fairbrother, who was one of the best one-day batsmen in the world at that time. Yet he couldn't get Frank away and the only bad ball he bowled was turned into a yorker by Neil, as he came down the wicket at him!

Dominic Cork played a fantastic innings that day and he was the sort of guy who thrived in that kind of game. He was feisty and competitive and someone who you would always want in your team.

I understand that part of the plan was to leave Mike Atherton batting for as long as possible?

It wasn't pre-planned, but once we saw Mike wasn't in the best of touch, we made a conscious effort to bowl tight lines and tie him down. We had well-set fields to frustrate him and were well aware that the danger man was Fairbrother.

We knew that if we could limit the time that he had at the crease and ensure the run rate was high enough to put him under pressure when he did get in, we had a chance.

A couple of questions about your international career: you produced the greatest spell of bowling by an England fast bowler in the 20th century, with 9-57 against South Africa at The Oval in 1994. What do you recall of that day?

It was magical. The best I ever bowled and everything just came out right. Everything just clicked that day. The crowd was fantastic, I had rhythm and was totally in the zone. I was following through and in the batsmen's faces and they couldn't handle me.

Your comment of 'you guys are history' is much quoted. The anger of that afternoon was in stark contrast to your perceived placid demeanour at times. Was that a factor?

You know, I often got told that I looked laid back and that it came across as if I didn't care.

I did. I was always passionate about my cricket. It hurt when I dropped a catch, but there was no point getting caught on camera swearing, as I felt I had responsibilities as a role model to young children and families.

There was a lot going on at that time and I had been previously dropped by England without being told and there were mixed messages from the coaching staff. I went back to Derbyshire and took a lot of wickets in a handful of games.

When I got hit on the head by a bouncer from Fanie de Villiers, who only had to pitch it up to have me in trouble, I just thought, 'You know what, I'm going to do things my way for once and see what happens.' It could well have been the last match I played for my country, so I decided just to do what came naturally.

They recalled me to the side because they needed a match-winner and I am glad that I was able to do just that.

Yet your England career stuttered and I suppose the nadir was the South African tour of 1996/97, with a supposed fall-out with Ray Illingworth. Was that the low point?

Undoubtedly.

Did it hurt you, as by that stage an established county and international bowler, that they tried to change your style?

It was ridiculous. I had demolished South Africa in 1994 and was now being told that the new management team wanted me to change how I bowled.

It was disruptive to my and the team's preparation and completely ruined the tour for me. If I wasn't right for them, maybe they shouldn't have picked me, but to try to change the way I bowled on a tour, after a good few years of success, was just silly and very hurtful.

Had it been any other tour I would have walked away, without question.

Yet when I thought of what Nelson Mandela and the people of South Africa went through, it would have been defeatist to do so. I

199

could have been nasty and controversial in my response to it, but I tried to maintain my dignity, despite considerable provocation.

A lot of players told me that they couldn't have handled things as I did, which was gratifying. Again, I bear no grudges, but it was very poorly handled.

Of the many great batsmen you bowled at, who were the best?

I bowled against Sachin Tendulkar when he was a young boy and thought he was going to be special when he grew up. That proved an accurate prediction!

Viv Richards was the most intimidating. He wanted to dominate you and just wouldn't back down, no matter how fast you bowled or how well you were bowling.

The best? Brian Charles Lara. He was just a run machine and when he got to 20, you would look at each other and say 'uh-oh', because the next you knew he was on 120. He never stopped wanting to score runs either. He was a wonderful player, with all the shots and an amazing ability to pick the gaps in whatever field you chose to set.

And what now for Devon Malcolm?

I run DEM Sports Ltd and we manufacture and sell cricket field equipment, such as sight screens, rollers, covers and mobile practice cages.

We also produce the Devon Malcolm Concertina Cricket Net System, which enables cricket to be played safely in any small space without the worry of a ball flying all over a playground or sports field. It takes very little space and is a development that I am very proud of.

Anything that can be done to promote the wonderful game of cricket is fine for me and I hope that such developments might inspire and give opportunity to the next generation of young cricketers.

I am also a proud father of three girls, all born in Derby, and a son, Jaden, who is nine and bowling pretty fast in the Northamptonshire Academy.

If he develops as I hope he will do, he will be playing county cricket for Derbyshire or Northamptonshire, that's for sure!

Kevin Dean
(1996–2008)

THERE WERE times, during a county career of some 13 summers, that Kevin Dean looked good enough for international consideration.

That he did so was a tribute to his consistency, because the locally-held belief is that Derbyshire players need to be much better than their counterparts elsewhere to get an opportunity at national level. Many Derbyshire bowlers over the years can be used as evidence to support such an argument, but Kevin was a worthy continuation of an illustrious line of Derbyshire seam bowlers that can be traced back to the 19th century.

Like so many of his counterparts, his biggest issue was injury. At 6ft 5in there were problems with his back and hamstrings at times, perhaps too often to allow him to really push those claims. Nor was he especially quick and there were those who suggested that he would have been cannon-fodder at a higher level on better pitches. Yet lesser bowlers of similar pace have been picked over the years and some have done well, somewhat defeating the argument.

What Kevin could do was swing a ball better than most, which helped him to take 170 wickets at an average of 22 before his 25th birthday. Even this wasn't enough to get him on to an England A tour, something that was both frustrating and disappointing in equal measure. There were days when you arrived at the ground, sniffed the air and realised that the conditions were ripe for Kevin's talents. A little early moisture in the wicket helped, his angle as a left-armer did too, but his opening spell was usually one that needed keen concentration to survive. The one across the right-hand batsman kept the slips interested, but the one that swung in late was the wicket-taker. Any batsman slow on his feet or stuck on the back foot was in danger and his broad smile, never far away, was the indicator of yet another victim.

His era for the county was marked by a number of fine seam bowlers who were available at the other end. With Dominic Cork, Devon Malcolm and Phil DeFreitas in the same attack, he might have been the perceived weaker link, the less-known bowler. That didn't last for long and when his body allowed it, he was as good as any of them.

He took 401 first-class wickets, including two hat-tricks, and 582 dismissals in all forms of the game, which made him the most successful Derbyshire-born bowler of his generation. He was also the club's Professional Cricketers' Association representative for ten years and is now the cricket advisory director on the club's Advisory Board.

A Derbyshire man through and through, I caught up with him on a pleasant day at the County Ground. Closing in on his 40th birthday, he still looked fit enough to be opening the bowling, which he still does for Ockbrook in the Derbyshire Premier League.

Kevin, you were born in Derby – how did you get into the game?

I was, but I was brought up in Colton, near Alton Towers in Staffordshire. I replied to an advert in the local newspaper, where Cheadle Cricket Club were looking for players. I played for the same Staffordshire under-16 side as Vikram Solanki and Scott Ellis, who was on Worcestershire's books for a while.

Then I was told I wasn't good enough to play for their under-19s, so I moved to Derbyshire, where I played for the colts side.

Your great asset as a bowler was an ability to swing the ball. How hard was that for you to develop or did it come naturally?

I don't think you can teach that sort of thing and certainly no one taught me! I could always get it to swing, much in the same way that

Angus Fraser could naturally move it both ways off the seam. Perhaps a really good bowling coach can do it, but my ability to swing the ball was something that was always there. Importantly it went late – a lot of people swing it from the hand, but mine used to be straight till around halfway down the wicket, then swing one way or the other, depending on my grip and the hand/wrist position.

You were never a quick bowler, like Mark Footitt, but when conditions were in your favour, a real handful?

I was always told to stand up tall when I released the ball, but pace is an innate thing. You can add a yard or two with muscle and strength as you develop, but you can't bowl quickly if your body doesn't allow you to do so. You just use what you are given to the best of your ability. Like all bowlers, I worked out quickly what I could and couldn't do. You need to know what your stock ball is, then work on the variations that will get you wickets by the surprise element. After that, you get to know your opponents. Cameron White, for example, liked the ball on his pads, so I would bowl five that went across him, followed by the (hopefully surprise) in-ducker.

These days they have video analysis, of course, so bowlers are less reliant on their memory!

You made your debut in 1996, when Dean Jones almost led us to the County Championship. That was a special summer?

I always say that was the best thing I ever did, walking into that dressing room. There were some great cricketers in that side and at the start of the summer I was actually 11th seamer! There were 25 players on the staff and for the first game of the season there were 12 players went with each of the first and second teams and I was told to go and play for my then club side, Langley Mill, and report back on the Monday morning.

Were you overawed?

Not really. I'd been at the nets where they all were, so I knew them all, some better than others of course. Playing under Dean Jones was quite an experience though.

In what way?

He was a great player but didn't suffer fools gladly and could be quite abrasive. I was 12th man at Old Trafford that year and took drinks out to Dean and to Kim Barnett, who didn't get along, during a stand of 200. They never spoke to one another through the entire partnership and I had to take a drink to either end of the wicket, which was quite awkward.

Dean was a tremendous competitor, but so were Chris Adams, Phil DeFreitas and Dominic Cork. The rest of us were dragged along and it was a magical summer to be a part of. I remember one Sunday game when someone threw the ball in on the bounce and I shouted, 'Keep it up, I'm trying to swing it.' Quick as a flash Dean was straight back at me, 'I don't want you f...g swinging it and bowling wides. Just bowl straight.' It made his point quite succinctly.

Yet it all went wrong so quickly afterwards. What happened?

In many ways it was similar to the England dressing room of recent vintage. While you are winning it is all fine, but as soon as results go against you, everyone starts pointing the finger at someone else and all hell breaks loose.

Dean was abrasive but Les Stillman, the coach who came over with him, was very influential on Chris Adams. Les smoothed things over when Dean went off on one and pulled us all together. He brought over diet sheets and the players were expected to adhere to them. Prior to that, most dined on McDonald's and were happy to have a few beers at the end of the day.

That was a world away from today's ice baths, recovery shakes, pool sessions and stretches at the end of play – and it was only 20 years ago!

So what happened in 1997, when Dean left early in the season?

It was lots of little things. There was a fire alarm at a hotel we were staying in one night and two of the players weren't there. Then there was a game when we started with 12 on the pitch, because Dean hadn't made it clear who was 12th man. Telling that player to get off the pitch, fairly bluntly, didn't help morale either. Lots of little things built up and eventually he decided that the best thing to do was to go home.

> **Your career coincided with those of Dominic Cork, Phil DeFreitas and Devon Malcolm, so getting the new ball was not always a possibility?**

The fact I was left-handed helped, as the others were all right-arm bowlers. The wind used to blow across the ground and they all wanted the end that helped their out-swinger, whereas I wanted to bowl so it helped it go the other way.

> **The breakthrough came in 1998, with over 70 wickets, then there were injury issues the following year?**

It helped that Corky, A.J. [Andrew] Harris and I were all trying to swing it and so we had a shared desire to keep the shine on the ball and not keep hitting the deck too hard. The ball swung well for most of the summer too, which helped!

Then I had a stress fracture in 1999 and had two screws put in my back. The club physio, Anne Brentnall, had left and we didn't replace her very quickly. I had to drive down to Essex, believe it or not, for treatment! I went there on a Monday morning and came back on Thursday or Friday. I stayed in what had been Danny Law's house and Robert Rollins was there, the Essex player, as was Graham Napier, who had the same operation as me the week before, so we did our rehabilitation together. Then I did the re-modelling of my action with Geoff Arnold. It was all over the place, with my shoulders going one way and my hips the other.

> **Didn't anyone say anything about that before?**

No, because I was taking wickets. No one changes something that works, although they tried to do that at England level with a few bowlers over the years.

> **Did you ever feel that an England call was close? In 2002 you must surely have been in contention, with 83 wickets at 23 each?**

I played with MCC at Chesterfield that year against Sri Lanka, when James Kirtley, Simon Jones and I bowled them out for 127. I took 3-29 but I never heard anything else. To be fair, out of what was a pretty good team, only Andrew Strauss and Simon Jones went on to have Test careers of note.

Thinking back, 2002 was probably my favourite summer. We won five out of the first six matches, with Corky, Graeme Welch and I swinging it around. A little Pakistani guy turned up at the nets in a tracksuit one day and asked if he could bowl and when he put his spikes on, bowled at the speed of light from a ten-yard run-up.

Mohammad Ali really only had that one summer of success because the novelty value soon wore off and injuries took a toll, but he was seriously quick and put a few people in hospital that year, which gave rise to a few fairly obvious newspaper headlines!

After that summer, the wicket haul started to decline. What happened?

The following year they changed the type of ball being used and the new one simply didn't swing as much. Once the first layer of lacquer wore off, the ball went pink! There were a few bowlers complained, I can tell you.

Any favourite matches? Presumably the one-wicket win over the Australians in 1997, when you helped avoid the follow-on in our first innings then came in as last man with 11 runs to win as we chased 371?

Yeah, that's my favourite. Chris Adams was given out lbw in the first innings, having flicked Shane Warne's flipper down to fine leg for four. Warney had a strangled appeal and was as astonished as anyone when Chris was given out. Poor old Chris then got fined for hitting the same boundary board that the ball had hit with his bat as he walked off.

In the second innings, he scored a brilliant 91 from just 76 balls, which hopefully made up for it to some extent.

We needed 11 off nine balls to win the game when I went in and I think I genuinely closed my eyes and swiped my first ball from Warne over midwicket for four. That was when Ian Healy piped up from behind the stumps, 'Is that your highest score, mate?'

Then I tried to sweep Warne and must have been close to leg before and took a one off the last ball of the over, leaving six off the last.

Brendon Julian bowled the last over and I kept thinking he was going to bounce me. I hit one to mid-off and ran, but was not even close when Greg Blewett's throw missed the stumps and, with no one backing up, went for an overthrow. I was still waiting on the short ball, because I never played the hook, when he bowled another one pitched up that I squirted through the covers for the winning runs.

Warne took seven wickets?

Yes, he was coming back from a shoulder operation and bowled a long spell. He was a great bowler, no doubt about it. A fantastic competitor too.

Did you have favourite grounds to bowl on?

Anywhere it swung! My best figures came at Canterbury and at Taunton, neither of them wickets where bowlers traditionally flourished. I enjoyed bowling at The Oval too, where I got a bit of bounce from my height.

My least favourites were Bristol, where the wicket was usually quite abrasive and scuffed the ball up and The Riverside at Durham, where it rarely seemed to swing over the years.

Who were the best batsmen you bowled to?

Initially Robin Smith, who was a really fine batsman. I always thought I might get him with late swing, but he seemed to have an answer for most things!

Latterly Kevin Pietersen. Some people don't like him, but you cannot deny that he is a fantastic player who, on his day, is almost impossible to bowl to. I think he scored five hundreds, including a double, against us in my time and when he made the England team and was hitting world-class bowlers around, I breathed a sigh of relief that it wasn't any real inadequacy on our part, just a brilliant batsman at work!

What about the bowlers you looked up to?

As a kid I used to operate the small scoreboard at Derby, for £3 a day! Doing that enabled me to watch the likes of Ole Mortensen and Michael Holding, who were wonderful bowlers.

I always admired Wasim Akram too. He had such astonishing natural talent and I watched his Sky Sports master class, when he was still swinging it prodigiously from two or three paces in his mid-40s. He was an extraordinary bowler.

Then again, I was lucky to bowl at the opposite end to Devon Malcolm's extreme pace, Dominic Cork's many variations and Phil DeFreitas's out- and in-swingers. All fine bowlers who you could learn from.

When you finished with Derbyshire, you started a property development business?

I started that in 2005, with my brother-in-law. We are still doing that, him doing all the skilled work and me doing all the other stuff that is required in such a business! We have renovated and sold on around 30 properties now – in fact I just sold one this morning!

Didn't I see you on *Homes Under The Hammer*?

Yes, that was in 2005, one of the first properties we did. The first bit was done in June, when I was looking pretty good and had the 'cricketer's tan'. Then the 'reveal' of the property revamp was done later in the year, the day after the PCA Awards Dinner, when I looked like something the cat dragged in!

I also do a bit of work for Betfair, having worked for Ladbrokes for a number of years in the close-season. That was in the days when cricketers were on a six-month contract and had to find their own work in the winter months.

Times have changed on that score.

Oh yes, without doubt. My first season on the Derbyshire staff, I earned £4,500, then when I got my September pay slip I had a £2,000 bonus for our finishing second in the league. I couldn't believe it, not far off what I earned all summer, after the tax came off!

You still play regularly in the Derbyshire Premier League, a role that lets you cast an eye over young local talent?

Yes, if I see someone who is worth a trial, then I point them towards the club and vice-versa. I hope to keep doing that while the body still allows me to do so without too much pain afterwards! My eldest son is seven and enjoys Kwik Cricket, so hopefully at some point we will meet in the middle, me on the way down and him on the way up.

The standard of the Derbyshire Premier League is high?

Without a doubt. In 2014 we won the league and Sandiacre won the national knockout. Their attack is as good as that in any county second team.

There are some very good overseas players too and 90 per cent of clubs have Derbyshire staff players on their books, so it is both competitive and very good quality cricket.

Finally, can you tell me about your current role on the club board?

I am cricket advisory director, so maintaining links between club cricket and the county side is important. We want a progression to the county side from the best club players who are interested and good enough for a career in the game.

I also liaise with Graeme Welch, because in the role I am representing Derbyshire members. I am his friend, because we go back a long way, but I also have to be prepared to ask difficult questions when the need arises, such as why we lost a particular game, or why player X isn't getting a game. If they are questions members might ask, I need to be prepared to ask them.

It is a wide and varied remit but I have to ask questions that will help us to get to the status in the game that everyone involved aspires to.

We will get there.

Graeme Welch
(2001–2006)

THE GINGER Warrior. We called him that for two very obvious reasons. One, that he was (and is) undeniably ginger in colouring. Two, because if you were a captain going on to a cricket pitch and looked back at the team that was following you, Graeme Welch was a man you would want to be among them.

As a batsman, he could score runs quickly, but was willing and able to graft for the cause if the need arose. He and Ant Botha rescued a few such causes and won a few games with late-order partnerships. Graeme struck a clean ball and there was always a chance of something being pulled from the fire when he was batting, or if you knew he was still to come.

As a bowler, he became one of the most respected seamers on the circuit. He went from a largely bit-part player at Warwickshire to an integral member of the side at Derbyshire, simply because he was appreciated and given that precious commodity named opportunity.

He responded well. On his arrival, he was part of a strong seam attack that was in the finest of Derbyshire traditions. With Dominic Cork and Kevin Dean, we had an attack that would take full advantage of a wicket offering help. Latterly he became the one constant in the seam attack, the man you knew would make batsmen think on a good wicket, as well as getting them out when the cards were better stacked in his favour.

Perhaps more than anything, he looked like he was enjoying himself. For all of its challenges, the life of a professional cricketer is one that is envied by thousands, the opportunity to play the game AND be paid for it one that most would consider body part donation to do. Welch seemed to realise this more than most, a smile seldom far from his face, his demeanour impeccable and his interaction with supporters always appreciated.

I wanted to see if that was still there, now he had a different role. I recall a lengthy chat at a pre-season game many years ago, when my son was the proverbial knee high to a grasshopper and somewhat overawed by a sportsman chatting easily to his Dad.

Graeme asked him a couple of questions, which made him feel special, then offered to take his autograph book into the dressing room for the other players to sign. It was a simple, yet hugely appreciated gesture that even now sees my son refer to him as a 'really top bloke'. Many would love such an accolade, but it needs to be worked for.

I met Graeme during the final game of a challenging 2015 season. We sat in his office at the 3aaa County Ground in Derby, following the action on the wall-mounted TV screen as we chatted, all this after he had made me a coffee. The challenges of his current role as elite cricket performance director seemed obvious, but he was as approachable as I remembered and gave each question due consideration before answering.

One of the most highly regarded bowling coaches in the country, my time with him gave a fascinating insight into a career that completely justified the use of the word 'professional'. It is one that can have various connotations in sport.

In the case of Graeme Welch, it can be used for the very best of reasons. He is a man who knows what he is doing and how he has to go about his work.

It made for a fascinating interview.

Graeme, anyone listening to you is in no doubt that you are from the north-east. Why were you not picked up by Durham, prior to making your first-class bow with Warwickshire in 1994?

I joined Warwickshire in 1990, when I was just 17, whereas Durham were only awarded first-class status in 1991. I went down for a trial in 1989 and it was perhaps the worst trial ever! The ball was coming too quickly, anything that could go wrong did. I was only 16, but Bob Cottam must have seen something, as I was offered a two-year contract. The first year, I enjoyed the bright lights of the big city too much. I had come from a small village up north and it was a huge change for me.

Is that where the nickname comes from?

Pop? Yeah, the Welch family through the years has had a liking for a pint, but it is one of those names that is passed through the generations and I have no idea how it got to Birmingham.

So you wasted the first year then?

Yes and it was only in the last six weeks of the season that I got my act together and realised what I had to do to be a professional cricketer. From that moment on, I knew how much work was involved.

You had some great years at Warwickshire, at a time when they were by a distance the best team in the country?

[In] 1994 [it] wasn't a bad year to break through! I was playing alongside Brian Lara, Dermot Reeve, Gladstone Small and Tim Munton, as well as lesser names like Dominic Ostler and Andy Moles. All of them were very good cricketers.

Brian Lara! What was it like being in the same team as one of the all-time greats?

It was like a circus to be honest, with cameras everywhere. Manoj Prabhakar was supposed to be the overseas player and he pulled out through injury. There were footballers in the changing rooms, we were invited to film premieres, got into nightclubs free – it was a whole new world for us. He came back late from a visit to Trinidad, then took his mobile phone on to the pitch against Somerset, which made the news at the time. It is fair to say that Bob Woolmer and Dermot Reeve struggled with him, because he largely did what he wanted.

But he scored 2,000 runs that year, at an average of 90, so he didn't let us down.

Was he the best player you played with or against?

With? Probably that year, when he was at his absolute peak. I played against Graeme Hick, Mohammad Azharuddin and Allan Lamb, all were wonderful batsmen, but in 1994 Brian was probably the best.

It was great to have him at slip too. 'Caught Lara, bowled Welch' still looks nice on the scorecards!

You had a really good year in 1997 with Warwickshire, taking over 60 wickets and scoring almost 500 runs. Then the returns dropped and in 2000 you barely featured for them. What happened?

It was strange really. Dermot preferred Dougie Brown in the side over me, but when he was unavailable and Tim Munton became skipper, he liked me in the side, rather than Dougie! Maybe it was competition, but I found myself missing more and more cricket and at the end of it I knew I had to do something.

How did the move to Derbyshire come about?

It was funny really. I was left out of the NatWest Trophy Final at Lord's and in the bar, after a few beers for Dutch courage, I said to the captain, Neil Smith, that I felt my time was up. He told me to speak to Bob Woolmer, who in turn directed me to Dennis Amiss, the chief executive, to ask permission to speak to other counties.

I saw him on the Monday morning and he said that there was a committee meeting in two weeks, when a decision would be made. Two days later he phoned me and said it was okay, I could go. So the writing was very much on the wall and I put myself out there to other clubs.

There were eight interested in signing me, but I had just become a father and wanted to stay in the Midlands. Tim Munton was by that time captain at Derbyshire, a man who I knew well and respected and he made the decision very easy for me.

From 2001 you became one of Derbyshire's most popular and consistent players. By that stage you were a time-served cricketer of 29. Was that experience a reason for success?

I had a good grounding at Warwickshire, with team-mates and coaches I could learn from. I matured late but for the first time I felt that I was valued and all cricketers like that. You know your game at that stage though and I knew what I could and couldn't do.

Was it hard to move from a winning environment?

It wasn't at all, because the most important thing for me was that I was playing all the time. That meant a lot to me and I revelled in it.

Isn't that a frustration of the modern game, where counties are rewarded for playing home-reared players only to the age of 26? Don't counties now miss out on the late developers?

No, because with 12-month contracts and constant working on their game, players are now 'ready' earlier than they used to be, if they are going to make it at all. By 25 or 26 you now know, in most cases, if a player is going to be up to the standard. You look at Billy Godleman, who has just had the best season of his career. He is 26 and has worked hard at his game. He knows it now, knows what works and what he has to do to maintain the standard. He's been in the game for a few years, but has now got there. Now it is a case of maintaining that.

There were some good players in that Derbyshire side, but results were never consistent. Looking back on it now, with a coach's eye, why was that?

It was the seam bowlers. When I started with the club, there was Dominic Cork, Kevin Dean, Tom Lungley and myself, not a bad attack. When the first two left and started to have injuries respectively, we had no real experience. Paul Havell, Ian Hunter, Wayne White and a few others came in and out but there was no one who really grabbed the opportunity. Mohammad Ali had one good season, but then opted for a big-money move that didn't work out.

There was no pace in our wickets at that time, so we really needed a top spinner. They were just as scarce as they are now and we struggled as a result of that.

> **Was the dressing room a happy place? There had been a number of years where the winter saw the departure of various players of big reputation and lots of stories.**

It was a decent dressing room but I would say a difficult one to manage. We had people from all over the globe and although they were good players, there were times that we didn't pull together as a team, with the inevitable consequences.

> **You once walked off when you were on 99, despite Luke Sutton wanting you to get the run for your century, to allow us time to bowl out Somerset at Taunton. A selfless gesture?**

Not really. Luke had decided that we would declare at a certain time or when we lost a wicket, whichever was the sooner. We lost a wicket so I walked off, that was it. I like to think that I was always a team player and personal success should always be secondary to that of the 11.

I could have stayed out there for another hour or so, because I then took five wickets and we won with plenty of time to spare, but getting a win was all important and I would have done it again in a heartbeat.

> **Your career ended with a nasty Achilles tendon injury. I recall seeing footage of it being irrigated. That looked nasty.**

I did it for the first time in pre-season 2007. I felt I had been kicked in the back of the leg and my Achilles tendon was shredding, leaving me with a big lump at the back of my calf. I had three months in plaster, then three months in a moon boot. A week after that came off, it went again, so I had to repeat the entire six-month cycle. I was very close to depression, as it is very tough to deal with that sort of thing when your livelihood depends on your being fit. I wasn't sure if I would lose my house or my car – there's a million thoughts race through your mind, but ultimately things happen for a reason.

You moved into coaching with Essex in 2008. How did that come about?

That's when the irrigation was done. I felt it when I was playing football with my son and got a nick on it, then when we got to Dubai for pre-season it got infected. Two holes appeared and there was infection coming out of them, though surprisingly after that it healed okay and has been fine since.

I had completed my Level 4 coaching certificate with Derbyshire, where I was set to move into coaching when I retired. I was resigned to the fact that my playing career was over and was filling in insurance claims to get some compensation. I saw Ronnie Irani of Essex on television, talking about degenerative and acute sporting injuries and realised that he must be in the same situation as me, so I called him up for some advice.

He told me that they had just been talking about me and asked if I would be interested in doing some coaching down there, possibly as bowling coach. I knew Paul Grayson, having been to New Zealand with him for a few years, and applied for the role.

I had two great years there, from February 2008. We won a couple of trophies and gained promotion, in a period of my career I look back on with great fondness.

Then of course, a return to Edgbaston as assistant coach in 2010?

That happened when Allan Donald wanted to move back home. He had an eight-year-old son back in South Africa who was missing him, so decided that he had to leave. My son was the same age, at home in the Midlands, so it was perfect for me. I called up Ashley Giles, asked about the role and it turned out there were only two applicants!

Of course, I knew the club, knew Ashley and Dougie Brown, as well as a lot of the players, so it made the move easy.

I have to say that Essex were great about it, which was appreciated.

When Ashley Giles moved to the England set-up, the press suggested that there was discord at Edgbaston, with players firmly in your camp or that of Dougie Brown, who eventually got the job. Was it the awkward period that was portrayed in the press?

Yes, it was. You should understand that as bowling coach I had been around the first team, while Dougie was second-team coach. The only other candidate was Ottis Gibson and there were those who felt that I had the best credentials. Obviously there were others – and the ones making the decisions were among them – who felt differently.

I felt that Ashley and I had laid the groundwork for us to dominate for the next five years, but it wasn't to be.

So did the move to Derbyshire take long to think about?

No. I had done a lot of work with bowling 'units' at two counties and had success, so I wanted to see if I could translate that to a team and develop other players. It was the next stage for me as a coach.

It is hard work, but hugely enjoyable. I have tried to change the culture and the environment and test the players, challenge them to think about what they do and need to do to improve.

I love it.

When you took on the role, did you have in mind the coaching set-up that is now in place, or did that evolve?

No, the improvement pathway, as it is called, had been put together by the chairman and chief executive. They had wanted to cover all the disciplines and take things to the next level. The players have everything that they need to succeed and what we have done is to take away the excuses for failure.

With these things in place, given time, the players will develop.

Which of the coaches that you played under or worked alongside had the biggest influence on you?

I think I have taken bits out of everyone. Neil Abberley, my first coach at Warwickshire, taught me the discipline – wear the right clothes, be on time, respect the badge and your team-mates – and was a big influence.

Bob Woolmer's forward thinking and ability to think 'outside of the box' was another, as was Dave Houghton's laid-back attitude and management style. Dave encouraged you to go out and express yourself, something that some players forget to do.

You need different things at stages of your career and you try to ensure you use the acquired skills when the need arises.

What is the hardest part of a coaching role?

It is getting players to open their minds and understand that what you are trying to do can and will improve them as players. Sometimes they think they are fine as they are and can continue and be okay, when in fact you know that you can improve them by ten to 15 per cent and make them into something much better, possibly something quite special.

There are times when you hit a core of resistance, where a player just doesn't want to listen and that can be frustrating, because you know they aren't being the best they can be.

It is like being a teacher. You are always giving, but don't always get something back. If a bowler gets 70 wickets, or a batsman scores a thousand runs, they rightly get the plaudits, but the coach who helped them to get there can be overlooked.

It is one of those things that you learn to accept.

Presumably, in this modern era, the comments on social media, blogs and forums can't make for an easy life. Or do you just not read them?

I don't bother reading them to be honest, but I hear things from those who do. There are plenty of people out there who will always be quick to criticise, but they are the same ones who will be shouting from the rooftops as soon as you win a few games.

When you moved to Derbyshire, it was reported that you felt there were better seam bowling prospects at the club than you had seen at Warwickshire?

Definitely. Both Ben Cotton and Tom Taylor are going to be 'proper' cricketers. They have hit second season syndrome this year and now realise how much work is needed to take wickets at this level, once the novelty value has gone when you first play.

But Greg Cork and Will Davis both have great potential, though are a little further back in their development. So too has Harry White. I remember him when I was at the club before and he was around 5ft 8in. Now he is 6ft 4in, has long levers and is similar in build and style to Mitchell Starc. He has all the attributes and we now need to find if he is willing to work at his game to succeed.

> **Your two summers so far have seen personal tragedy affecting a player and the club, players quitting due to pressure and a chronic spate of injuries. That's a lot to deal with and still deliver results?**

Yes it is. When I arrived at the ground to start the job, I had four or five issues to deal with which I had no prior knowledge of, so they all needed sorting. It has taken us nearly two years to get the squad that we want, to have a group of players that we firmly believe, over the next couple of years, will kick on.

Last year was a baptism of fire and we were thrown in at the deep end, but we have come through it and this winter's work will be important for their continued development.

> **You must be proud of the number of young players who are now progressing through the ranks as the structure bears fruit?**

Yes. Because of the club's financial position, it is important that we develop our own, if for no other reason than there's not the money to do otherwise. For me though, developing a 'siege mentality' among a group of players who grow up through the age groups, enjoy each other's company and succeed together is the way forward for this club.

> **Yet how do you balance and reconcile the need to develop and encourage them, with the need for results to retain the support of the board and supporters?**

It's hard and I won't pretend otherwise, but it's not about me, it is about what is best for the long-term future of the club. There are a few players who have had knocks this year, but they will work on their games and come back stronger for that.

We have had people asked to do things beyond them this season, batting too high in the order and bowling at times because there were no options. The addition of Hamish Rutherford and Neil Broom from New Zealand will make a big difference next year, as will those experiences that the young players have had, especially the bad ones.

You can look at it from one angle and say we didn't qualify through the T20 and the Royal London One-Day Cup, as well as finishing second-bottom of the championship. You look the other way and see some talented young players have been given early experience that I believe will benefit them and the club in the long term.

The chairman called it a five-year plan and we have just completed the second season, but first full winter of coaching.

We kick on from here.

And what of the future for Graeme Welch?

I see myself here for the long haul. I love the club and the environment and the work we are doing now is the start of what I hope will be a long stay at the club.

Hopefully, other people see things the same way!

James Pipe
(2006–2009)

AFTER CAREFUL consideration, I don't think I have met someone so enthusiastic about his chosen career as James Pipe.

I spent a couple of hours with him on a warm, sunny, non-match afternoon at the County Ground. We sat on the pavilion balcony, watching the ground staff busy in their preparations for the game the following day and the conversation flowed like the water from the groundsman's hosepipe.

I had a set of questions prepared, but plenty of additional ones came to mind as we chatted easily about his two careers, cricket and life in general.

Derbyshire wicketkeepers have almost as good a lineage as the seam bowlers. Harry Elliott, George Dawkes, Bob Taylor, Karl Krikken…there are fine names in that sequence and James proved to be a worthy addition to it.

His glovework was solid and dependable, all you could wish for. At times it extended to the spectacular, but his footwork, like that of the best of his trade, was excellent and the dives that normally justify such terminology were only occasional in their use. He was vocal too; not quite of the Karl Krikken standard, but always urging his team-mates to renew their efforts, especially towards the end of a long, hot day in the field.

It was his batting that set him apart. Just as Bob Taylor remains the Derbyshire gloveman *non pareil,* so James was probably the best batsman among those who have donned the gloves. Luke Sutton was good, especially in his first spell at the club, but the latter's approach was less vigorous, more functional.

Once he was in, James really hit a cricket ball. Sometimes his approach resulted in an early demise, his dismissal met by audible disappointment from the local faithful, eager to be entertained. A career batting average of just under 30 suggests a more tempered approach may have brought dividends on occasion. Yet just as there were plenty of times when he entertained, enlivened a day and helped to win a match, so there were gritty rearguard knocks that highlighted his battling qualities.

His retirement came too soon for supporters, but made eminent sense for the man. Throughout it all he has retained a ready and winning grin, given only to a man at ease with his lot in life. As you will see, he enjoyed his cricket, loves his more recent career and is a devoted family man.

He even took the time, at the end of the interview, to show me his new physiotherapy facilities.

They were impressive, just as he was himself.

James, how does a Yorkshire lad from Bradford end up starting his career at Worcestershire?

Well, I played all of my age-group cricket for Yorkshire from nine years old and was invited to play for the Yorkshire County Cricket Club Academy at the age of 16. I spent two years there and it was a great grounding, playing a bit of second-team cricket and improving both my game and self-discipline.

The problem was that Richard Blakey was the established first-team keeper and Colin Chapman was regarded as one of the best wicketkeeper/batsmen on the second-team circuit, so there was nowhere for me to go.

I started looking around and Ismail Dawood had moved from Worcestershire, where he was understudy to Steve Rhodes, to Northamptonshire.

I went for one training session and then Damian D'Oliveira called the next day to offer me a one-year contract. I accepted without even asking how much I would be paid, I was so excited. I'd have done it for a tracksuit!

You were on the staff there for a good few seasons without really establishing yourself?

I was there for nine seasons and made some lifelong friends along the way. The first few years were great and I learnt a lot about wicketkeeping working with Steve Rhodes, for which I was grateful. I was extremely fortunate to work with Damian D'Oliveira throughout my time at the club, undoubtedly one of the best coaches, but more importantly one of the best blokes I have ever met.

He helped me survive and grow into a first-class cricketer and we became great friends over the years. There was a lot of competition for places, opportunities were limited and I found it impossible to get a consistent run in the first team, no matter how I performed. I remember scoring 104 not out against Hampshire and then getting dropped for the next game!

However I am proud and honoured to have represented the club. I made some great mates, had some amazing experiences and developed my game.

So how did the move to Derbyshire come about?

Luke Sutton was moving from Derbyshire to Lancashire and they were in the market for a replacement. I was lucky in getting a few runs down the order for Worcestershire in a televised game and the next morning got a call from the Derbyshire coach, Dave Houghton. He had been at Worcester previously and when he started talking to me, it just felt right. Steven Davies was coming through at Worcestershire and I felt I had to get first-team cricket at that point.

It was quite funny, I met Tom Sears, the Derbyshire chief executive, in a pub in Worcester and went through to a back room for some privacy, to talk terms. The next thing we knew, two of the Worcestershire committee walked in, knew both of us and put two and two together! So much for a discreet meeting.

❚ Did you remember to ask about the money this time?

I did, yes!

❚ Were you always a 'dasher' with the bat, or is that something that you were encouraged to do by Dave Houghton?

I like to think I was adaptable, depending on the match situation, but I did prefer to take the game to the opposition. Dave Houghton helped me to believe that I could score runs consistently at first-class level. There were a lot of similarities between him and Damian at Worcestershire and we clicked straight away. He got me thinking, playing like a batsman and valuing my wicket more. He reinforced a few technical components of my game, but more importantly he taught me how to score runs.

I also enjoyed batting at seven. It's an important position in four-day cricket and I loved the responsibility. I found myself coming in either early on, when the team was in trouble, or later in the innings when the bowlers were returning for their third or fourth spells so you could really put your foot down.

The new ball would often be taken around that time too and the combination of a harder ball and attacking fields provided some great opportunities to cash in on a few runs. Most teams had the same plan for me, tending to bowl short or back of a length, with two men back on the hook, as I had a reputation for taking on the short ball. I had been dismissed a couple of times playing the hook early on in my career, but I worked hard with Dave Houghton on controlling the shot and developing other scoring options against the short ball. I saw this tactic as a massive advantage, especially when the team was in trouble and I had to go in early. Teams would often go away from bowling the areas that had been successful for them, to bowling short. On occasions I was able to get myself in, score at a decent rate and change the momentum and direction of the game.

❚ We had some good players in your playing career at the club, but never seemed to string together results consistently?

When I joined Derbyshire we hadn't won a home championship game for four years. It was hard to believe, with players like Graeme

Welch, Kevin Dean and Michael Di Venuto in the side. Steffan Jones and Graeme Wagg joined the club at the same time and we arguably gave the team a bit more depth. We started to compete and became a 'scrapping' side, one that others knew would make them work.

In 2007 we signed Simon Katich and Ian Harvey, two very fine Australian players, and we started well. Then unfortunately Ian became ineligible to play for us and 'Pop' Welch picked up an Achilles tendon injury that ultimately ended his career. There were other injuries too and I often wonder what might have happened had we had better luck that year.

In 2007 and 2008, you really emerged as a batsman and played an innings of 133 at Chesterfield against your old county, that is still spoken of by those that saw it.

I was sitting on the balcony at Chesterfield watching Simon Jones bowl his quick, skiddy, back of the length stuff. He got Wavell Hinds caught behind, with one that clipped his glove as he threw his hands up in front of his throat.

It's not what you want to see when you are in next and of course, I was getting plenty of comments from the Worcestershire lads as I walked out to bat. I went back to my old philosophy and focused on the fight between the bowler and myself, blanking out everything else.

I got away quickly with a few boundaries and it went on from there, on a small ground with a quick outfield. Graham Wagg and I got a stand going and while the comments kept coming, we managed to take the game away from them.

Author note: The two players added 145, as James scored his runs from just 121 balls.

Who were the best bowlers that you kept to over your career?

I was extremely fortunate at Worcester to play with Glenn McGrath, who was both a wonderful bowler and a great professional. He was also a great team man. It didn't matter how many overs he had bowled or how he was feeling, he was the first man out on the balcony to support the batters, every game. I also enjoyed keeping to the off-spinner Gareth Batty, who I had kept to since the age of nine!

Keepers and spinners generally get on pretty well in most teams. I learnt to read his game over the years and we developed a good understanding. He was an aggressive, attacking spinner who went hard at the batsman and I always felt like I was in the game.

My move to Derbyshire gave me the opportunity to keep to other fine bowlers. Two that spring to mind were Charl Langeveldt and Graeme Welch. Both had the ability to land the ball in great areas and build pressure, but had dangerous attacking variations in their armoury. I always admired the work ethic and professionalism of Steffan Jones and the skill and aggression of Graeme Wagg. I also kept to some unbelievable spells of bowling from Tom Lungley, that would have troubled any batsman in the world.

When did you start to think of a career in physiotherapy?

Quite early on, actually, as even at school I was interested in science. I had a few injuries over the years, which gave me an insight into the body's response to injury and the rehabilitation process.

In 2003, I suffered a serious head injury while batting in the nets at Worcestershire and sustained damage to the retina in my right eye. It was career- and sight-threatening and I was sidelined for months. I started to think then that I had to prepare for a life outside the game and although I had an interest in strength and conditioning, I opted to go down the physiotherapy route.

Worcestershire was a great environment for extra-curricular learning, with Vikram Solanki and Phil Weston studying for degrees at that time and most other players having working interests outside of playing cricket. I was offered a place to study physiotherapy at the University of Salford and enjoyed every minute.

How long did that take you, allowing for a career as a professional cricketer?

It took five and a half years to graduate as a chartered physiotherapist. It was challenging at times managing the two careers, but it gave me a good balanced lifestyle. It allowed me to completely switch off from cricket and provided the security I needed at that time in my life, while playing in a ruthless environment. I felt more relaxed and enjoyed playing cricket even more than previously, which probably reflected in my performance.

After I graduated, I was determined to continue developing my physiotherapy knowledge and skills alongside my professional playing career. Fortunately I achieved this through an internship at Sale Sharks rugby club and an NHS outpatients post, working in the Lincolnshire Trust.

Presumably you had mixed feelings when you stopped playing?

No, not really. I felt a bit emotional as the end came, but I was at the start of an exciting career, which made the transition a lot easier for me. I had hit my peak and there comes a time for everyone and the time was right for me. I got to challenge myself against the best players of that era, travel the world, experience different cultures, make lifelong friends and create some great memories along the way. Even now, though, I still have days when I miss playing. Your playing days are special and can never be replaced.

I am extremely fortunate to have an amazing wife who supported me all the way through and two beautiful daughters who are our world.

How did the offer of the new job at the club come about?

Quickly, as I only had a week's notice! The club were in the market for a new physiotherapist as the man in post, David Beakley, was offered a job with Cricket Australia. My playing contract was up at the end of the season and when the club offered me the head physiotherapy position, I jumped at it. It was what I had worked for and, so early in my career, was more than I had dared hope might happen.

Opportunities like that come along once in a blue moon. My ambition when I finished playing was to work in sport and have my own private practice and to be able to do both, right at the start of my career, was and is a dream. I feel extremely fortunate and honoured to be in the position that I am in and love working at Derbyshire CCC.

In your new career, what were the biggest challenges?

I guess coming to terms that I wasn't going to be taking the field with the lads anymore. It was enjoyable and easy to watch when the team were performing well but I found myself getting frustrated that I couldn't contribute and change anything on the pitch when we were up against it.

Another big challenge was that I had always worked in a team of physiotherapists together with other health care professionals and when I first started at Derbyshire I was on my own! Having experienced different sporting environments, I felt the situation at Derbyshire was unhealthy and I didn't want to work in isolation. Over the years we have developed a strong team of health care professionals and medical referral pathways to support the players. This has created an open environment that allows us to develop, support and challenge each other to ensure best practice.

My ambition is for Derbyshire to have the best sports science and medicine department in the country and we are working steadily towards that.

Does it help that you have experience as a top player, compared to others in the field?

Thank you, but I am not sure that I was ever a top player! My past experiences definitely help me relate to the players. Having been in similar situations, I can empathise and appreciate what they are going through and support them to the best of my ability.

I hear supporters complain about the lack of information at times on player injuries. Would I be right in saying that there are confidentiality issues to observe?

Yes, we operate under a code of professional conduct. All medical information is 100 per cent confidential. If the player wants to share information with the media, it should be completely at their discretion.

Early in the 2015 season there were three bowlers who went down with knee injuries. Was that the result of too much winter work?

Although we do everything in our control to prevent injuries, nobody has yet designed a crystal ball. We are extremely reflective and analytical when we get an injury though. Two of these knee injuries were from what are called 'traumatic onsets'. Unfortunately, the nature of sport exposes players to potential traumatic injuries and we certainly don't want to wrap them in cotton wool. In this instance we try to confirm the diagnosis as quickly as possible and plan an appropriate rehabilitation programme.

We do all we can to maximise availability and optimise the performance of the players and this is a really exciting area. First, we profile each player, looking for imbalances and weaknesses. We then use this data, along with their past medical history and input from coaches and players, on the technical and functional areas of their game. This enables us to construct an individualised physical preparation and strength and conditioning programme.

In addition, we continually monitor the workloads of each player to help reduce any risk of injury or drop in performance and guide the amount of physical training we do. We investigate the stress response of each individual in training and the different formats of the game by taking swabs from players' mouths and by using GPS units. We can detect from the GPS data how hard they are working and if they are getting tired, which is useful in working out player 'threshold'. Of course, a captain will still ask a bowler how he's feeling and if he can do one more, but it helps to spot things that might alleviate a potential problem down the line.

Your role combines with that of a medic too, at times, especially on tour. Was that tough to handle?

Not really. It is important for me as a physiotherapist to work inside my scope of practice.

If a player presents with a medical issue or something outside of my scope, I refer on to the appropriate person. We all have our areas of expertise and I am fortunate to have a great network of medical and surgical colleagues to help me out!

We plan and regularly practise to prepare for the worst-case traumatic on-pitch scenarios. In addition, I must achieve an annual, ongoing re-accreditation in advanced life support and pitchside trauma, that I gained through the Rugby Football Union.

You must work long hours, especially with the injury list this year?

Yes, but then again I am doing my hobby for a living, so cannot complain too much!

What are the key things in keeping people fit and fresh for what is an arduous and dangerous sport?

Keeping a close eye on personal injury data, monitoring workloads closely and talking to players regularly are the main things. Yet if they twist a knee in the field, or break a finger when they are batting or taking a catch, there's nothing you can do. Sometimes, like this year, you have a spate of these things and you have to take it on the chin and sort it out. You need luck, that's for sure.

It is also important to have a solid medical referral pathway. If we cannot clinically diagnose an injury immediately, we get a second opinion from our chief medical officer, Dr Roger Hawkes, and then decide on the requisite tests and scans. We have a network of orthopaedic specialists for different parts of the body and we bring them in early, when required.

How did you go about building up a strong network of specialists? I have heard that you are already highly regarded in the game, with an extensive contacts book?

It is partly luck, partly research. Dr Hawkes is an acclaimed sports physician and is also chief medical officer for the PGA European Tour. He is based 20 miles down the road and is a massive support to me. You get reliable contacts from such people.

We don't just have 'a knee guy' but ones who specialise in specific procedures, again with a view to getting players fit quickly. The same goes for other parts of the body.

How has the game changed in the period even since you started playing?

It has progressed tremendously over the past six years since I retired. The tolerance for players carrying excess fat now is much lower from coaches. It slows you down and increases the risk of injury, so the goal is to ensure that players are fit within expectations. There are so many variables in cricket and fitness is probably one of the few things that you can control.

We now call them 'cricketing athletes' and that's what most of these guys are now. They are robust and look after themselves seven days a week, 365 days a year. I think there is probably a correlation between the fitness levels of the modern day player and the quality of fielding. The standard now is breathtaking and it just keeps getting better.

Yet, to use bowlers as an example, there have always been fast bowlers like Harold Larwood, Keith Miller and an array of them in the 1970s and 80s. They didn't have access to such facilities and monitoring.

No, but they would have been fit and strong, perhaps had manual jobs to maintain that and crucially had the physiological make-up that enabled them to bowl faster than others in their era, as well as their rhythm and skill levels.

Finally James, what of the future for you?

I want to complete my Masters in muscular and skeletal medicine, which I am about a third of the way through at present. I also want to drive excellence in player care, both at Derbyshire and across the country, through the Physiotherapists In County Cricket group, of which I am currently chairman.

Most of all, as a family man, I want to be able to enjoy my two daughters growing up and still manage to find enough time to spend with them and my wife!

Wayne Madsen
(2009–present)

IF ONE takes some outstanding overseas players from the discussion, in any consideration of the best Derbyshire batsman in the post-war era, Wayne Madsen would need to be included in the debate.

From his first game in the county colours he has impressed, not just with the runs he has made, but the way in which he has done so. A stylish player, he exudes a calmness in the middle that has all too rarely been the preserve of Derbyshire batsmen, while at his best his organised technique suggests he might never be dismissed once he gets in.

Truth be told, his county's batting has at times been overly-reliant on his success, most notably in the summer of 2013 when he was the first player in the country to 1,000 runs and shone like a beacon against top-division attacks that exposed the rest of a somewhat flimsy batting line-up.

He has all the shots, but rarely hooks, preferring to concentrate his efforts on those shots offering a better percentage of success. Having opened the batting for some time, he is comfortable against pace, but his real forte is against spin bowling, where his quick feet and hands enable him to handle most that comes his way. As he explained in the interview, the hockey skills of his youth enable him to be one of the few batsmen I have seen who plays the reverse sweep with grace, making it look an almost natural shot in the process.

He has grown into captaincy. There are demonstrative leaders out there and others who display a quiet authority and demeanour. Wayne is very much in the latter camp and always manages to do so with a smile never far from his lips.

Therein lies perhaps his greatest talent. As a figurehead for the club, meeting and greeting sponsors, having a word with supporters and posing for photographs, there can be few better men in the game. Indeed, in many years of following professional sport, I don't think I have met a more approachable man, which left me optimistic that my request for an interview might receive a positive response.

What I didn't expect was an invitation to carry it out at the lovely house he shares in the heart of the Peak District with his delightful wife, Kyla, followed by a convivial evening that centred around a typically South African braai. The conversation flowed as easily as the runs from his bat, he seemingly as interested in me as I was in him, a gift given only to the most sociable of people.

A very special man is Wayne Madsen. South African by birth and most definitely by accent, but as you will see, his heart and future is now very much centred on his adopted home in Derbyshire.

Wayne, tell me about your background in South Africa?

I grew up in a strong sporting family and my parents, Paddy and Adele, were both international hockey players. I was the seventh Madsen to play hockey for South Africa – there are now nine! As well as that, I have a few uncles, Trevor and Mike Madsen and Henry Fotheringham, who played first-class cricket there, so the talk was often of sport and you effectively grow up at the side of a sports field.

I always played a lot of sport, but gave up rugby at age 13. From then I largely played hockey in the winter and cricket in the summer, though I played individual sports like squash, tennis and a bit of golf. I loved the camaraderie of team sports, so that's where my focus always lay.

You made your first-class debut in 2003/04, then exploded on to the scene the following year with an average of 63. At the age of 20, were you being 'talked up' as a future international player?

Not really. I had just got into the Dolphins side and looking back it was a year in which both my cricket and hockey took off, so juggling the demands of each sport was tough. The head of the cricket academy was good enough to allow me time off to prepare for hockey.

In February 2004 I played for the Dolphins in the Supersport Series, having done well for Kwa-Zulu Natal, and that was a week after I played in midfield for the South African hockey team! It was a really hectic time and as soon as the cricket season ended I was selected to go to Australia with the South African hockey squad.

You missed the following cricket season?

Yes, because I was playing so much hockey. I simply couldn't fit it all in.

Do you find that helped your cricket subsequently, especially with the reverse sweep, which you play more gracefully than most?

Definitely. I started to play the reverse sweep when I was at school and few youngsters were playing it at that stage. Now, it is something that they work on, but it was always a huge shot for me in one-day cricket and remains so. The advent of T20 has made it very popular and I use it a lot. At times I get out playing it, but like any other shot you play, it is a case of balancing risk and reward.

When I bat in T20, there are almost always two men behind square on the off side, so if I get it right, I can manipulate the ball through midwicket and keep the scoreboard ticking over, even if it isn't an especially bad ball.

How and when did the opportunity come to play in league cricket in England?

I had just played the hockey World Cup in Germany in 2006 and got home to a crossroads in my life. I was coming to the end of my Bachelor of Commerce degree in Financial Management and either had to find a job that would enable me to play hockey, or take up cricket full-time. At that stage it was a planned sabbatical from hockey, although it hasn't turned out that way!

Kyla was also finishing her degree and said that she wanted to go over to England to do some work for a while. So I agreed to go over with her and play some club cricket for a year. I was fixed up as professional with Unsworth Cricket Club in the Central Lancashire League, who had strong South African connections. They proved to be very welcoming, a fantastic bunch of people, but I quickly realised that if I didn't perform, we would lose games. I either had to score big runs, or take wickets, because it was too much to expect of the amateurs to do that. It was a time that improved me as a player and as a person, because people depended on me and I didn't want to let them down.

How long did you play there?

I had three fantastic years at the club. When I finished with them, they presented me with a lovely photo book, commemorating what they called 'The Madsen Years'. They were terrific people and I learned a lot in my time there.

Didn't you go back as a guest professional at one point?

I was meant to. I was lined up to play a game for them when Derbyshire had no game and was contacted by Middleton Cricket Club, asking me if I could fix them up with a professional for their game that weekend. So I got Tim Groenewald to go along, then he told me that Middleton were actually playing Unsworth! I was tempted to get on the phone and say, 'Sorry, Tim's not available now!'

Then it was rained off, after all that.

How did the opportunity come to trial with Derbyshire?

I knew Clive Rice from South Africa and he let John Morris know that I might be worth a look at. At the same time, I was doing some coaching with Luke Sutton, the Derbyshire wicketkeeper, and he suggested I speak to Karl Krikken, who was the Derbyshire Academy coach at the time.

John Morris got in touch and invited me to Derby for a trial in August 2008. I had a ten- to 15-minute net against Charl Langeveldt, Greg Smith and Ian Hunter and at the end of it, John told me he liked what he had seen and asked me how I could play in this country. I knew I could get an Italian passport through my ancestry and Kyla had an Irish passport, which would also have enabled me to play.

John suggested we moved to this country sooner, rather than later, to get the requisite qualifying days out of the way. We got married in South Africa in December 2008 and moved to England in the January. I trained through the winter here, played for Unsworth and had some second-team cricket for Derbyshire.

In fact, that was when I first met Chesney Hughes. He had just arrived in this country and we played at St Annes together against Lancashire. He made 30 in no time and then called me for a quick single. I sent him back and, because he was wearing 'flats' with no spikes, he slipped, ended up flat on his back and was run out.

Sadly, it wasn't the only time we have had running issues.

How did you think then the county game compared with the level you had played back home?

That's a good question. I asked Hashim Amla what he thought when he played for us last season and he felt, like me, that the opportunity to bring talent through is better in England. While you are diluting the standard a little, with 18 teams, it means there are many more good ones coming through and gaining top level experience. In South Africa there are only six franchise sides and while it is a good standard, it doesn't give you a huge pool to choose from.

My game also suits English wickets better too. I play spin well and I tend not to hook much, so the faster, bouncier South African wickets would be less suited to my normal game.

Do you see more South African players coming over to this country using similar routes to you?

One hundred per cent. In the next couple of years, the revised quota system will see an exodus of cricketers from the country. From September 2015 each side at franchise level and below will have to select six players of colour, three of who have to be of black African origin.

Of course, they will need to have played either the necessary international matches, or have a European passport in order to do so, but some of those players will hold considerable appeal for English counties, there's no doubt about that.

For Derbyshire, as long as they can teach good habits and bring the right ethic to the club, I see no reason why we shouldn't potentially field one, or even a couple, alongside our own, home-grown talent.

Author note: The day after this interview was conducted, Roelof van der Merwe was announced as signing a two-year contract with Somerset, using his Netherlands passport in order to do so.

You had a memorable county debut with an unbeaten 170 against Gloucestershire?

I did! The day before I had played for Unsworth and made a hundred, during which I tweaked a hamstring. Kyla and I drove down and got to Bristol around 11.30pm, by which time my team-mates were all in bed.

We were doing warm-ups before play and started a game of football. I went in goals but when I had to kick the ball I could feel the hamstring, so asked the physio to strap it for me.

I was dropped early and then made only seven in the first innings, at which point Kyla had to go home for work the next day. So she missed my second innings, when I was put down a couple of times, but I played my natural game and made a big score against James Franklin, Steve Kirby and Jon Lewis, a pretty good seam attack.

Cheltenham is such a lovely ground and to bat with Chris Rogers and Wavell Hinds was such a huge thrill.

At what point did you decide that you wanted to make your life in this country and qualify for England?

That was in the winter of 2007/08. I was captain of the Kwa-Zulu Natal side, which was selected by a panel without any involvement from me. I didn't notice that we only had four players of colour in the side, instead of the required five and 15 overs into the game there was a wave from the dressing room.

The coach came on and said that one of our bowlers had to go off. The 12th man came on and, of course, could neither bat nor bowl, while the bowler, Nick Hewer, sat kicking his heels down on the boundary.

On the Monday, I got a letter from the person in charge of playing affairs, who was also the convenor of the selection panel, saying that I had disgraced the cricket union for going on the field as captain in such a manner when I knew the rules and had brought the game into disrepute.

He was effectively covering his own back and while I was naive in not checking the team sheet, I had done nothing wrong.

So after eventually clearing my name, I asked them to pay me what I was owed and told them that I would not be available for selection thereafter.

Did your wife's growing business success help in that decision?

It helped to confirm that I had made the right decision, but it wasn't the deal-breaker. Her sports coaching business has gone really well though and I am really proud of how well she has done with it.

You took over as Derbyshire's captain in 2012. How did that offer come about?

It was strange in a way. I had some indifferent form at the end of 2011 and dropped to the second team for a few games. At the end of the season, we all went our separate ways on holiday and then reported back for training. Luke Sutton was skipper, of course, and he wasn't around for a couple of weeks when we started back.

Just before Kyla and I were flying back to South Africa for Christmas, Karl Krikken, the coach by that time, called me into his office, I thought to remind me to train while I was out there. Instead he told me that Sutts was retiring with immediate effect and he wanted me to take over. I didn't have to think twice about it, to be honest, called my wife and accepted.

The news actually broke when we were on the plane to South Africa and I only gave one interview before we came back a month later.

Everyone was very supportive though and it made it easier than perhaps it could have been.

> **Of course, you then led Derbyshire to the Division Two championship that summer.**

Yes, that was a great summer. In the first over of the first game of the season, Martin Guptill hit Chaminda Vaas, who was playing for Northamptonshire at that stage, on to the roof of the marquee at Derby. We all looked at one another and thought, 'Well, that's set the tone.'

It all snowballed from there really. We got on a winning streak and the confidence grew throughout the team.

By halfway we had built up a big lead and just had to keep our composure to get promoted. There were a few worrying moments but we came through eventually.

> **How would you describe your captaincy style?**

I like to lead from the front and set the tone with my own performances, then on the field try to set an example and show guys how I want things to be done. I'm not especially demonstrative and I neither enjoy nor look for conflict, but you learn from good times and bad in cricket and in the time since then there has been a fair proportion of each.

> **The following summer you were the first batsman in Division One to reach the coveted 1,000-run landmark. That must have been a source of pride in a disappointing summer for the team?**

It helped the acceptance of my captaincy, but it was a disappointing first half of the season.

We really only started to play in mid-season and had we done so sooner, we might have stayed up. That I scored runs was satisfying, but to be relegated was frustrating.

Phil Russell, who was Derbyshire's coach for a while, was at one time my coach in South Africa and he told me that first and foremost as a captain you get your own job right, then attend to everything else. When you bat, you get ready to bat, then you look after the team. I understand now what he meant, because in difficult times you are then at least seen to be doing as much as you can.

You won an award for sportsmanship in 2013, after walking in the match against Yorkshire at Chesterfield when the umpire had given you not out. That seemed to swim against the tide of the modern game and, with respect, that of South Africans over the years! Was it something you have always done and would do again?

Yes, I've always done it. My parents instilled in me that you should always play fair and be honest, as did my school coaches. Sometimes you get given out when you're not, but there have probably been times when I have been lbw and it hasn't been given.

I am a firm believer in walking if I hit it and would do it again in similar circumstances.

In the summer that just passed, Graeme Welch decided to split the captaincy and make Wes Durston the one-day skipper. Was that a decision reached after chatting with you?

Yes, definitely. My championship form dipped during the T20, which is mentally and physically draining. Every ball is an event and there is no opportunity to switch off, so I chatted to Graeme and said that I could do without it.

We decided at the end of the season that I wasn't going to do it, but it was a case of seeing who we could get for the overseas roles in T20, just in case there was someone who might enjoy that challenge. When we knew that role was going to be split, it was always Wes Durston's role after that.

He's a fine one-day player and he did a very good job. I helped if it was needed, but Wes is a very experienced cricketer and captained the team intelligently.

At the end of a season, is the mental or physical tiredness the biggest thing for modern players?

Your body gets used to playing every day and, while there are aches, pains and niggles, you can generally handle them. The mental side is tougher, without doubt, and being able to switch off in October is quite nice and really needed after a long season.

> **What about social media? Do players read stuff on Twitter and/or blogs/forums, or do they normally give them a wide berth? They can be merciless at times.**

Some do, some don't. I stay away from Twitter and don't have an account.

I don't tend to focus on what other people think, when they don't know the many factors that go into decision-making. You might not want the other team to know that someone has a niggle, or maybe there's other things going on in the background.

At the end of a day's play, it is time to unwind, not read what others might think.

> **Are there still characters on the circuit? Any stories you would care to share?**

There are but the game has changed and some of the, perhaps, less professional things of days gone by don't happen now.

Graham Wagg is funny. When Glamorgan played Derbyshire last year at Chesterfield, I threw a braai at our house for the South Africans in their team.

Waggy got to hear of it and, when I went out to bat the next day, started shouting, 'Here he is, here's the chef.'

As we came off for tea there was a nice picture published showing him with his arm around my shoulders. What it didn't show was Graham saying to me, 'Thanks for the invitation chef, what happened to mine, by the way?'

He's a really top cricketer, he dishes it out on a pitch, but is happy to take it in return.

> **You have shown great loyalty to Derbyshire in the face of interest from elsewhere. Do you regard yourself as settled in the area now?**

Very much so. We have been living here for five years now; we love Derbyshire as an area and it is a great, family club to play for. I wouldn't like to move away and we can both see ourselves staying here for a very long time.

In the recent season, wheels went full circle and you became director of hockey at Belper Hockey Club. A winter project for you?

It is more an ambassador role than a coaching one, simply because of my cricket commitments. I am doing my Level 4 cricket coaching qualification over the next couple of winters and that won't leave much time. However, when I have the time I will help as much as I can and advise on hockey matters, whether it is in the progression of juniors or the development of the club as a whole.

We want to get the club back into the National League, so there's a lot of work to do!

And what of the future? By the end of your current contract a well-deserved benefit will be in sight.

Well, that would be great! I have been playing for the club for seven seasons now and if that happened I would be very grateful. I've always given my best for the club and hope that I am able to do so for a good few years yet.

It's been a great time!

Chris Grant
(2010–present)

YOU DON'T need too long in the company of Derbyshire County Cricket Club's chairman, Chris Grant, to understand how he has made such a huge success of his career.

He is extremely articulate and combines that with a ready smile and a tangible energy that has swept through the club since he first became involved, late in 2010. That energy and a desire to succeed helped him make a great success of a career in the City, so much so that he was able to retire, comfortably before the age of 40. The finance world's loss is very much Derbyshire's gain and at times it is hard to remember what the club was like before he came on the scene.

Without meaning to offend anyone involved over those years, his work ethic, positivity and desire – perhaps demand is more apposite – to be the best has transformed the place. Irrespective of results, a visit to the club these days is some way removed from those when admission to the game required circumventing stewards who my Dad was convinced once held key roles in the Third Reich.

It is all about friendliness, smiles and welcome, something that has been noted – and commented upon – by people from other counties that I have met on my travels. The visitor feels that their attendance is appreciated, not an unfortunate intrusion on the day's other work.

It would be hard to find anyone who had a bad word to say about the chairman's impact, one that had a very quick reward with a trophy in 2012, the first in too many years, truth be told. There have been challenges in the intervening period, on and off the field, but the vast majority of supporters and members remain grateful for his efforts and confident that the remarkable off-field transformation will soon be matched by greater on-field success. If this is the result of a youth policy that has seen a succession of promising local talent emerge, then there will be even greater reason to rejoice. For too long the club became home to soldiers of fortune, some of whom had long since relinquished their weaponry.

He is a busy man and several attempts at an interview had to be aborted as his many commitments took him away. At the last game of the season – indeed, on its very last day – I had resigned myself to plan B in closing the book when he called and invited me to his private box in the Lund Pavilion at the 3aaa County Ground.

There he proved the perfect host, offering me a drink and then sitting down with me in comfortable armchairs to watch the closing session of a summer that had not gone to plan. For a man who idolises the late Sir Winston Churchill, his team's failure to 'fight them on the beaches' too many times had proved a frustration.

We finished the interview just before Derbyshire made another mess of what earlier good batting had turned into a routine run chase on the last day. Near-defeat from the jaws of victory – it wasn't the first time it had happened and the frustration for each of us was obvious to the other.

Yet as I walked out of the 3aaa County Ground for the last time of the summer, I was heartened by a chat that covered his work and career, and left me even more convinced that the club is in the safest of hands.

Chris, five years down the line from when you took over as chairman from Don Amott. How has the job met your expectations?

It has been hugely challenging. I had a successful career in the City but this is massively different.

It is a voluntary role and you put in as many, or as few hours as you can. I threw myself into it and was effectively executive chairman until we got Simon Storey on board, when I was able to draw back a little. I enjoy it, though the days we play badly and are beaten affect me as much as any other supporter. I am passionate about taking this club forward: preserving its first-class status but then developing it. I want to leave the club in a better state than I inherited it, on and off the field, and the occasional setback will not detract us from that.

We had a huge loss to contend with at the end of that first year, one that threatened the very survival of the club, but since then we have recorded successive small profits, transformed off-field facilities and improved the overall perception of the club. We now need to kick on and do better on the field, the trophy that we won in 2012 being a bonus that we must now aim to repeat.

Yet overall, for all its challenges, it has been wonderful.

Tell me about your early life and how you became interested in the game.

I was born and brought up in a council house in Alvaston, very much to a working-class family. I used to watch the cricket on TV and my parents rang the local council to ask if there was a club I could go to.

They directed me to Alvaston and Boulton and a chap named George Schofield gave me some coaching. He was a lovely bloke and used to put tuppence on a length, or on a stump, then if you hit it, you got it. It used to buy a bottle of Mandora shandy, which at eight or nine years old was living the high life!

I played there a while, then moved to Spondon, where I played alongside Johnny Owen, a very good cricketer who should have made it in the first-class game after early success in his time at Derbyshire.

You were a decent player yourself, I believe?

I was a good club player but never more than that and my studies took priority. I played for Loughborough University and then, when I moved down south, for Bromley Common in the Kent League. I was a left-arm seamer, but not in the Mark Footitt or Kevin Dean class!

My career was testing, though, and I hardly played after my late 20s, before we moved back to Derbyshire and Swarkestone in 2008.

> **Your career in the City was a massive success, enabling you to retire at a very young age. Can you tell me about that?**

I did a Banking and Finance degree at Loughborough and then started as a research analyst, writing reports on companies with a view to them publishing the report and investors buying and selling shares in that company.

My father and grandfather had worked for Rolls-Royce in Derby and my mother was a driving instructor, but from a very young age I only wanted to be a stockbroker. I recall trips to London with my Mum, where I pleaded to go to the visitors' gallery at the Stock Exchange, rather than Madame Tussauds!

I joined a subsidiary of Barclays in that capacity, then moved to Deutsche Bank for a while, before becoming chairman of the European equities and head of global research for the Dutch bank, ABN Amro, the position I retired from at the end of 2008.

> **At what point did you make the decision to call it quits and move back to live in Derbyshire?**

The company was at the centre of a bidding war between Barclays and the Royal Bank of Scotland. Our share price prior to the bid was around 14 euros and the price was driven up to around 38 euros. I realised then that given the number of shares I owned, at 38 years old I never needed to work again.

Yet I think back and know that I worked very hard to get to that stage. I would be up for work at 5.15am and wouldn't get home some nights until midnight. I once flew to Australia for a one-hour meeting to win a deal, then got the next plane back home! I gave it my all for 15 years and in return it gave me the chance to devote myself, ultimately, to Derbyshire County Cricket Club.

> **You then became heavily involved in your local club at Swarkestone?**

I started to play third-team cricket there and after an early game I turned on the shower and the water started coming through the light fittings. They wanted to build a new pavilion and had a 'Buy a Brick' scheme that was not doing especially well.

I knew the chairman, Dave Corner, who was a close family friend and I wanted to give something back, so I bankrolled the pavilion for them.

So how did the approach to join the Derbyshire committee come about?

Well, I knew Don Amott, the then chairman, pretty well and sat with him in the directors' box at Derby County. In August 2010 he invited me down here for lunch, to sound me out about coming on to the committee.

Soon after I came on board, the senior members of that committee had a bust-up and Don left the club. The following March, I was elected chairman.

What was the state of the club when you took over?

Well, I should first say that Don Amott and Keith Loring, the chief executive, had done a good job by and large, but the wheels came off in 2010. When I came on board, it was evident that the club was going to make a loss, but it spiralled into a calamitous one of £187,037.

The ECB had introduced PRFP (Performance Related Fee Payments) for clubs playing young, England-qualified players and we hardly had any who were near to the first team. We hadn't massive debt, but we didn't own the ground and we had little in the way of financial reserves. We ran an overdraft and that level of loss was simply not sustainable.

One of my first tasks was to drill down in minute detail through the entire accounts and take out a lot of unnecessary expenditure. My background helped me to do that and the fact that I had the time to do so was important. Keith and I got the club back into the black in 2011, at which point he told me of his plans to retire.

The focus every year is not to lose money, which as a non-Test match club is a tough thing to do. You can illustrate that in that last year, on a business with a £3m turnover, we made a £1,000 profit. It can be done, but you have to make sacrifices, especially in the playing budget. Ours is still one of the smallest in the country and the constant aim is to generate more in advertising, marketing and sponsorship revenue that we can plough back into the playing side of the club.

The more we can utilise the ground and its facilities when we are not playing, the better chance we have of becoming competitive on the field.

> **When you took up the post, one of your early comments was on your desire to deliver a 'marquee signing', an Eddie Barlow-type player to galvanise the club. Do you regret that comment now?**

No, I don't. Back in 2010, a former club legend made the comment that the club resembled the League of Nations. We had become a county that offered a last pay cheque, while we also brought in too many Kolpaks and British passport players. Among the English counties we had a reputation for low salaries and poor facilities and for any player worth signing we were never going to be the first choice of employer.

My vision was of a largely home-grown team, but with a figure-head player who could take them forward. We put in 28 days' notice on Paul Collingwood, who we saw as doing a Barlow-type job and I was told by someone involved in the club at that time that Derby-shire would never again sign a big-name player. It was as if there was resignation to our lot as the 18th of 18 counties and I wouldn't accept that.

Now? Well, we have signed Shiv Chanderpaul, Martin Guptill, Hashim Amla and Tillakaratne Dilshan. There have been mixed results, but there is no player in the world now that Derbyshire does not have the resources to sign and would not, I think, be impressed by what we are trying to do here.

> **You revealed the club's nine-point strategy in 2011 – are you happy with progress?**

That was a blueprint of how we were going to run the club and there were some good things in there. Historically, we had not treated players well and we invited all the players, for the first time, to enter the pension scheme. The cost of doing that was £70,000–£80,000, but it was all about caring about and looking after the players, creating a better working environment, if you like. It gave an idea as to how we would operate and ensured that everyone knew what we were working towards. Interestingly, when we won promotion in 2012, both Northamptonshire and Surrey asked for a copy of the plan. I heard that David Ripley at Northamptonshire pinned a picture of our side on their dressing room wall as motivation. Like us, they have subsequently backed youngsters and created a better dressing room environment as a result.

The thing is, had we been doing well, on and off the pitch, it wouldn't have been necessary. Has every element been a success? No, but on balance it gave us a route map for the future. We have won a trophy, had a player selected for an England squad and enjoyed five years of financial stability.

Put it this way. Had we continued to lose money as we did in 2010, there would have been a Tesco built on the County Ground now.

That Division Two championship in 2012 looked to herald a bright new dawn. Do you think mistakes were made in the euphoria of that success?

Yes. You have to look back and say that we showed undue faith in some players in the length of contract issued, more than their performances justified. Yet in doing that we were fulfilling what we said we would do, in backing home-grown players.

We wanted to secure players we saw as key to our future, but it didn't work out. Had we not done so and they had moved on, we would have been blamed by the members and supporters. It was a classic 'damned if you do, damned if you don't' scenario, because for a variety of reasons, those players largely didn't build on the promise that they showed in that summer.

There have been tough decisions in that time, including two coaches leaving the club?

I should say first of all that I don't take pleasure in that side of the business. I came with a reputation as having worked in a cut-throat industry, where people are hired and fired all the time. That is actually incorrect, because you are generally on a long-term contract in the finance world and as long as you perform, you can work there until you are 60, should you choose to do so.

In sport, usually you are on a short-term deal and I came into a club where results were poor, morale was low and I did what anyone worth their salt would do. I evaluated the results and talked to people who worked with and for the coach, John Morris, and had to make a decision.

At my very first committee meeting, I was asked to give John the answer to his question as to whether his contract would be extended. Having gathered all the feedback, I acted decisively. The timing, in the middle of a championship match, was far from ideal, but we had been boxed into a corner and we had a contingency plan of Karl Krikken taking over. That led to one of the best seasons in recent memory and the title win of 2012.

In 2013, having gained promotion, we came straight back down. We hadn't worked out, I think, that to get out of Division Two you have to win games, but to stay in Division One you have to avoid losing. When we lost, we lost badly, despite winning more games than two teams who stayed up.

At the end of the season, we instigated a cricket review and opted for a different structure. I felt that we weren't ready for that level, with other clubs having specialist coaches and analysts. While he had the opportunity to do so, Karl Krikken opted not to apply for the new role.

I have nothing bad to say about either man. John Morris was the best 'spotter' of a player I have known, bringing Wayne Madsen, Wes Durston, Chesney Hughes, Tony Palladino and Mark Footitt to the club. Karl was great with young players and very popular, but the bottom line is that neither departure was the result of my decision alone. The club is certainly not run as a personal fiefdom.

Has the lack of success in T20 been a frustration for you? It is, after all, the biggest 'earner' in the game.

We have the worst record in the country at T20 and we have tried hard to sort that. We have brought in some big names, but with mixed results. It has been the single most frustrating thing for me, as the competition gets the club the most exposure. If you are doing badly, it shows the club in a poor light, irrespective of what you are doing well for the rest of the time.

Yet let's not forget that we compete in a very tough northern group, containing five Test match counties. That's not an excuse – Northamptonshire made it to Finals Day, Leicestershire have won it three times. We have to improve and are looking closely at how to do that and who can make a difference for us.

We are constantly looking at how we can improve our fortunes in the competition and won't rest until we have done so.

> ## The creation of the club management board came in 2014. How important was that for the club's continued development?

I think the changes we made in corporate governance, moving from a members' committee to a supervisory board, will be seen in years to come as the most significant action in the management of the club over many years.

It was painful to achieve, with some people resistant to change, but the club was being run by, largely speaking, a well-meaning group of amateurs. There were some professionals, but others were just people with time to spare. I use a simple analogy – when you are going on your holidays, you want the pilot to be someone who is qualified to do that job, just as if you go to the dentist.

To get on to the new board, you have to be first of all a member, but also have to prove you have the requisite skills and experience for the role that you are applying for. If more than one person does so, then an election can take place.

Members will hate me saying this, but I firmly believe that the biggest ball and chain around English cricket is in the way that clubs are constituted and run and the influence that members have. That's controversial, I know, but the reality is that the opinion of county members is largely out of synch with that of cricket lovers elsewhere in the world, especially India, which is the new power-base of the game.

We have to brace ourselves for change. It is as simple as that.

> **You have made remarkable strides off the pitch, with ground development plans transforming the club. How important has Simon Storey, the chief executive, been to that? The two of you go back a long way?**

Well, Simon and I first met at Loughborough University in 1989. He went off and developed his career with Johnson and Johnson and was happily living in Switzerland, when Keith Loring told me he was going to retire. I went through my telephone contacts and came up with his name, then after chatting with him, encouraged him to apply for the advertised role.

I purposely wasn't involved in the interviews as I wanted the successful candidate to get the job on merit, but I was thrilled that we were able to attract someone who already had a huge role and a significantly bigger salary than we could ever afford.

It speaks volumes for him that within weeks of [Simon] taking up the role, Giles Clarke called me and said he wanted to second him on to an ECB committee. We work well together, discuss a lot of things, disagree on some of them but work very well together as the public face of the club.

> **Has criticism of results in social media hurt you, or do you have to become immune to it or ignore it?**

I'd love to say that I ignore it and take no notice, but because of my passion for the club I do read it. To be honest, I dismiss 95 per cent of it as ill-informed rubbish, but people are entitled to their point of view, if at times being unkind in the way that they express it.

There's no hiding from the fact that we have had a bad season in 2015 and I cannot expect them to be saying nice things all the time as a result of that. To answer your question though, yes, it does hurt me at times, I can't deny that.

We need the players to learn from some disappointing, under-performing displays this summer and turn things around in 2016. We will all be pulling together and working towards that and I hope that people have much less to moan about.

What of the future for the club? Are you still as confident that we can become established in Division One of the County Championship?

That's the aim, though of course it isn't an easy objective. There are a lot of counties who can spend around twice what we can on their playing budgets and to a great extent it is David versus Goliath when we play one of the big, Test ground counties.

It is not as bad as football, because thankfully we do have the salary cap in cricket, but if that should ever be removed, it will kill the 18-county system. There will always be those with more resources, but the financial disparities are not always insurmountable. That's why you get the likes of Gloucestershire, Leicestershire and Northamptonshire doing well in one-day competitions and we want to do that and think that we are capable of doing so.

That Gloucestershire won the Royal London One-Day Cup as the joint lowest paying county, against Surrey, who have the biggest playing budget, showed what can be done, so hope springs eternal!

And for you?

Well, I was re-elected chairman until March 2017 and there's still a lot to do. There is the second phase of ground redevelopment and then we need to improve from this season on the pitch.

I enjoy the role and while I would be happy, if invited at some point, to serve on the ECB board, we need to get Derbyshire right and to the position that we all think is possible before that happens.

Epilogue

SEVENTY YEARS have elapsed since Walter Goodyear returned to the County Ground after the war. There have been ups and downs aplenty in the intervening period, but there are encouraging signs of a bright future, the club perhaps in a better position financially than at any time in its 145-year history.

A month or so before the 2015 season ended, I had the great pleasure of watching a session or so of play with Edwin Smith, this book's first playing subject and a man whose career had begun 64 summers earlier. It tied in with the release of my biography on him and the club had looked after us well, as we undertook a successful signing session.

Listening to him was fascinating stuff, the kind of history that should be on a curriculum. He explained how the ground used to be laid out and regaled me with stories of his times, many of them uncomfortably chilled, on what was for many years a sporting space, rather than cricket ground. It was why, he told me, people disliked coming to Derby for so many years.

'This,' he said, looking over the late-season turf, bathed in sunshine, with a wistful look in his eye, 'is a world apart from what it used to be. My generation would have given their eye teeth to have played on a ground like this and with these facilities.'

The shake of his head told its own story.

As an indicator of progress, as well as conclusion to a book, it could not have been bettered.